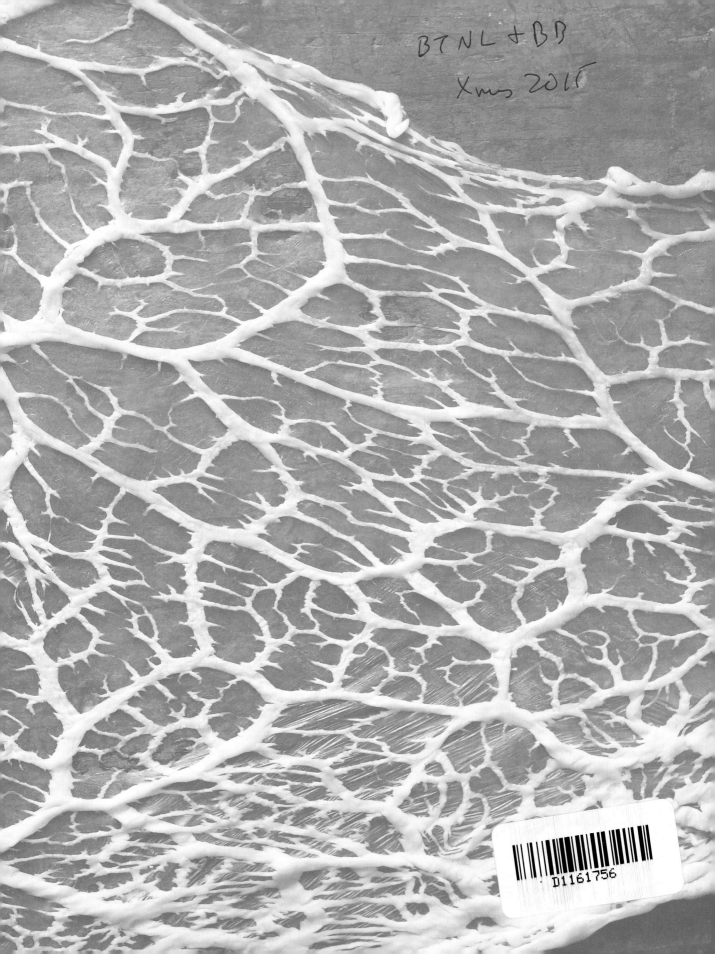

BTNL + BB
Xmas 2015

D1161756

fat

fat

An Appreciation of a Misunderstood Ingredient,
with Recipes

Jennifer McLagan

Photography by Leigh Beisch

TEN SPEED PRESS
Berkeley

Copyright © 2008 by Jennifer McLagan
Photography © 2008 by Leigh Beisch

Excerpt from "Bogland" from *Opened Ground: Selected Poems 1966–1996* by Seamus
Heaney. Copyright © 1998 by Seamus Heaney. Reprinted by permission of Farrar,
Straus and Giroux, LLC.

Library of Congress Cataloging-in-Publication Data

McLagan, Jennifer.
  Fat : an appreciation of a misunderstood ingredient, with recipes / Jennifer McLagan ;
photography by Leigh Beisch.
     p. cm.
  Includes bibliographical references and index.
  1. Oils and fats, Edible. 2. Cookery. 3. Lipids in human nutrition. I. Title.
  TX560.F3M35 2008
  664'.3—dc22

                                                2008009378

ISBN-13: 978-1-58008-935-7 (hardcover)

Printed in China

Cover and text design by Betsy Stromberg
Food styling by Dan Becker
Prop styling by Sara Slavin

12 11 10 9 8 7 6 5 4

First Edition

For all the Jack Sprats out there—
you're wrong!

contents

introduction: A MATTER OF FAT

I love fat, whether it's a slice of foie gras terrine, its layer of yellow fat melting at the edges; rich, soft marrow scooped hot from the bone; French butter from Normandy, redolent of herbs, flowers, and cream; hot bacon fat, spiked with vinegar, wilting a plate of pungent greens into submission; a slice or two of fine ham eaten just as its fat begins to turn translucent from the warmth of the room, sweet, nutty, and salty all at once; or a piece of crunchy pork crackling, delicious either hot or cold. I love fat: I love the way it feels in my mouth, and I love its many tastes.

As a cook and a person who loves food, I can't imagine my food without fat. I grew up in suburban Australia in the 1960s, and there were always at least three different fats in our refrigerator: butter, lard, and dripping. Close to Christmas and during the winter there would also be suet in the freezer, waiting to be mixed into mincemeat or transformed into dumplings and pudding. The butter had its own special dish, complete with a lid to protect its delicate flavor from any strong odors lurking in the refrigerator. The snowy-colored lard came from our butcher packaged in a white, waxed cardboard container, and next to it sat a ceramic jar filled with meat dripping. The dripping was homemade, the fat from roasted meats carefully poured into a bowl and left to solidify, forming a creamy beige layer suspended on top of dark jelly. That dripping was an essential base for a roast beef sandwich.

These fats were indispensable in our kitchen: we used lard and dripping to cook, while the butter was for bread, toast, and cakes. On the weekends, breakfast began with thick rashers of bacon cooked until they became crisp and oozed their fat into the pan. Then the eggs and, best of all, thick slices of day-old bread were added. Cooked in bacon fat, the bread became crunchy and full of the smoky, salty taste of bacon. We ate dumplings and puddings made with suet, fried our vegetables in beef dripping, and enjoyed buttery cookies. Once or twice a month we

> "Can you inform me of any other pleasure that can be enjoyed three times a day, and equally in old age as youth?"
>
> CHARLES MAURICE TALLEYRAND PÉRIGORD

1

stopped at the local fish-and-chip shop to indulge in hand-cut potatoes and thick slices of golden battered shark, euphemistically called "flake," which was cooked until crisp in hot, bubbling tallow and served with pickled onions. We ate fat with pleasure, and although we weren't a family of supermodels, none of us had a weight problem. We ate sensibly and, despite living in the suburbs, we walked.

Today, most people live more sedentary lives, driving instead of walking, and eating processed or take-out food more often than freshly cooked. As our lifestyles changed we gained weight, and it was easy to blame fat. Fat, we reasoned, was why we packed on the pounds and got ill, so we banned animal fat from our lives. Butter and lard disappeared from our kitchens, and we cut the fat off our meat. We've replaced traditional animal fats with vegetable oils, and we gobble up everything with a "low-fat" label. We have sacrificed all that taste and pleasure, yet we haven't lost weight or improved our health. When I say "we," I am generalizing: it is in North America in particular where eating is often seen as a necessary evil and fat is the most frequently demonized. Cultures that celebrate the pleasures of the table appear able to enjoy fat while still maintaining a healthy lifestyle. The French, for example, are cited as lucky people who can eat tubs of fat yet still maintain a normal body weight. But it's their love of food, combined with modest portion sizes and no grazing between meals, that is keeping them thin. They are both

> "Never before have so many people believed that the shape of their lives depended on the shape of their bodies."
>
> ROBERTA POLLACK SEID

SOME NOTES FOR THE COOK

Cooking is an art, not an exact science, and the ingredients and equipment one cook uses will never be exactly the same as those of another. While I have carefully tested all the recipes in this book, the cooking times may vary, and the number of servings a recipe yields will depend on your personal preference for portion size. Approach these recipes as you would any recipes—with a good dose of common sense.

The recipes in this book use sea salt, because it has the best flavor and is free of additives. Although volume measures are provided in this book, cooking by weight is the most accurate method. I strongly advise buying a kitchen scale if you don't already own one. This will take the guesswork out of the recipes and greatly improve your pastry. In several recipes where a specific amount of salt is required, only a weight measure is given.

Think carefully about what you buy, cook, and eat, and start with fresh, high-quality products, and you will be on the way to eating well in every sense of the word. Basic recipes like the Simple Roast Chicken (page 138) completely depend on the quality of the chicken, the butter, and the herbs. Meat and fat are a product of what the animals eat, so buy the best you can afford—naturally raised animals from small producers often top the quality charts. Get out of the supermarket and shop in markets that sell real food. Most important of all—*cook*.

a model and a warning. As the French youth adopt the bad habits of snacking, eating on the run, and consuming industrial foods laden with hidden fat, guess what? They're gaining weight, too.

We have never been more obsessed with diet, exercise, and cutting the fat out of our food as we are in the new millennium, and never have we been fatter or unhealthier. Our approach to food is schizophrenic: if we enjoy a meal that has a lot of flavor, and therefore fat, we punish ourselves with a salad and a low-fat dressing from a bottle. There is something fundamentally wrong when, in a society of plenty, we fear what is on our plate, seeing our food as a poison (or, alternatively, as a medicine). I would argue that we are not just frightened of fat, but we are also fearful of pleasure. Eating is essential to life, and it is a pleasure that we can share with friends and enjoy in public. It should be a happy experience, not a torturous trial. How did we come to this?

> "And take your father and your households, and come unto me: and I will give you the good of the land of Egypt, and ye shall eat the fat of the land."
>
> GENESIS 45:18

How Fat Lost Its Luster

From the beginning of human history until the middle of the last century the word *fat* had positive connotations. People lived off "the fat of the land" and everybody was happy to receive a "fat paycheck." Fat was valuable and useful. The best meat was well marbled and had a good coating of fat, and only the plumpest chicken was selected for the pot. Fat was an integral part of our diet, and those who didn't eat enough were sickly and often died. People living in extreme conditions, like the Inuit and the Masai, survived only because their food was high in fat. Eating fat and being a little plump was a sign of prosperity and health; no one wanted to be thin.

According to Jean-Anthelme Brillat-Savarin, the early-nineteenth-century French epicure:

> Every thin woman wants to grow plump: that is an avowal which has been made to us a thousand times. Therefore it is in order to pay homage to the all-powerful sex that we are going to try here to tell how to replace with living flesh those pads of silk and cotton which are displayed so profusely in novelty shops, to the obvious horror of the prudish, who pass them by with a shudder, turning away from such shadows with even more care than if it were actuality they looked upon.

How odd Brillat-Savarin's advice sounds to us today, when it seems that everyone is on a diet or watching his or her weight. Fat is no longer seen as valuable, and being plump is considered a health risk. Fat is no longer admired or associated with wealth, and, worse still, the fat in our food is now inexorably linked to the fat on our bodies. So our fear of getting fat makes us choose low-fat meats and eat lean chicken. How our view of fat was turned on its head in just a couple of generations is a complicated story.

One strand of the story is rooted in a concern for our health. In the 1950s, coronary heart disease emerged as a leading cause of death. Scientists searched for reasons to explain this phenomenon, and one hypothesis suggested that the increase in heart disease might be related to the cholesterol levels in our blood. Soon a theory was advanced suggesting that increased consumption of animal fat raised our cholesterol levels and resulted in heart disease. The link between cholesterol, saturated fat, and heart disease was only associative, not causal, and it did not account for the fact that some populations that eat diets high in animal fats (such as the French and the Inuit eating their traditional diet) don't have high rates of heart disease. During the following two decades science failed to prove conclusively that there was any direct connection between eating saturated fats and developing heart disease, but the theory persisted. Then, in 1977, the theory gained widespread credence when the U.S. Congress endorsed it. Americans were urged by no lesser authority than their government to reduce their fat intake for the sake of their health. Thousands of years of human history showing the importance of animal fat in our diet were overlooked, and instead it was labeled the greasy killer. While many experts still promoted a diet including eggs, meat, and animal fat, their voices were drowned out by industry and science. "Low-fat" and "nonfat" became the new mantras, and since none of us wants to die any sooner than is absolutely necessary, we also obediently replaced the cholesterol-containing animal fats in our diet with new, man-made ones.

The first man-made fat was margarine, created in 1869 to replace butter. Although it was cheaper than butter, it wasn't an immediate hit. At the beginning of the twentieth century, lard, tallow, chicken fat, and butter were the top four fats in our kitchens. With the discovery of how to extract oil from plants and the development of the hydrogenation process, the number of industrial fats multiplied, and they became even cheaper (see page 18). These new fats were slow to gain widespread popularity, but the food industry loved them. They were inexpensive and extended the shelf life of baked and fried products, so they were soon incorporated into food products and prepared foods. When animal fat came to be associated with heart disease, these new oils and spreads were marketed as a healthy alternative, and their sales took off. By the end of the twentieth century, not one animal fat made the list of the most popular fats for cooking; they had all been replaced by vegetable oils.

The campaign against animal fat was very successful, and it didn't stop with cooking fats. The obsession with low-fat spread to our meat. We rejected marbled beef, fatty pork, and plump birds, so producers responded by breeding leaner animals. Today few of us can look at a slice of pork belly or consider a well-marbled steak without a pang of guilt or, worse, fear, even though that pork belly and steak are much leaner than they were thirty years ago. We lack the positive flavor memory that fat should trigger. This fear of fat extends to everything—especially butter. Recently scientists announced they have successfully bred a cow to give low-fat milk. Does that mean no more cream or butter?

Fat was also attacked on a second front. Not just bad for our health, fat became socially unacceptable. In North America, we are surrounded by cheap, plentiful food, and since in a society of plenty anybody can get fat, being plump no longer represents wealth. "You can never be too rich or too thin," the Duchess of Windsor is quoted as saying, and being thin has become the new ideal. To be thin is to be beautiful, rich, successful, and powerful, a message reinforced daily by advertising, movies, and the fashion industry. Your weight reveals on which side of the divide you stand: rich or poor, powerful or impotent, with or without self-control. Fat has become entangled not only with health concerns but also with aesthetics, politics, and morals.

Bombarded from all sides by the food industry, medical celebrities, science, the government, and the media, how could we not be convinced? The amount of animal fat in our diet has declined, and we eat less than a quarter of the butter and a fifth of the lard that we ate in 1900, and low-fat proponents claim this is why there are fewer deaths from heart disease today. However, a closer look at the data reveals that it is improved medical care that is responsible for the decline. The actual rates of heart disease haven't abated, and obesity, diabetes, and cancer rates are all on the rise. What went wrong?

Fat Science

The relationship between what we eat and how our bodies react to it is very complex, and it wasn't smart to dismiss thousands of years of empirical evidence. Eating animal fat didn't kill our ancestors, and there is no proof that a low-fat diet improves our health or lengthens our life, let alone makes us beautiful, rich, or powerful. The best computer projections generated by fat researchers reveal that a low-fat diet may add a mere two weeks to our life. Is it worth it? I don't think so, though an existence without flavorful fat would *seem* very long indeed.

We need to rethink our relationship with fat. After decades of low-fat propaganda, most of what we think we know about fat just isn't true:

All animal fats are saturated. Wrong.
Eating fat makes us fat. Wrong.
A low-fat diet is good for us. Wrong.

To understand the role of fat in our food we must understand the science of fat, so here is a very simplified science lesson. All fats are lipids, which is to say they don't dissolve in water: this is why we can skim them off our stock. There is no such thing as a completely saturated or completely unsaturated fat: every fat is a combination of both saturated and unsaturated fatty acids. These fatty acids are simply chains of carbon atoms with pairs of hydrogen atoms attached at each link. If each link in the chain has its two hydrogen atoms, it is a saturated fatty acid; if the chain is missing one pair of hydrogen atoms, it is monounsaturated; and if it is missing two or more pairs of hydrogen atoms, it is polyunsaturated. The location in the chain of the missing hydrogen atoms is important both to scientists and to our bodies. An omega-3 fatty acid is missing its pair of hydrogen atoms three links from the end of its chain. (Since scientists love Greek, and omega is the last letter of the Greek alphabet, you can see why it is called an omega-3 fatty acid.) An omega-6 fatty acid has no hydrogen atoms attached to the sixth link from the end of its chain. These two fatty acids are usually singled out for special mention because they are what are known as essential fatty acids, or EFAs. The body makes other types of fatty acids, but not EFAs, so they must be ingested. The length of the fatty acid's chain is also important. Fatty acids with short and medium chains are quickly metabolized, while the body tends to store fatty acids with longer chains.

Because saturated fatty acids have a chain complete with all its pairs of hydrogen atoms, they are firm at room temperature and very stable. Saturated fatty acids, like stearic acid, a common saturated fatty acid found in beef and lamb fats, are less vulnerable to heat and oxygen and don't turn rancid easily. Monounsaturated fatty acids are softer than saturated fats at room temperature because they are missing a single pair of hydrogen molecules, but they are almost as stable and slow to turn rancid. The most common monounsaturated fatty acid is oleic acid, which is found in pork and beef fats. Polyunsaturated fatty acids have two or more pairs of hydrogen atoms missing from their chains, making them liquid at room temperature. They are very fragile and turn rancid quickly.

"I've been fat and thin so many times in my life. People aren't allowed to be fat anymore. You can be an addict or go to prison, and that's socially acceptable, but being fat? That's not socially acceptable."

SHARON OSBOURNE

The final group of fatty acids is the trans fatty acids. These are the fats everyone is talking about. They are created when liquid or polyunsaturated fatty acids are made solid at room temperature by the addition of hydrogen. These are all man-made, except for the one natural trans fatty acid, conjugated linoleic acid, or CLA, which is found in butter and fat from ruminants. This natural trans fat is good for us, credited with fighting cancer and preventing weight gain and heart disease. CLA was the only trans fat we ate up until the twentieth century, but now we consume huge amounts of man-made trans fatty acids in prepared food products. While it is possible to hydrogenate any fat—lard is sometimes hydrogenated to prolong its shelf life, for example—most of the trans fatty acid we eat is in hydrogenated vegetable oils.

Finally, we need to take a look at cholesterol, because it is always linked to animal fat. Cholesterol is often described as a fatty substance, but it is actually a sterol or type of alcohol found in all animal protein. Our cell membranes and much of our brains are made of cholesterol. Our vital organs need cholesterol to work, and our bodies use it to repair themselves. Cholesterol is important to our health, and recent studies have linked low cholesterol levels with certain diseases, depression, and an increased risk of infection. Our understanding of cholesterol is continually evolving, and the ideal cholesterol level is hotly debated, as is the net effect of dietary cholesterol on blood or serum cholesterol, whether high-density lipoprotein (HDL), the so-called good cholesterol, or low-density lipoprotein (LDL), or "bad" cholesterol.

Why Fat Is Important in the Kitchen

So now we understand that there is no such thing as a completely saturated or unsaturated fat, and that all fats are a combination of the two. Butter contains 50 percent saturated fat, while lard is only 39 percent saturated and duck fat a mere 33 percent. But why should we care about the saturation of fat at all? And why don't we just cook and eat without fat?

Since humans made their first fire, fat has been an important cooking medium. Cooking without fat is very difficult; fat keeps our food succulent in the heat of the oven and stops it from sticking to the pan. Fats that can be heated to high temperatures are indispensable for frying; they make our food appetizingly brown, adding caramelized flavors and a crisp texture. The best fats for all these roles are those higher in saturated and monounsaturated fatty acids because, unlike vegetable oils, which are typically high in polyunsaturated fatty acids, they are stable and don't

"For millennia people have known how to make their food. They have understood animals and what to do with them, have cooked with the seasons and had a farmer's knowledge of the way the planet works. They have preserved traditions of preparing food, handed down through generations, and have come to know them as expressions of their families. People don't have this kind of knowledge today, even though it seems as fundamental as the earth."

BILL BUFORD

turn rancid easily when heated. Fat is also critical to the flavor of our food: without it, meat has no real taste. In addition, without marbling and external fat to baste and tenderize them, lean meats become tough and dry as you cook them. Many aromas and flavors are soluble only in fat, so unless you use fat in your cooking, they are not released. Fat, then, adds, carries, and helps us taste flavor. Fat's molecules are big, round, and smooth and they feel good in our mouth; think of the pleasurable sensation of butter melting on your tongue. Fat is the body's preferred fuel, providing us with more than twice the amount of energy as the same quantity of carbohydrates and protein. It helps the body to absorb nutrients, calcium, and the fat-soluble vitamins A, D, E, and K. Fat and protein are found together in nature because it's the fat that helps us digest the protein, so it makes good sense to eat a well-marbled steak, or a roast chicken with crispy skin. Because fat is digested slowly, eating it leaves us feeling sated, and we're less likely to snack between meals. Eat the right fats and you'll probably lose weight! And, as we all know, fat tastes good. Scientists now believe that we may have a taste receptor for fat and speculate that fat is the sixth taste. Fat may belong alongside salty, sweet, sour, bitter, and umami (a savory taste associated with amino acids, the building blocks of protein), the five tastes that govern the flavor of food.

Whether or not it's the sixth taste, I rest my case: fat is fundamental to the flavor of our food and essential for cooking it. So let's cook our French fries in lard, spread our bread with butter, make our pastry with real animal fats, grill a well-marbled steak, and enjoy them all.

Why Fat Is Good for Our Health

Fat is just as indispensable to our health as it is to our cooking. Every cell in our body needs fat, our brain and hormones rely on fat to function, and fat supports our immune system, fights disease, and protects our liver. Fat promotes good skin and healthy hair, and it regulates our digestive system and leaves us feeling sated. Yet after more than 30 years of reducing our intake of animal fats, we are not healthier, but only heavier. Diets low in fat, it turns out, leave people hungry, depressed, and prone to weight gain and illness. We reduced the animal fat in our diet but increased our intake of sugars and other refined carbohydrates, then were surprised when we got fat. We shouldn't have been. Up until recently, everyone understood that fat and protein were satisfying and starches and sugar made you fat. Animals are fattened for slaughter by feeding them grains, and the same applies to us. Jean-Anthelme Brillat-Savarin, the famed French food writer of the early nineteenth century, once wrote, "The second principal cause of obesity lies in the starches and flours which man uses as the base of his daily nourishment. As we have already stated, all animals who live on farinaceous foods grow fat whether they will or no; man follows the common rule." Dr. Robert Atkins, perhaps the most famous modern proponent of the idea that fat doesn't make you fat, carbohydrates do, became successful advocating a diet based on this old truism.

All fats, however, are not equal. We have reduced our intake of animal fats, but at the same time the total amount of fat in our diet has increased. We have replaced animal fats with man-made hydrogenated fats, which are full of trans fats. These trans fats are difficult for our body to process, so instead it stores them as fat. They adversely affect our cholesterol levels by increasing LDL and lowering HDL, and they interfere with insulin production, promoting diabetes and obesity. It is now understood how dangerous trans fats are, and in 2002 the Institute of Medicine declared that there is no safe level of trans fat in our food.

The other dietary fats we've been using to replace animal fats are polyunsaturated salad and cooking oils. Polyunsaturated fats that are not hydrogenated are very unstable and oxidize easily, especially when heated, so they are not good to cook with. Oxidized fat makes us sick and damages our cells' DNA. Polyunsaturated fatty acids are also dangerous because they suppress our immune system, and our increased consumption of them has affected the balance of the essential fatty acids omega-6 and omega-3 in our bodies. An ideal ratio would be around two to one—twice as much omega-6 as omega-3—but by replacing animal fat with vegetable oils rich in linoleic acid, an omega-6 fatty acid, many of us now consume up to twenty times more omega-6 than omega-3. An excess of omega-6 has been linked to cancer, heart disease, liver damage, learning disorders, weight gain, and malfunction of the immune, digestive, and reproductive systems. While our consumption of omega-6 has skyrocketed, our sources of omega-3 fatty acids are vanishing. Meat and butter from grass-fed animals contain omega-3, but animals raised on a diet high in grains are full of omega-6 fatty acids. Too much omega-6 in our diet also inhibits our intake of omega-3.

In the last hundred years our diet has changed more dramatically than at any other time in our history. As food has become cheaper and more plentiful we've increased our caloric intake, and the sources of those calories have changed radically. We now eat more trans fats, more sugars, more processed foods, and large amounts of vegetable oils. We need to stop and think about what we are eating and why. Animal fat was an important part of our diet until quite recently. Our experiment with reducing it hasn't

"Now, eating little fat although plenty of it is available, and managing—through an aristocratic combination of expense, pride, and self control—not to be fat, has attained the kind of ineffable prestige which was once accrued to soft hands and clean linen. Our sedentary lives and access to various sources of calories have induced us to shudder at the thought of the unctuous and quivering lumps of fat for which Homer's gods lusted. Most of us do eat a lot of grease, but less than a third of it is actually seen and tasted as fat; compound and processed foods effectively disguise the rest."

MARGARET VISSER

1 butter: WORTH IT

What could be better than a slice of fresh bread slathered with butter? Rich, buttery shortbread, perhaps? A fish doused in a bath of brown butter and capers? Or simple pan juices enriched with a swirl of butter? In the kitchen, butter is a tasty and very useful fat. Butter melts at just below body temperature, giving it a luscious sensation on the tongue, and it imparts a rich, creamy taste. Just a little butter adds flavor to everything we eat. Butter is also an excellent flavor carrier: spike it with garlic and herbs or sugar and orange and it delivers those flavors to everything it touches.

Butter is unique in the world of fat. Unlike other animal fats, it doesn't require that we kill an animal to obtain it, and without us it wouldn't exist. But just what *is* butter, exactly? The science behind the transformation of liquid milk into a solid fat is not completely understood. Anyone who has been distracted while whipping cream knows how quickly it can turn to butter. Whipped too long, cream changes from a stable foam into a combination of fatty globules and a watery liquid, or buttermilk. Those fatty globules are not pure fat, but an emulsion of butterfat, water, and milk solids. The fat content of butter is naturally about 82 percent—this is the European standard for butter—although it can range up to 86 percent, depending on the cow and its diet. In North America, butter's minimum fat content is set at 80 percent, so water is often added to lower the butterfat to the legal minimum. What's in the other 20 percent of butter? Mostly water—around 18 percent, which explains the sizzle when butter hits a hot pan—and the rest is milk solids. Those milk solids will burn in the pan if the butter gets too hot, which is why butter is not the best fat for frying.

Butter is a very complex fat, containing more than 500 fatty acids and 400 volatile compounds, all of which determine its flavor. The breed of cow, its diet, and the season all affect the taste, texture, and look of butter. Most of us have forgotten that butter, like many foods, is seasonal.

Like a hot knife through butter

66Leave the butter in the pie crust, but take a smaller piece of pie.99

SHIRLEY O. CORRIHER

13

Butter one's bread
on both sides

**"Guns will make
us powerful; butter will
only make us fat."**
HERMANN GOERING

Love is like butter.
It is good with bread.
(Yiddish)

In spring and early summer, butter is a deeper yellow because the cows eat grass at this time of year, which has a high percentage of orange and yellow carotenes. The pasture is also filled with herbs and flowers, which gives the butter floral and herbal notes. In winter, the cow's diet is supplemented with silage, so the butter is pale, higher in fat, firmer, and milder in taste. There is a direct link between what the cow eats and the flavor of its butter, but most of us have never tasted herbs or flowers in our butter.

Before the advent of refrigeration, butter shipped to towns and cities was highly salted to preserve it, but it still often went rancid and was sometimes adulterated. Only those who lived in the countryside and churned their own enjoyed the taste of fresh butter. Thankfully, our butter is no longer adulterated, since it is highly regulated and mass-produced, but the same system that guarantees a certain standard also results in a uniformity in both the butter's color and (lack of) flavor. Our butter is often frozen for long periods of time and may be months old before reaching the store. Butter's delicate flavor is so easily overwhelmed that most of us don't know what good, fresh butter from grass-fed cows tastes like.

Good butter is smooth, unctuous, and creamy under the knife and bursts with myriad flavors in the mouth. These flavors, which range from clean, delicate, and sweet to tangy, ripe, and complex, are determined by the taste of the cream and how it is handled and churned. Butter made with fresh cream is milder in flavor, so it is often called "sweet." It is not sweet like sugar, but it has none of the tang and depth of cultured butter. Cultured butter is made from ripened cream, or cream that has lactic cultures added before churning, giving the butter a more complex taste that is nutty and mildly acidic. These flavors occurred naturally in butter in the past, before pasteurization, but now they must be added back. The longer the cream is ripened, the more developed the butter's flavor will be. Both sweet and cultured butter can be salted to add taste and to help preserve it. Salt is sometimes also used to mask off tastes. The amount of salt added varies from almost nothing to 3 percent. Salted butter can have a lower fat content than unsalted, and for that reason unsalted butter is often specified in recipes. Higher-fat butters, with their lower water content, are firmer and better for cooking and baking. Using unsalted butter also allows the cook to control the amount of salt added to a recipe. Salted butter is often regarded as inferior, but this is not always true. A small amount of salt, used in what the French call *demi-sel*, or lightly salted, butter, can enhance the flavor of both the butter and whatever is mixed with it. If you doubt it, try lightly salted butter on toast with jam; the way the salt in the butter intensifies the fruit's sweetness is a revelation. There is a long tradition of salted butter in Brittany, the only region of France that uses salted butter exclusively, even for baking and desserts. Salted butter is currently enjoying a renaissance elsewhere, too. It's not just fine sea salt that can be added to butter; large, irregular salt crystals can be folded into the butter at the end of the churning, giving the butter an almost gritty texture. When this butter melts in your mouth or on your fish or potatoes, those salt crystals burst on your tongue, highlighting the butter's taste.

French butter has long been considered the butter benchmark, and several French butters have achieved AOC (Appellation d'Origine Contrôlée) status, like many French wines and cheeses. These butters express what the French call *terroir*, or a unique essence of place, and you can tell them apart by their taste. These AOC butters, which come from the regions of Charentes-Poitou and Normandy, are made using the cream from pasture-fed cows that is ripened for a minimum of twelve hours. The cream is churned slowly in small batches and is often finished by hand, giving the butter a superior flavor and texture. Many gourmets regard Echiré butter, which is still made in wooden churns, as the best butter in the world. The French, however, don't have a monopoly on good butter, and many small producers in other European countries and the United States are producing high-quality, distinctive, and tasty butter.

Rich, fatty, and full of calories and cholesterol, butter hasn't received any good press in a long time. Butter is a mainly saturated fat (see below), and unless it is clarified (see page 23), it is less useful for cooking than other mainly saturated fats because of its milk solids. Although those milk solids limit the usefulness of butter for cooking, they are the reason butter is such a flavorful fat. Many of butter's saturated fatty acids are short- and medium-chain ones, which means our body uses them up quickly rather than storing them on our hips. Many of butter's fatty acids are also very good for us: lauric and butyric acids boost our immune system, while stearic and palmitic acids lower our LDL cholesterol. Butter contains the fat-soluble vitamins A, D, E, and K, plus copper, zinc, chromium, selenium, iodine, and lecithin, so butter is actually good for us.

> "Werther made butter poetical. It was while watching Charlotte buttering bread for the children that he was overcome by that fatal passion which ended with a pistol shot. Goethe was right; children like nothing as much as buttered bread, except if it is bread and jam."
>
> ALEXANDRE DUMAS

Fat	% Saturated	% Monounsaturated	% Polyunsaturated
BUTTER	50	30	4

Note: These figures are approximate and vary with the breed and diet of the cow. The numbers don't total 100, since butter also contains water and milk solids.

To enjoy the benefits of butter you must eat the best you can buy. Good butter not only tastes better, but it is better for you. Butter from pasture-fed cows has omega-3 fatty acids, which we need more of in our diet. Butter has the natural trans fat conjugated linoleic acid (CLA), which behaves like omega-3 fatty acid in our body and is reputed to protect against heart disease, cancer, and weight gain. Butter shouldn't taste only of fat, but also of what the cows ate. We should be able to savor the grass, the herbs, and the flowers. While we are all willing to spend a small fortune on deluxe olive oils, we grab a pound of butter without thinking.

Next time you eat butter, really taste it. Cut a thick slice, smell it, and place it on your tongue. Let it melt in your mouth and savor its taste. Remember how special butter is in the world of fat.

Keeping and Using Butter

To fall on your ass in butter: to strike it rich or be lucky (Dutch)

Whether salted or not, butter is perishable, and it begins to slowly deteriorate from the moment it is made. Although it is mainly saturated fat, which tends to turn rancid more slowly, those milk solids in butter speed up the process.

Freshly churned butter once had a cachet, and many food lovers went to extreme lengths to make sure they could enjoy it daily. In Normandy, butter was churned very early every morning, then rushed to the breakfast tables of discriminating and no doubt late-rising Parisians. Today, you probably won't be able to taste truly fresh butter unless you know someone who makes his or her own butter or you churn it yourself (see page 21).

If you take the cow's milk and butter, you must accept her kicks, too. (Indian)

Homemade or not, your butter should be refrigerated and well wrapped to protect it from light and any strong odors. Butter will absorb any odors that are circulating in your refrigerator. If your refrigerator is full of truffles from Périgord, you'll end up with truffle-flavored butter, which would be great, unless you were planning to bake shortbread. As for using the butter compartment in your refrigerator: don't. By keeping the butter at a warmer temperature than the rest of the refrigerator and exposing it to oxygen, it just speeds up the butter's decline. Butter can, however, be frozen.

A History of Butter

Humans have been eating butter for a very long time. The domestication of goats, sheep, and cows began in Mesopotamia and Romania sometime between 9000 and 8000 B.C. Although these animals were initially raised for their meat, those keeping them no doubt quickly learned how to use their milk. The leap from herding animals for meat to milking them is a big one, however, and no one is sure exactly when it happened.

Sumerian temple friezes from 2500 B.C. depict scenes of butter churning, so it has generally been accepted that butter is at least 4,500 years old. However, science has recently proved that butter is even older than that. Traces of butterfat found on pottery fragments have been dated to 4000 B.C., proving humans have been making butter for at least 6,000 years. There is no way to know how butter was first discovered, and its genesis is part of food folklore. A popular legend relates how a traveler carrying milk arrived at his journey's end not with the thick, creamy milk he'd started with, but a thin, watery liquid full of lumps of fat. His bumpy journey had churned his milk into butter. While butter's discovery was probably just such a lucky accident, it was also a momentous one. That a liquid could be transformed into a solid bestowed on butter a very special status. From its very beginnings butter was never simply a food; it was also considered a formidable medicine and a useful cosmetic. Many thought it had magical powers and was a worthy sacrifice to the gods.

Although butter keeps longer than milk does, it is still highly perishable, especially in warmer climates. Ever resourceful, humans discovered they could prolong butter's life by cooking or salting it. In India and the Middle East, butter was heated and the milk solids removed, preventing it from turning rancid. In India, ghee is as important for its role in religious ceremonies as it is as a food. Around the Mediterranean, where other fats and oil were available for cooking, butter was often reserved for external use. In fact, in many cultures the idea of eating butter was ridiculous; it was considered something only a barbarian would do. In his *Natural History*, Pliny discusses butter's medicinal properties and refers to it as "the most delicate food among barbarous nations" (though he points out that it is not something a Roman would eat). The majority of people who ate their butter in its solid state lived in the cooler climes of northern Europe and the grasslands of Central Asia, where butter lasted better and the abundant pastures provided food for the animals. The Vikings and Celts who spread butter culture throughout northern

"Du beurre! Donnes-moi du beurre! Toujours du beurre!"
FERNAND POINT

Butter spoils no meat. (Danish)

butter   17

Europe also valued butter's medicinal qualities, and their word for "butter" and "ointment" was the same. Even though butter kept longer in northern Europe, it still went rancid, and there was a continual search for ways to prolong its freshness. By 1000 B.C. the Celts were mining salt in Central Europe and realized that adding salt helped their butter keep, while those living in Ireland, Scotland, and Scandinavia preserved their butter by burying it in peat bogs (see page 35).

Eating butter created a rough divide across Europe, with butter lovers to the north and butter skeptics to the south. Although we might think of butter as a luxury item, it was for a long time considered peasant food, especially among northern Europeans, who were prodigious butter eaters. Readily available, butter was ignored by the nobility, who had good supplies of meat. Early cookery books reveal butter's lowly status; in an edition of Taillevent's *Le Viandier*, dated 1450, fewer than 2 percent of the recipes contain butter, and lard is the preferred fat. The growth of a middle class in the fifteenth century boosted butter consumption, as did the Reformation, one result of which was that butter was no longer banned during Lent or on fast days. Butter appeared in a third of the recipes published in sixteenth-century cookery books, and by the nineteenth century it had become the basic building block of classic French cuisine. As butter's culinary status grew, it ceased being a peasant food and was commandeered by the rich.

Northern Europeans took their love of butter with them to the New World. North Americans, South Africans, Australians, and New Zealanders all developed a love of butter that was supported by vast grasslands. A French traveler to America in the 1900s remarked, somewhat disgustedly, that everything was served with a sauce of melted butter.

Since the turn of the last century, however, butter has been under siege, first by fake fats, and then by the fear that it would kill us. Butter consumption in North America dropped from around 18 pounds / 8 kg per person at the turn of the twentieth century to a mere $4^1/2$ pounds / 2 kg today.

Butter is unique, not only in its taste, but also in how it is made. No matter how we try, we cannot replicate it.

Margarine

Just as nineteenth-century French chefs were creating a classic cuisine based on butter, one of their fellow countrymen was busy inventing margarine. During the middle of the century a cattle plague had swept

Fine words butter no parsnips.

To promise more butter than bread: to promise the best (French)

Let there be ghee and sugar in your mouth: said in reply to a compliment or to say you hope something comes true (Hindi)

To look as if butter wouldn't melt in one's mouth

through Europe, making butter scarce and expensive, and so the French navy was looking for a substance to replace butter on long sea voyages. They required a cheap fat that was high in calories and would not turn rancid. Napoleon III offered a prize for the invention of a butter substitute. The winner was the French chemist Hippolyte Mège-Mouriés, who had already been awarded the Légion d'honneur for improving the French army's bread yield. In 1869 Mège-Mouriés was granted a patent for *"certain corps gras d'origine animale,"* or margarine. This new fat, which had a butterlike texture, was pale in color and was made from an unappetizing combination of chopped sheep's stomach, suet, cow's udders, potassium carbonate, water, and some milk for flavor. It was not the first attempt at creating a butter substitute, but it was, despite the list of ingredients, apparently the first palatable one. Mège-Mouriés named his invention oleomargarine, believing that it contained a substance called "margaric acid"—which was itself a misnomer. Another Frenchman, Michel Chevreul, had identified a pearly colored substance in animal fat in 1813. Believing it to be a new fatty acid, he called it margaric acid, after the Greek word for pearl, *maragon*. He was wrong—his margaric acid was not new, but simply a combination of stearic and palmitic acids—however, the name "margarine" stuck.

In 1870, the Franco-Prussian War broke out, making it impossible for Mège-Mouriés to capitalize on his invention, so he sold the patent to the world's leading butter producers of the day, the Dutch. Perhaps he also realized that his fellow countrymen would never replace their delicious butter with his invention. This new oleomargarine was cheap to make, and by 1880 large amounts were being produced in Europe and the United States. In his *Life on the Mississippi*, Mark Twain recorded the following conversation overheard on a Mississippi river boat:

> "Now as to this article," said Cincinnati, slashing into the ostensible butter and holding forward a slab of it on his knife-blade, "it's from our house; look at it—smell of it—taste it. Put any test on it you want to. Take your own time—no hurry—make it thorough. There now—what do you say? Butter, ain't it. Not by a thundering sight—it's oleomargarine! Yes, sir, that's what it is—oleomargarine. You can't tell it from butter; by George, an EXPERT can't. It's from our house. We supply most of the boats in the West; there's hardly a pound of butter on one of them.
>
> We are crawling right along—JUMPING right along is the word. We are going to have that entire trade. Yes, and the hotel trade, too. You are going to see the day, pretty soon, when you can't find an ounce of butter to bless yourself with, in any hotel in the Mississippi

As easy to get butter out of a dog's mouth as money out of a lawyer

The Dutch were called butter boxes or butter mouths by the English because of their love of butter and their habit of always traveling with their own box of butter.

and Ohio Valleys, outside of the biggest cities. Why, we are turning out oleomargarine NOW by the thousands of tons. And we can sell it so dirt-cheap that the whole country has GOT to take it—can't get around it you see. Butter don't stand any show—there ain't any chance for competition. Butter's had its DAY—and from this out, butter goes to the wall. There's more money in oleomargarine than— why, you can't imagine the business we do. I've stopped in every town from Cincinnati to Natchez; and I've sent home big orders from every one of them."

So useless he couldn't put a dent in a pack of butter (Dutch)

You didn't invent the tool for cutting butter: you're not that smart (French)

Twain's businessman was overly optimistic; although margarine was cheaper than butter, butter's flavor kept it popular. At the beginning of the twentieth century, French and German scientists developed a method to solidify oil called hydrogenation. Vegetable oils could now replace the animal fat in margarine, making this new oleomargarine even cheaper and giving it a longer shelf life. While this made it popular with food manufacturers, it was still slow to catch on with consumers, and the powerful dairy industry lobbied hard against it, preventing manufacturers from coloring margarine to improve its unappetizingly pale color and persuading the government to tax this new product. It took the butter rationing imposed during the two world wars to convince people to try it again. The abolition of the ban on coloring and the promotion of margarine as a "healthy" alternative to butter boosted sales, and North Americans eventually embraced margarine. From the mid-1960s until the early 1990s, they ate up to three times more margarine than butter.

Today the dangers of hydrogenated fats are better understood, and margarine consumption has dropped. Work is being done to solidify oils without creating trans fats, which interests food manufacturers, who, just like the French navy, want a fat that is cheap and won't turn rancid. Margarine's high water content, however, makes it of little use in the kitchen, and the few calories you may save when spreading it on your toast do not compensate for its lack of taste.

Homemade Butter

The simple act of making butter will give you an insight into the magical transformation of cream into butter and show you just how good very fresh butter can taste. Unlike Alexandre Dumas, you won't need a horse (see quotation at right)—just an electric mixer, a sieve, and the best cream you can lay your hands on. Whipping cream with 35 percent butterfat will work, but if you can get cream with a higher fat content, it will produce a richer butter.

Pour the cream into a bowl of a stand mixer and let it warm up to about 60°F / 15°C. Using the whisk attachment, whip the cream on medium-low speed. The cream will thicken, become stiff, and then start to break down. After 7 to 15 minutes, depending on the cream, it will separate into a milky liquid and globules of fat, and the latter will collect on the whisk. Stop whisking.

Remove the pieces of butter from the whisk and place them in a fine-mesh sieve. Strain the liquid from the bowl through the sieve. This liquid is true buttermilk, and you can drink it. Rinse the pieces of butter under cold running water until the water runs clear. This rinses off the remaining whey, which could turn the butter rancid.

Using your hands, squeeze the butter hard to remove the excess water. Place it on a work surface and knead it with your hands and a dough scraper to remove any remaining water.

If you prefer salted butter, work the salt into the soft butter with your hands. Using your hands, shape the butter as you like, wrap it well, and refrigerate. The butter will keep for up to a week.

Makes about 3/4 cup / 6 ounces / 175 g

2 cups / 500 ml good-quality high-fat whipping cream

1/2 teaspoon / 0.17 ounce / 5 g fine sea salt (optional)

"In a few countries where I have traveled, I have always had freshly made butter, made on the day itself. Here for the benefit of travelers, is my recipe; it is very simple, and at the same time foolproof.

Wherever I could find cow's or camel's milk, mare's milk, goat's milk, particularly goat's milk, I got some. I filled a bottle three quarters full, I stoppered it up and hung it around the neck of my horse. I left the rest up to the horse. In the evening, when I arrived, I broke the neck of the bottle and found, within, a piece of butter the size of a fist which had virtually made itself."

ALEXANDRE DUMAS

Clarified Butter

Clarified butter, also called drawn butter, is often served with steamed lobster as a dipping sauce. Much of butter's flavor is in the milk solids, so don't throw them away. Instead, add them to vegetables, rice, or any dish in which you would use butter.

Cut the butter into small pieces and place them in a small, heavy saucepan over very low heat. Once the butter has melted, skim any foam from the surface.

Remove the pan from the heat and let the melted butter stand for 5 minutes. The butter should separate into a clear golden liquid and white milk solids, which will fall to the bottom of the pan.

Carefully strain the golden liquid through a fine-mesh sieve lined with a double layer of cheesecloth into a clean glass jar, leaving the milk solids behind. When cool, cover the container and store the clarified butter in the refrigerator.

Makes $3/4$ cup / 6 ounces / 175 g

1 cup / $1/2$ pound / 225 g unsalted butter

"If you are afraid of butter, as many people are nowadays, just put in cream."

JULIA CHILD

CLARIFIED BUTTER AND USILI GHEE

I used to lump clarified butter and ghee together, thinking that they were the same thing, but I was wrong. Although the two terms are often used interchangeably, and they both begin with melted butter, they are actually quite different.

Because butter isn't a pure fat, it will burn at the relatively low temperature of 250°F / 121°C. To remedy this, butter can be clarified, or melted over low heat, so that it separates into butterfat and milk solids. When the butterfat is poured off, leaving the milk solids behind, this clarified butter can be heated to a higher temperature. It also keeps better than regular butter does. However, much of butter's distinctive flavor is in those leftover milk solids, so clarified butter doesn't have the same taste as melted butter.

Although butter keeps better than raw milk does, it still spoils quickly in hot weather. This is why butter made in warmer climates has traditionally been clarified. (Both clarified butter and ghee can be kept without refrigeration, but they have a longer life if refrigerated.) Originally made with water-buffalo butter, most ghee today comes from cow's-milk butter. The Indians have a long history of making ghee, and it has played an important role in their culture and religion. The Indus-Saraswati civilization (2600–1700 B.C.) was renowned for the quality of its rich, cream-colored buffalo ghee and the beauty of its copper artifacts created by their skilled craftsmen. Their ghee was exported as far as Oman in exchange for the copper, the raw material for their art. In the Rig Veda, the oldest Hindu Veda, dating from around 1500 B.C., there is a hymn praising ghee, while another Veda describes rivers of ghee flowing to heaven. The Vedas refer to ghee as a source of strength and an excellent food for the brain, so it is common practice for Indians to give their babies and young children a daily spoonful of ghee to ensure their health and intelligence.

Ghee is not only considered brain food, but it is also thought to have the power to redeem sinners. It plays an important part in many religious ceremonies, and it is often poured onto funeral pyres and burned in temple lamps. Ghee, especially aged ghee, is reputed to have healing properties. Ghee can be stored for very long periods of time; *kumbhaghrta* ghee can be anywhere from 10 to 100 years old, while *mahaghtra* ghee is over 100 years old. According to the Hindu religion, any food cooked in ghee becomes complete and pure, or *pukka*. This has a practical application in the complicated Hindu caste system, as it allows a person of higher caste to eat food cooked by a lower-caste person as long as the food is cooked in ghee. Ghee is also linked to fertility and sexual power: in Hindu wedding ceremonies the male guests attempt to prove their virility by eating large amounts of ghee.

Ghee—correctly called *usili* ghee to differentiate it from *vanaspati* ghee, which is made from vegetable oil—begins like clarified butter. The butter is melted, but then it is cooked so that the water is boiled off and the milk solids turn brown. As a result, ghee can be heated to an even higher temperature than clarified butter can be, around 375°F / 190°C, and it keeps longer. Ghee also has more flavor than clarified butter, since the brown milk solids infuse the ghee with their characteristic nutty flavor. The browning of the milk solids creates antioxidants that help delay rancidity. Sometimes herbs and spices, such as mint, curry leaves, chile, fresh ginger, cumin, cardamom, and cloves, are cooked with the butter to impart extra flavor. After the ghee is poured off, the browned milk solids are kept to flavor rice, breads, and desserts.

In other warm climates, such as the Middle East and North Africa, butter is also clarified to prevent it from turning rancid. In the Middle East it is called *samneh*, *samn*, or *samna*, and in North Africa, *smen*. It, too, can be flavored with herbs and spices. Further south, in Ethiopia, they make a spiced clarified butter called *nit'r k'ibe* (see page 25).

Paula Wolfert, in her *Couscous and Other Good Food from Morocco*, describes how *smen*, which is often kept buried in jars, acquires a strong smell and a taste similar to that of Gorgonzola cheese. This aged butter is often brought out for special occasions, but it was not appreciated by early English travelers to the region, who described *smen* as rancid and nauseating.

Ghee

Makes about 3/4 cup /
6 ounces / 175 g

1 cup / 1/2 pound / 225 g
unsalted butter

All is not butter that comes
from the cow. (Italian)

Although ghee is available at Indian grocery stores, it is very simple to make yourself. The milk solids left over from making ghee are particularly tasty, so save them to add to rice and vegetable dishes.

Cut the butter into small pieces and place them in a small, heavy saucepan over low heat. Once the butter has melted, increase the heat just until the butter simmers. As the butter simmers, a layer of white foam will form on the top and the butter will bubble and spit as the water boils off. After about 10 minutes the spitting and bubbling will stop.

Now the milk solids on the bottom of the pan will begin to color. Watch the butter carefully at this point, using a spoon to push aside the foam to check the color of the milk solids. When they turn brown and you smell a sweet, nutty aroma, remove the pan from the heat and let it stand for 10 minutes, allowing the flavor of the browned milk solids to infuse the ghee.

Carefully strain the ghee through a fine-mesh sieve lined with a double layer of cheesecloth into a clean glass jar, leaving the browned milk solids behind. When cool, cover the jar and keep the ghee refrigerated for up to 6 months. It can also be frozen.

To butter up: to flatter excessively

Spiced Ethiopian Butter

I admit my knowledge of African cuisine is pretty much limited to the Mediter-ranean coast. However, my quest for butter recipes led me to this Ethiopian spiced butter. I met Marcus Samuelsson, the well-known Ethiopian-born New York chef, at a food event in Michigan and discovered he loved oxtail. He had just written a book on African cuisine, and this is a riff on his recipe for nit'r k'ibe, Ethiopian-style spiced butter. I use it to flavor rice and steamed vegetables and cook my Cape Malay–Style Lamb Shoulder (page 197), and my husband brushes it on his grilled corn. Like any clarified butter, it keeps well.

Cut the butter into small pieces and place them in a small, heavy saucepan over low heat. Once the butter has melted, add the shallot, garlic, ginger, cardamom, cinnamon, clove, oregano, and turmeric. Increase the heat just until the butter simmers. A layer of orange foam will form on the top, and the butter will bubble and spit as the water from the butter, shallot, and ginger boils off. After about 10 minutes the spitting and bubbling will stop.

Continue to simmer the butter and spices gently, stirring and scraping the bottom of the pan often. Watch the color of the milk solids: when you see brown flecks at the bottom of the pan or in the foam, remove the pan from the heat and set aside to allow the milk solids and spices to settle.

Carefully strain the butter through a fine-mesh sieve lined with a double layer of cheesecloth into a clean glass jar, leaving the solids behind. Discard the solids. When the butter is cool, cover and refrigerate for up to 6 months. It can also be frozen.

Makes about 3/4 cup / 6 ounces / 175 g

1 cup / 1/2 pound / 225 g unsalted butter

1 shallot, chopped

2 cloves garlic, peeled and crushed

1 tablespoon peeled, finely chopped fresh ginger

4 cardamom pods, crushed

One 3-inch / 7.5-cm cinnamon stick, broken into pieces

1 clove

1/2 teaspoon dried oregano

1/4 teaspoon ground turmeric

BUTTER MUSLIN

A simple fine-weave natural cotton material, cheesecloth, also known as butter muslin, is very useful in the kitchen. Its advantage over paper towels is that it won't disintegrate when wet, and it is reusable.

Flavored Butters

Remember flavored butter? In the 1970s garlic butter was so popular that everyone was slicing baguette-shaped "French" bread, spreading it with garlic butter, and then baking it in the oven, or melting maître d'hôtel (parsley butter) over every steak. Of course, flavored butter predates the 1970s, and my 1961 Larousse Gastronomique *has more than forty different recipes. Simple to make—just soften the butter and add the flavorings—flavored butters deserve to be restored to our culinary repertoire. There is an endless variety of options, including garlic, chile, herbs, anchovy, lemon, lime, and foie gras (see page 159). Flavored butters can even be sweet (see page 27).*

To make a basic flavored butter, add 4 rinsed anchovy fillets, or $1\frac{1}{2}$ tablespoons of chopped herbs, or 1 tablespoon of blue cheese to $\frac{1}{4}$ cup / 2 ounces / 60 g of softened unsalted butter. Add some lemon juice or zest, a teaspoon of Dijon mustard, and season with salt and pepper (omit the salt if you're using anchovies). Combine all the ingredients in a small bowl and blend with a fork until they are thoroughly mixed.

Shape the butter into a roll using parchment paper and then refrigerate until firm. I prefer to make smaller amounts of flavored butters and use them up, but you can easily double these recipes and freeze them. The slices can be placed on grilled meats, fish, and chicken, or added to vegetables. Flavored butter can also be swirled into a sauce or added to soup; in short, use it anywhere you'd use butter.

PORCINI BUTTER

Makes about $\frac{1}{2}$ cup / 4 ounces / 115 g

$\frac{1}{2}$ ounce / 15 g dried porcini mushrooms

$\frac{1}{2}$ cup / 125 ml boiling water

$\frac{1}{3}$ cup / $2\frac{1}{2}$ ounces / 75 g unsalted butter, softened

Fine sea salt and freshly ground black pepper

A squeeze of lemon juice

I like to serve this strongly flavored butter on crackers or bread, sometimes topped with shavings of aged Comté cheese, but it also goes well with a grilled steak or an omelet. Try stirring it into sautéed mushrooms or mushroom soup just before serving, or toss it with pasta.

Place the mushrooms in a small bowl. Cover with the boiling water and leave to soak for 1 hour.

Remove the mushrooms from the water and squeeze out the liquid. Strain the soaking liquid through a fine-mesh sieve lined with a double layer of cheesecloth, discarding any sediment and dirt. Set the liquid aside and chop the squeezed mushrooms finely.

Melt 1 tablespoon of the butter in a small frying pan over medium heat. When the butter is hot, add the chopped mushrooms and season with salt and pepper. Lower the heat and cook gently, stirring, until you can smell the mushrooms and they begin to stick to the pan. Add the strained soaking liquid and continue cooking, stirring, until most of the liquid has evaporated and the mushrooms are moist and shiny but not dry. Remove from the heat and set aside to cool.

Blend the mushroom mixture into the remaining softened butter, add a squeeze of lemon juice, and taste, adjusting the seasoning if necessary. Cover and refrigerate.

RADISH BUTTER

I never liked radishes until I went to France. There I discovered elongated pale pink radishes with white bottoms. Milder than the big, bright, red ones I was familiar with, they inspired love at first bite. I also like the French habit of eating them with butter and salt as a starter. I tried serving radishes with butter and salt with drinks before dinner, but it was too messy trying to dip them in the salt and eat them with buttered bread, so I turned them into a spread.

To make this I use the two-toned radishes often called French breakfast radishes, which are about half the size of my pinkie. You can use the big, bad peppery ones if you like, but you'll need less; $^{1}/_{2}$ cup of chopped radishes should be about the right amount.

Spread the butter on thin slices of baguette or crackers to serve as an appetizer, or use when making sandwiches. It's especially good with an egg, smoked fish, or salty ham filling.

Trim the radishes and place them in the small bowl of a food processor. Add the leaves. Process until very finely chopped. Add the butter and process until well blended, scraping down the sides of the bowl as necessary. Add the salt and lemon juice and process again.

The finished butter will be slightly chunky and more like a spread than a butter. Cover and refrigerate for several hours before serving.

Makes about $^{1}/_{2}$ cup / 4 ounces / 115 g

15 French breakfast radishes

6 radish leaves (optional)

3 tablespoons unsalted butter, softened

$^{1}/_{2}$ teaspoon fleur de sel (see below)

A squeeze of lemon juice

RUM BUTTER

Flavored butters don't have to be savory. This rum-flavored one, usually served with Traditional Christmas Pudding (page 211), can also be made with brandy. You need a high-quality aged rum for this recipe, preferably the same rum you use to set your pudding alight. This butter isn't restricted to plum pudding, however. Serve it with hot waffles and pancakes, or just spread it on bread for a snack. You can also use it to sauté fruit such as apple slices.

Combine the butter, sugar, and rum in a bowl and, using a wooden spoon, mix until well blended. Transfer to a serving dish and refrigerate until ready to use.

Makes about $^{1}/_{2}$ cup / 4 ounces / 115 g

$^{1}/_{3}$ cup / $2^{1}/_{2}$ ounces / 75 g unsalted butter, softened

$^{1}/_{3}$ cup / $1^{1}/_{2}$ ounces / 40 g confectioners' (icing) sugar

2 tablespoons aged rum

This is the French name for the first harvest of salt produced in the coastal regions of France by evaporating seawater in a series of ponds. Harvested by hand, *fleur de sel* is prized for its crunchy texture and delicate taste. Full of minerals, this expensive salt is used only as a condiment, not for cooking. The most famous *fleur de sel* comes from the salt marshes of Guérande and the islands of Noirmoutier and Ré.

FLEUR DE SEL

Browned Butter Sauce

Makes about 1/2 cup / 125 ml

1/2 cup / 4 ounces / 115 g unsalted butter

2 tablespoons freshly squeezed lemon juice

2 tablespoons chopped flat-leaf parsley

Sea salt and freshly ground black pepper

Traditionally this sauce accompanies pan-fried sole, but there is no need to limit it to fish. It also makes an excellent sauce for vegetables, such as asparagus, broccoli, and steamed potatoes, and of course it's delicious on pasta (see page 33).

Cut the butter into small pieces and place them in a frying pan over low heat. When the butter is melted, increase the heat to medium and cook until the milk solids start to brown and you smell a nutty aroma.

Remove the pan from the heat, add the lemon juice (the butter will bubble and spit), and stir to combine. Stir in the parsley, season with salt and pepper, and serve immediately.

VARIATION To make an excellent sauce for poached skate, brains, or eggs, replace the lemon juice with red or white wine vinegar and add 2 tablespoons of chopped, rinsed salt-packed capers.

BROWN AND BLACK BUTTER

Making brown butter is similar to making ghee. You cook the butter until the milk solids caramelize and turn golden brown, but you don't strain them out. The caramelized milk solids give the butter its characteristic nutty aroma and flavor, which is why it's called *beurre noisette*, or hazelnut butter, in French. Often a little lemon juice is added at the end to stop the cooking and balance out the richness. Black butter, *beurre noir*, is not really black at all: if you cooked the butter until the milk solids blackened, it would be acrid. Instead, black butter is simply brown butter cooked for a few seconds longer and finished with capers and vinegar. It is helpful to have a bowl of ice water near the stove that you can dip the base of your pan into to stop the butter from turning too dark. Browned butter is more than just a sauce. With its nutty flavor it makes a great salad dressing (see page 29), and you can add it anywhere you'd add butter for depth and richness. Don't limit brown butter to savory dishes. It shines in Brown Butter Ice Cream (page 50) and Burnt Butter Biscuits (page 52).

Double Butter Salad

Popular in Flanders, the region in southern Belgium where they love butter, this dressing gets its luscious texture and nutty taste from browned butter. And the perfect lettuce for this dressing? Butter lettuce, of course! Boston and Bibb are both "butter lettuces," and although they are sweet and delicate, I am not sure why they merit the name. I don't find them buttery in any way. This dressing, however, will remedy that, and its lack of acidity will help preserve the lettuce's soft leaves. This lettuce must be at room temperature before dressing the salad; cold leaves will cause the butter to set.

Rinse the lettuce leaves and spin dry. Place them in a salad bowl and allow them to reach room temperature.

Cut the butter into pieces and place them in a small frying pan over low heat. When the butter is melted, increase the heat to medium and cook until the butter begins to brown. Remove the pan from the heat, add the vinegar (the butter will bubble and spit), and stir, scraping the bottom of the pan to incorporate all the browned bits. Stir in the chives and season with a little salt and lots of pepper.

Let the dressing cool slightly, then pour over the lettuce leaves. Toss well and serve the salad immediately.

VARIATION Try this dressing on steamed asparagus, warm potato salad, and grilled or sautéed vegetables.

Serves 4

1 small head Boston or
2 heads Bibb lettuce

$1/4$ cup / 2 ounces / 60 g
unsalted butter

1 tablespoon cider vinegar

1 tablespoon chopped chives

Sea salt and freshly ground
black pepper

To have one's bread
buttered for life

When the Japanese first encountered Europeans, they were disgusted by their smell. Europeans ate large amounts of animal fat, giving them a different body odor, which the Japanese found very offensive. Believing butter was the cause, the Japanese derisively called all Europeans *bata-kusai*, or butter stinkers. During the last century the term *bata-kusai* was also used pejoratively in Japan to describe people or objects that were obnoxiously Western in style. With the rise and acceptance of American culture, however, the term has dropped out of common usage.

BUTTER STINKERS

Spicy Buttered Popcorn

Makes 8 cups / 1.75 l

8 cups / 1.75 l popped popcorn

1 cup / 180 g firmly packed brown sugar

$1/2$ cup / 4 ounces / 115 g butter

2 tablespoons corn syrup

$1/2$ teaspoon fine sea salt

3 tablespoons puréed chipotle peppers in adobo sauce

$1/2$ teaspoon baking soda

Popcorn at the movies was ruined when they replaced the real butter with that odd-tasting "butter-flavored" topping. Popcorn really has no flavor, and it's only made edible with butter and salt, or, even better, with a flavored butter. This spicy-sweet popcorn is my version of a savory snack served at a popular Toronto tapas bar to accompany pre-dinner drinks.

Preheat the oven to 250°F / 120°C. Line a rimmed baking sheet with parchment paper and spread the popcorn on the paper. Set aside.

Combine the sugar, butter, corn syrup, and salt in a saucepan and place over medium-low heat. Stir until the butter and sugar melt and the mixture comes to a boil. Stop stirring and boil until it reaches 250°F / 120°C on a kitchen thermometer. Remove the pan from the heat and stir in the chipotle peppers and baking soda.

Pour the mixture over the popcorn, and stir with a spatula until the popcorn is evenly coated.

Bake the popcorn for 35 minutes, stirring 2 or 3 times. Let cool and store in an airtight container.

MAFIA BUTTER

Ever since butter was first sold it has been subject to tampering. Marigolds, carrot juice, and annatto were all added to improve its color, while lard and water were incorporated to make it go further. Today butter for sale is highly regulated, but it is still not immune from tampering.

Between 1997 and 1999 more than 16,000 tons of adulterated butter were distributed in Europe. Most of this "butter" contained no milk products whatsoever and was made instead from a mixture of tallow, animal carcasses, chemicals, and petroleum by-products, and some of it posed a real health risk to the consumer. Through a combination of bribery and threats, a Neapolitan mafia family, the Camorra, had taken control of one of Italy's largest butter manufacturers and produced this cheap fake butter. The scam gave them access to the generous agricultural subsidies paid by the European Economic Union.

Buttered Eggs

Serves 4

$1/3$ cup / $2^{1}/_{2}$ ounces / 75 g
unsalted butter, softened

2 slices cooked bacon, diced

1 tablespoon chopped chives

4 eggs

Freshly ground black pepper

Fleur de sel (see page 27)

Shirring eggs, or cooking them in individual ramekins, is a great method that has almost been forgotten. This simple method makes it easy to cook a large number of eggs at once. In this recipe the eggs are cooked in a bath of herb butter spiked with bacon. It makes a perfect breakfast dish and also a great appetizer.

For breakfast I serve shirred eggs with fingers of crisp toast (toast soldiers, as I called them as a child). For dinner, accompany the eggs with some just cooked asparagus, which are great for dipping into the eggs in their ramekins.

Preheat the oven to 350°F / 180°C.

Use about $1/2$ teaspoon of the butter to grease four $1/2$-cup / 125-ml ovenproof ramekins.

Place the remaining butter in a bowl and blend in the bacon and chives. Break an egg into each ramekin and then divide the bacon butter among the ramekins. Season each egg well with pepper.

Place the ramekins in an ovenproof baking dish, then fill the dish with enough hot water to come halfway up the sides of the ramekins.

Bake the eggs until the whites are barely set and the yolks are just beginning to cloud, about 15 minutes. Look at the edge of the ramekins to see if the whites are set (the layer of melted butter can make it look as if they aren't set yet). The eggs will continue to cook in the warm ramekins. Transfer the ramekins to individual plates and serve with the *fleur de sel*.

Butter and egg man:
a wealthy but unsophisti-
cated man who spends
his money freely

BUTTERED EGGS

When most people think of buttered eggs, they think of fresh eggs gently cooked in lots of butter, seasoned with salt and pepper and perhaps some fresh herbs. But butter was once used to preserve eggs as well as cook them. A layer of butter or fat on foods forms a seal that prevents contact with the air, providing protection against light, oxygen, and bacteria. In southern Ireland, around the city of Cork, freshly laid eggs used to be rolled in butter while they were still warm. The butter was absorbed into the shell, and as the egg cooled it formed a protective coating, stopping the air from passing through. The eggs could be stored in a cool place for up to six months, ensuring a supply through the winter, when the hens laid fewer eggs. Not only did the butter preserve the eggs, but it also imbued them with flavor. Now *those* eggs would make wonderful buttered eggs!

Spaghetti with Butter and Sage

Travel both broadens the mind and opens up new culinary horizons. I love trying new dishes when I travel, and before each holiday I usually compile a long list of restaurants and foods to try. Once when my husband and I were in Italy, we made a last-minute decision to stop in the Tuscan town of Arezzo. It was lunchtime and I didn't have the name of even one restaurant to try! My husband has a skill of picking good restaurants without a guidebook, and he did it again. We ate spaghetti alla burro e salvia, *spaghetti with butter and sage, and it totally changed my opinion of this herb. I had always thought of sage as a rather musty herb, good for stuffing poultry but not much else. However, cooked in butter, sage loses its characteristic wooliness, turns crisp, and impregnates the butter with its sweet flavor. Great on pasta, this sauce is also good with veal and fish (see page 87).*

Bring a large saucepan of salted water to a boil over high heat. Add the spaghetti, stir, and return to a boil. Adjust the heat so the water boils gently and cook until the spaghetti is al dente, 10 to 12 minutes. Drain well.

While the spaghetti is cooking, cut the butter into pieces and place them in a large frying pan over medium-low heat. When the butter is melted, add the sage leaves and cook, turning once, until the leaves are crisp and the butter begins to brown, about 7 minutes.

Add the cooked drained spaghetti to the frying pan and toss to coat with the sage butter sauce. Season well with salt and pepper and serve immediately.

Serves 2

Sea salt and freshly ground black pepper

7 ounces / 200 g spaghetti

1/2 cup / 4 ounces / 115 g unsalted butter

20 to 30 fresh sage leaves

To make one's butter:
to make a pile of money
(French)

Puff Pastry

Many books warn their readers about the difficulty of making puff pastry. While it's true that it can't be quickly thrown together in a food processor, it is actually not hard to make with a little time and planning. The reason to make it from scratch is that it is often very hard to buy good prepared puff pastry. Most are not made with pure butter, and nothing else will do. If you don't own a kitchen scale, invest in one before making this recipe. This recipe only makes a small amount of pastry, so it is easier to handle and roll out. Puff pastry, which contains equal weights of butter and flour, is made in two stages. First, some of the butter is rubbed into the flour, and water is added to make a dough. After this dough is left to rest, the remaining butter is "wrapped" in the dough. The dough is then rolled to make layers of butter sandwiched within the dough and these layers are what make the pastry rise in the oven. For the best results, use a high-fat butter.

Don't try making this in the middle of summer unless you turn up the air-conditioning: the pastry must be made in a cool kitchen.

Sift the flour and salt into a bowl. Using your fingers, rub 2 tablespoons of the butter into the flour mixture until mealy. Add the water and the lemon

Makes about 1 1/2 pounds / 650 g

2 cups / 8 3/4 ounces / 250 g flour

1 teaspoon fine sea salt

1 cup plus 2 tablespoons / 8 3/4 ounces / 250 g unsalted butter

2/3 cup / 150 ml ice-cold water

A squeeze of lemon juice

BUTTER WRAPPERS

My mother always saved the wrapper from butter and I have continued the habit, since they are perfect for greasing a baking sheet or buttering a pan.

If your head is made of butter don't become a baker: if you are not cut out for the task, don't do it. (French)

Butter fingers: a clumsy person

juice and stir until incorporated. Turn the mixture onto a cool surface and knead, gathering up all the flour, until the dough comes together. Lightly flour the surface and continue to knead until the dough is smooth. Form the dough into a ball and cut a cross in the top. Wrap and refrigerate for 10 minutes.

Place the remaining butter between 2 sheets of parchment paper, and, using a rolling pin, beat the butter until it is pliable. Shape the butter into a 6-inch / 15-cm square. The goal is to have the butter and the dough cool and the same consistency. Test by pushing your finger into the dough and then into the butter. If necessary, refrigerate the dough for up to 15 minutes longer to achieve this.

Place the dough on a cool floured surface and roll out the 4 flaps of dough, leaving the center about 4 times as thick as the flaps. You want to make a rough square about 12 inches / 30 cm across to enclose the butter. Place the butter on top of the thicker dough center so that it sits as a diamond on the dough square, and fold the flaps over to enclose the butter completely and form 4 layers of dough on top of the butter. You should end up with a square of pastry with the butter sandwiched in the middle. Tap the pastry square firmly with a rolling pin to seal the edges and flatten it slightly. Then, starting from the center of the square, roll the pastry into an 18 by 6-inch / 45 by 15-cm rectangle. As you roll the pastry try to keep the sides straight. Fold the pastry into thirds, like you would fold a letter. You should now have a square again, composed of 3 layers of pastry. Turn the square 90 degrees, so that the open end faces you. Tap the pastry again with the rolling pin to seal and flatten, then roll out to a rectangle of the same size. Fold the pastry into thirds again, and press 2 fingers into the corner of the square to indicate the pastry has 2 turns. Wrap it in plastic wrap and refrigerate for 30 minutes or longer.

Bring the pastry to room temperature, then roll it out into a rectangle again, fold it into thirds, and turn it 90 degrees. Roll it again, fold the pastry into thirds, and use your fingertips to make 4 indentations in the corner of the pastry, indicating you have completed 4 turns. Wrap it in plastic wrap and refrigerate. Let the pastry rest in the refrigerator for at least 1 hour or overnight.

Bring the pastry to room temperature and roll it, fold it, and turn it twice more and refrigerate for 30 minutes. Now the pastry is ready to roll out according to the recipe directions. After cutting out the desired shape, turn the pastry over so that it rises more evenly.

Refrigerate for another 30 minutes before baking at 425°F / 220°C.

Use the pastry within 2 days, or freeze it for up to 6 months.

TIP If you know what you will be making with the puff pastry, roll out the pastry and cut it into the final shape before freezing it. This way you will only have to thaw the pastry to use it.

34   fat

Butter sunk under
More than a hundred years
Was recovered salty and white.
The ground itself is kind, black butter

Melting and opening underfoot,
Missing its last definition
By millions of years.

From "Bogland," by Seamus Heaney

In 1681, an English traveler in Ireland named Thomas Dinely described "Butter layed up in wicker baskets, mixed with a sort of garlic and buried for some time in a bog to make provision of an high taste for Lent." He was describing a practice that had been in use for at least 2,000 years, from Iceland to Finland, and that continued well into the nineteenth century.

Bogs are waterlogged peat, and they provide a cool, virtually airless environment that acts like a primitive refrigerator. The soil in bogs is highly acidic, making it perfect for preserving everything from ancient artifacts to bodies to butter. Butter (or, sometimes, tallow) was carefully prepared, either by wrapping it in cloth or animal skin, or by packing it into containers made from bark, wicker, or elaborately carved wood. Burying butter in a bog may have been a way to age the fat as well as a way to preserve it. Debes's *Description of the Faeroe Islands*, written in 1673, tells how, in these islands sheep tallow was buried to improve its flavor. Over time it tasted less like tallow and more like cheese.

Today, farmers and turf cutters routinely uncover white, waxy lumps of animal fat in bogs. One of the biggest discoveries weighed in at 110 pounds / 50 kg, while the oldest has been radiocarbon dated at 2,000 years old. Samples of bog butter are displayed in the Scottish and Irish national museums.

Freshly excavated bog butter is white or gray in color and has a waxy texture because of its high water content. As the butter dries out it becomes very granular and crumbly. Depending on its age and the nose of the discoverer, bog butter smells like strong cheese, like old socks, or just plain rancid. Some bog butter is edible, if not particularly palatable.

BOG
BUTTER

Mixed Spiced Nuts

Makes 4 cups / 1 pound / 450 g

4 cups / 1 pound / 450 g mixed unsalted nuts

$1/2$ teaspoon ground coriander

$1/2$ teaspoon ground cumin

2 tablespoons unsalted butter

2 tablespoons brown sugar

2 tablespoons chopped fresh rosemary

$1/4$ teaspoon cayenne pepper

$1 1/2$ teaspoons fine sea salt

This great snack proves that butter is the ultimate flavor carrier. You can use almost any combination of nuts, including cashews, almonds, macadamia nuts, walnuts, and pecans, although I'd avoid using Brazil nuts, as the coating never seems to stick to them. I am not a big snack-food person, but these are delicious and perfect for accompanying drinks. As with all good snacks, once you've eaten a couple, it's impossible to stop.

Preheat the oven to 350°F / 180°C.

Scatter the nuts on a rimmed baking sheet and bake, shaking a couple of times during baking, until they are browned, about 10 minutes.

Meanwhile, place a small, heavy pan over medium-high heat. Add the ground coriander and cumin and toast until aromatic, about 30 seconds. Remove the pan from the heat and add the butter, brown sugar, rosemary, and cayenne pepper.

Place the pan over low heat and stir constantly until the butter melts and the sugar dissolves, about 2 minutes. Stir in the salt and keep warm.

Transfer the nuts to a large warmed bowl, pour the warm spiced butter on top, and stir until the nuts are well coated. Taste and adjust the seasoning, adding more salt if necessary, and try to allow the nuts to cool completely before eating them. Store in an airtight container for up to 1 week.

BUTTER SAUCE BASICS

Butter is ideal for making a quick sauce: just whisk it into the pan juices after sautéing or roasting. Unlike cream, which has to boil for several minutes to reduce and thicken, butter instantly emulsifies with the pan juices to form a sauce.

Two sauces made almost entirely of butter are *beurre blanc* and *beurre rouge*, or white and red butter. *Beurre blanc nantais*, usually just called *beurre blanc*, was created in the Loire Valley to accompany the local specialty, poached pike. The French food writer Curnonsky, who was born in the Loire, credits the local housewives with its creation. It is a short step from adding a little butter to enrich the fish's cooking juices to adding a lot to make a rich butter sauce. *Beurre rouge*, however, does have a pedigree. Charles Barrier, whose eponymous restaurant is also in the Loire Valley, at Tours, wanted a butter sauce to serve with meat, so he began with a red wine reduction. Barrier no longer cooks at his restaurant, but his sauce lives on, inspiring many chefs to create new sauces based on whisking butter into the reduced cooking juices from meat, poultry, or fish.

Harold McGee explains the science behind butter sauces in his book *The Curious Cook*. Anyone familiar with *beurre blanc* recipes will know that the proportions of butter to the wine-and-vinegar reduction vary widely, and there is a lot of mumbo jumbo around the method that scares off novices. McGee's experiments show us that *beurre blanc* is an extremely flexible sauce whose only fault is that it is susceptible to heat and cold. As McGee points out, butter—a mixture of fat, water, and milk solids—is essentially a sauce in waiting. When you make a *beurre blanc*, you are turning your butter back into the thick cream it came from. This is why butter makes such a great last-minute sauce and no recipe is needed.

Two important things to remember when making butter sauces are to use a heavy pan that transfers the heat slowly and evenly and to keep the sauce between 100° and 130°F / 38° and 54°C. The addition of a little cream at the beginning will make the sauce more stable. If your sauce overheats you can let it cool down slightly, add a splash of water, and whisk it back together. Remember that butter sauce is a warm sauce, not a hot one, and it should be served as soon as it is made. You can hold it for a few minutes by placing the sauce in a pan of barely warm water, around 120°F / 48°C. If you have some leftover sauce, it cannot be used again as a sauce. Refrigerate it and then, when you are ready to use it, let it come to room temperature, whisk it, and use it like a flavored butter.

Beurre Blanc (White Butter Sauce)

Although originally created to accompany fish from the Loire River, this sauce is good with mildly flavored fish, scallops, lobster, shrimp, chicken, and vegetables. This is the time to seek out white peppercorns and put them in the pepper grinder: black pepper spoils the look of this sauce.

Combine the wine, shallots, and vinegar in a small saucepan and place over medium-high heat. Bring to a boil, then reduce the heat and boil gently until the mixture is reduced to about 3 tablespoons.

Strain the reduction into a small, clean saucepan, pressing on the shallots to extract the liquid. You should have about 2 tablespoons. Stir in the cream and season with salt and pepper.

Cut the butter into 12 pieces.

Place the pan over very low heat and slowly whisk in the butter, thoroughly incorporating 1 piece before adding another. While you're whisking, keep the sauce warm, but not hot, so that the mixture emulsifies and the butter doesn't melt into the sauce. When all the butter is incorporated, taste, adjust the seasoning, and serve.

VARIATION You can vary this sauce by adding one of the following: 1 tablespoon of chopped fresh herbs, 1 tablespoon of whole-grain mustard, or a peeled, seeded, and finely chopped tomato and some finely shredded basil leaves. You can also replace the reduction with orange juice or the cooking juices from a roast or sautéed meat, but add some lemon juice or vinegar to make sure there is enough acid to balance the butter.

Makes 1 cup / 250 ml

1 cup / 250 ml dry white wine

2 tablespoons finely chopped shallot

1 tablespoon white wine vinegar

1 tablespoon whipping (35 percent fat) cream

Sea salt and freshly ground white pepper

3/4 cup plus 2 tablespoons / 7 ounces / 200 g cold unsalted butter

To slip into the butter:
to get into something
very easily (French)

Butter-Poached Scallops

I first got the idea of poaching in butter while reading Thomas Keller's The French Laundry Cookbook. *I immediately made his butter-poached lobster. It was delicious, but far too much work even for me. It's the sort of dish best ordered in a restaurant, and perhaps one day I'll eat it made by Keller himself. The idea of poaching in butter stayed with me as I was rendering pork fat and cooking duck legs in their own fat. I realized that poaching in butter was similar to making a confit (no, I didn't consider cooking a cow in butter). Unlike Keller, I had no desire to make large quantities of* beurre monté, *an unflavored* beurre blanc, *so I decided to keep it simple and poach my scallops in plain butter. Serve this dish with a dilled cucumber salad or warm cooked spinach.*

Arrange the scallops in a saucepan that is just large enough for all the scallops to fit snugly in one layer. Add water so that it just covers the scallops. Pour the water into a measuring cup and place the scallops on a paper towel and pat dry. Season the scallops well with salt and pepper and set aside.

The amount of water in the measuring cup is the amount of melted butter you'll need. Dice the butter, place in a saucepan over medium-low heat, and clip a kitchen thermometer to the side of the pan. Heat the butter, stirring occasionally, until the thermometer reads 185°F / 85°C. Add the scallops and bring the temperature back to 185°F / 85°C. Cook the scallops, turning once, until they are cooked through, 2 to 4 minutes. Test a scallop by cutting it in half; it should be opaque in the center.

Using a slotted spoon, transfer the scallops to warmed serving plates. Drizzle the scallops with a little of the cooking butter and a squeeze of lemon juice. Serve immediately.

Serves 4 as an appetizer

12 sea scallops

Sea salt and freshly ground black pepper

About 1 1/3 cups / 10 1/2 ounces / 300 g unsalted butter

A squeeze of lemon juice

❝He shall eat butter and honey when he knows to refuse the evil, and choose the good.❞

ISAIAH 7:15

Buttered Parsnips and Rutabaga

I really dislike rutabaga. I find its taste assertive and bitter, but my husband loves it, so I keep trying to find ways to love it too. This is one answer: mix it with sweet parsnips and butter, which mellows its strong taste and smooths its hard edges. So while, as the saying goes, fine words butter no parsnips, butter certainly softens the rutabaga. If blood oranges are not in season, use a regular orange.

Peel the parsnips and rutabaga. If the parsnips are large, cut them in half, and cut the rutabaga into 1/2-inch / 1-cm pieces. Place the vegetables in a steamer and steam until they are very tender, about 10 minutes.

Purée the parsnips and rutabaga using the fine grill of a food mill into a saucepan. Finely grate the zest of the orange and add to the purée along with 3 tablespoons of the orange juice. Cut the butter into pieces. Place the saucepan over low heat and add the butter and ground cumin and season well with salt and pepper. Stir until heated through and serve.

Serves 4 to 6

1 pound / 450 g parsnips

8 ounces / 225 g rutabaga

1 blood orange

1/4 cup / 2 ounces / 60 g unsalted butter, diced

1/2 teaspoon ground cumin

Sea salt and freshly ground black pepper

FROM BUTTER BOAT TO GRAVY BOAT

The word *boat* has referred to an oval sauce dish since the seventeenth century. In the late eighteenth century, as butter became more popular on noble tables, this dish was filled with melted butter and called a butter boat. By the late nineteenth century it was just as likely to hold gravy as butter, and we now call it a gravy boat.

Poached Shrimp with Beurre Blanc and Spinach

Serves 4 as a main course, 6 as an appetizer

2 bunches spinach

1 pound / 450 g large shrimp (16 to 20), shelled and deveined

1/4 cup / 60 ml dry vermouth

4 cups / 1 l water

2 fresh bay leaves

2 sprigs flat-leaf parsley, stems only

1 slice onion

1 slice lemon

1 clove garlic, peeled

1 teaspoon coarse sea salt

1/2 teaspoon black peppercorns

1 recipe Beurre Blanc (page 37)

Butter, for reheating the spinach

To simplify the assembly of this dish, the spinach is cooked in advance and reheated, and the shrimp are poached while you make the sauce.

Rinse the spinach well, remove the stems, and place in a colander to drain. Place a large frying pan over high heat. When it is hot, add the spinach and cook, stirring, until the spinach wilts. Return the spinach to the colander and refresh under cold running water. Squeeze out the water and chop the spinach coarsely; you should have about 2 cups / 340 g. Set aside.

In a bowl, toss the shrimp with the vermouth. Pour the water into a saucepan and add the bay leaves, parsley stems, onion and lemon slices, garlic, salt, and peppercorns. Bring to a boil over high heat, then lower the heat and simmer the liquid, uncovered, for 5 minutes. Add the shrimp and vermouth to the saucepan and return the liquid to a simmer. Remove the pan from the heat, cover, and let stand until the shrimp are cooked, 3 to 5 minutes. While the shrimp are cooking, make the Beurre Blanc.

Reheat the spinach in a frying pan with some butter and divide it among warmed plates. Drain the shrimp and place them on top of the spinach, then top with the sauce. Serve immediately.

THE DISH ON THE BUTTER DISH

Before refrigeration, butter dishes were designed not only to present the butter but also to preserve it by keeping the butter submerged in salted water. Today there are dishes made of two sections—a crock and a bell-shaped dish—which can keep butter fresh at room temperature for several weeks. The butter is packed into a bell-shaped cup, then a little water is poured into the crock and the bell-shaped dish slips into the crock butter side down. The water creates an airtight seal and the butter is protected from both light and oxygen so it stays fresh and spreadable.

Beurre Rouge (Red Butter Sauce)

There is no doubt that Charles Barrier succeeded in creating a butter sauce to serve with meat (see page 36): this sauce goes well with beef, duck, and venison. However, many chefs since Barrier have turned back to fish and now serve beurre rouge with salmon. My favorite way to enjoy this sauce is with poached bone marrow (see page 180).

Place 1 tablespoon of the butter in a saucepan over medium-low heat. Add the shallot, carrot, celery, and bay leaf and cook until the vegetables have softened slightly. Add the wine and vinegar and bring to a boil. Reduce the heat slightly and boil until the mixture is reduced to $1/4$ cup / 60 ml.

Strain the reduction into a small, clean saucepan, pressing on the vegetables to extract all of the flavor; you should have about 2 tablespoons of liquid. Add the cream and season with salt and pepper.

Cut the remaining butter into 12 pieces.

Place the pan over very low heat and slowly whisk in the butter, thoroughly incorporating 1 piece before adding another. While you're whisking, keep the sauce warm, but not hot, so that the mixture emulsifies and the butter doesn't melt into the sauce. When all the butter is incorporated, taste, adjust the seasoning, and serve.

Makes 1 cup / 250 ml

3/4 cup plus 2 tablespoons / 7 ounces / 200 g cold unsalted butter

2 tablespoons finely chopped shallot

1 tablespoon peeled and finely chopped carrot

1 tablespoon finely chopped celery

1/2 fresh bay leaf

1 cup / 250 ml fruity red wine

1 tablespoon red wine vinegar

1 tablespoon whipping (35 percent fat) cream

Sea salt and freshly ground black pepper

THE HOLLANDAISE FAMILY

This is another family of sauces that slipped off the culinary radar when butter was deemed bad for us. The French name translates as "Dutch sauce," and it was named after those well-known butter lovers to the north. In England it was still called Dutch sauce up until the mid-nineteenth century. Hollandaise is the best known of a group of sauces thickened by egg yolks, but there is also béarnaise from the town of Béarn in southwestern France (duck and goose fat isn't the only fat they use in the south), and, my favorite, Maltaise Sauce (page 42), named for the blood oranges from Malta.

I've always made hollandaise sauce by cooking the egg yolks in a bain-marie or water bath, and then whisking in the melted butter, but after reading Harold McGee's *The Curious Cook*, I decided to try his method of throwing everything in the saucepan at once. It works so brilliantly that I won't be going back to the complicated and less sure method I learned in chef's school.

These sauces are more stable than simple butter sauces are, but they will break, or curdle, if they get too hot, so cook them gently and attentively.

Murgh Makhani (Butter Chicken)

Serves 4 to 6

2 onions, chopped

6 cloves garlic, peeled and halved

1/4 cup / 1 ounce / 30 g peeled and coarsely chopped ginger

8 cardamom pods

2 fresh bay leaves

2 teaspoons toasted cumin seeds

1 teaspoon black peppercorns

2 green chiles

1 dried red chile

3/4 cup / 175 ml water

One 3-pound / 1.4-kg chicken or chicken pieces on the bone

Coarse sea salt

2 to 3 tablespoons Ghee (page 24)

Two 3-inch / 7.5-cm cinnamon sticks

14 ounces / 398 g canned tomatoes

1/4 cup / 60 ml whipping (35 percent fat) cream

1/2 cup / 4 ounces / 115 g unsalted butter, diced

2 tablespoons chopped cilantro (coriander)

1 lime

Every Indian restaurant has its own recipe for butter chicken. It is an ideal restaurant dish, because it uses leftover pieces of tandoori chicken, cooked in a sauce enriched with tomatoes and butter. Although this recipe is not authentic, since it doesn't start with tandoori chicken, it is easy to prepare. I adapted it from a recipe by my friend Elizabeth, who began with a recipe by Madhur Jaffrey. I usually use a whole chicken, but legs and thighs, on the bone, also work very well. Be sure to use real cinnamon for this recipe.

Serve this dish with rice and Lamb Fat and Spinach Chapati (page 204), brushed with ghee rather than lamb fat.

Place the onions, garlic, and ginger in a food processor. Remove the seeds from the cardamom pods and add the seeds to the food processor along with the bay leaves, cumin seeds, and peppercorns. Remove the seeds from the green chiles and discard. Chop the chiles and add them to the food processor along with the red chile, complete with seeds. Add 1/4 cup / 60 ml of the water and process until the mixture forms a soupy paste. Set aside.

Cut the chicken into 8 pieces (see page 47) and remove the skin. Keep the skin for another use, like making Poultry Cracklings (see page 133). Season the chicken pieces with salt.

In a large frying pan with a lid, heat 2 tablespoons of the ghee over high heat and brown the chicken pieces in batches, adding more ghee if necessary. Transfer the browned chicken to a plate. Lower the heat to low and add the onion-spice paste to the pan. Using a wooden spoon, deglaze the pan, scraping up the browned bits on the bottom. Add the cinnamon sticks, the tomatoes with their juice, the remaining water, and 1 teaspoon salt. Bring to a boil, then lower the heat, cover, and simmer, stirring occasionally, for 30 minutes.

Add the chicken pieces and any juices to the sauce. Bring to a boil, then lower the heat to a simmer. Cover and cook, stirring occasionally, until the chicken is cooked through, about 30 minutes.

Transfer the chicken to a dish and keep warm. Remove the cinnamon sticks from the sauce, add the cream, and bring to a boil. Boil, stirring often, until the sauce thickens. Remove from the heat and stir in the butter pieces until they are melted. Return the chicken to the pan and stir to coat the pieces with the sauce. Sprinkle with the cilantro, add a squeeze of lime juice, and serve.

CUTTING SUPRÊMES

Buy a good-sized chicken just under 4 pounds / 1.8 kg; it will yield 2 *suprêmes* around 7 to 8^1/$_2$ ounces / 200 to 250 g each. Place the bird on a cutting board breast side up. Pull 1 leg away from the body and cut down through the skin, twisting the leg and cutting through the joint to release. Repeat with the other leg. Set them aside. Now cut along 1 side of the breastbone the length of the chicken. Keeping the knife close to the bone, remove 1 breast. When you reach the wing joint, cut through it to leave the wing attached to the breast. Repeat with the other breast. Remove the wing tip and the second joint from each breast, leaving only the first joint still attached. Grab the skin and pull it right off the breast. Scrape off the flesh from around the bone, being careful to leave the bone securely attached to the breast. Using a cleaver, trim the wing bone.

Chicken Kiev

Serves 2

^{1}/$_4$ cup / 2 ounces / 60 g unsalted butter, softened

2 cloves garlic, peeled

Fine sea salt and freshly ground black pepper

Fresh flat-leaf parsley, chives, and tarragon

1 teaspoon freshly squeezed lemon juice

2 boneless, skinless chicken breast halves with the first wing joint attached (7 to 8^1/$_2$ ounces / 200 to 250 g each)

1 egg

1 tablespoon milk

2 tablespoons flour

1 cup / 3^1/$_2$ ounces / 100 g fine dry bread crumbs

About 4 cups / 1^3/$_4$ pounds / 800 g lard, melted (see page 73)

A crisp chicken breast that releases a jet of flavored butter with the first cut, chicken Kiev is both delicious and fun to eat. I make no excuses that this recipe serves only two, no more. Chicken Kiev takes time to prepare and it needs plenty of attention, so it is difficult to cook in quantity. If your butcher is willing to prepare you true chicken suprêmes—*skinless chicken breasts boned except for the first joint of the wing, which is left in place—let him, but they are easy to prepare yourself (see above). The two* suprêmes *should be the same size, so they should be cut from the same bird.*

Serve this with a green vegetable—peas would be perfect. And although the thick crumb coating might seem to make potatoes redundant, a couple are excellent for mopping up that garlicky herb butter—but you'd better make them steamed ones. Make your first cut into the cooked chicken gingerly; you don't want to wear the filling.

Place the softened butter in a small bowl. Crush the garlic cloves with a couple of large pinches of salt and chop until they form a paste. Chop the parsley, chives, and tarragon to obtain 1 tablespoon of mixed herbs. Mix the garlic, herbs, lemon juice, and pepper into the softened butter until well blended. Divide the butter in 2 and place each half on a square of plastic wrap. Using the wrap, shape each piece of butter into a flat oval about 3 inches / 7.5 cm long and 1^1/$_2$ inches / 4 cm across at the widest point. Wrap the butter in the plastic wrap and refrigerate.

Remove the small piece of meat, called the fillet, attached to the inside of each chicken breast by a membrane; set the fillets aside. Place each filleted *suprême* with the bone side up, on a cutting board. Holding a small, sharp knife parallel to the work surface, cut a pocket in the thickest part of the breast, as long and as deep as you dare without penetrating the other side of the breast. You will insert the butter in this pocket, so ideally it will be longer and wider than your prepared butter. Place each *suprême* between

46   fat

2 pieces of plastic wrap and pound them with a meat mallet until they are an even thickness.

Remove the butter from the refrigerator; it should still be malleable. Check to see if it will fit inside the pocket. If necessary, increase the size of the pocket or change the shape of the butter by squeezing it. Refrigerate the butter, *suprêmes*, and fillets separately until the butter is firm, about 30 minutes.

When the butter is firm, insert a piece into the pocket of each *suprême*, and use the fillet to cover any exposed butter and press to seal it in; the fillet will stick to the breast.

Whisk the egg with the milk and pour into a shallow dish. Place the flour and bread crumbs in 2 separate shallow dishes. Season the flour and then the *suprêmes* with salt and pepper. Coat the *suprêmes* lightly with flour, then dip them into the egg mixture, and finally coat them with the bread crumbs. Transfer them to a plate and refrigerate for 30 minutes. Then coat the *suprêmes* with the flour, egg mixture, and bread crumbs again.

Heat the lard in a large pan about 10 inches / 25 cm wide and 2 inches / 5 cm deep; the lard should be 3/4 to 1 inch / 2 to 2.5 cm deep in the pan. When the temperature of the lard registers 350°F / 180°C on a kitchen thermometer, carefully slide the *suprêmes* into the fat. The temperature will drop; adjust the heat so that the lard remains around 325°F / 160°C. Cook the *suprêmes*, turning them occasionally, until dark golden brown, 12 to 15 minutes.

Drain the *suprêmes* on paper towels and serve immediately.

VARIATION Although garlic and herb butter is the classic filling for this dish, you could also use Porcini Butter (page 26), anchovy butter (see page 26), or even Foie Gras Butter (page 159).

To know which side your bread is buttered

Buttered: to be very drunk (French)

A Russian is still a Russian even if you fry him in butter. (Finnish)

Place the bird on a cutting board breast side up, pull 1 leg away from the body, and cut down through the skin. Using the tip of the knife, cut around the "oyster" of meat nestled in the backbone so that it remains attached to the thigh. Twist the leg firmly until the hip pops out of its socket, and cut between the ball and socket. Repeat with the other leg.

Next, cut from the top of the wishbone down the length of the chicken through the skin and meat to the breastbone. Using a knife or poultry shears, cut through the breastbone. Now cut down the length of the chicken through the rib bones to remove the breast halves from the backbone. Cut the backbone, with ribs attached, into smaller pieces and reserve for the stockpot.

Cut the leg pieces in half, separating the thigh and the drumstick, and then cut the breasts in half on the diagonal, through the breastbone. Remove the wings and reserve them for the stockpot.

CUTTING A CHICKEN INTO 8 PIECES

Brown Butter Ice Cream

Makes about 3 cups / 750 ml

1 cup / 250 ml whole milk

1 cup / 250 ml whipping
(35 percent fat) cream

$1/2$ cup / $3^1/2$ ounces /
100 g sugar

$1/2$ cup / 4 ounces / 115 g
unsalted butter, diced

$1/2$ teaspoon freshly squeezed
lemon juice

3 egg yolks

$1/8$ teaspoon fine sea salt

Butter hands: wooden
paddles used to shape butter

By giving butter, you give
your heart. (Breton)

I love making ice cream, and this one is rich, buttery, and delicious, perfect for anyone bored with vanilla. I like to experiment with ice cream and have succeeded in making avocado and mustard ice creams, so I thought making brown butter ice cream would be a snap. It wasn't, but after several attempts I realized that if you emulsify the butter into the egg yolks, like a mayonnaise, then the ice cream will stay creamy and smooth. When making ice cream there are two important things to remember: cool the cooked custard mixture quickly, and then let it rest overnight in the refrigerator so the flavors can meld. Like all homemade ice cream, this one is best eaten within a week . . . if you can keep it that long. Serve this ice cream by itself, or topped with the Salted Caramel Sauce (page 54).

Combine the milk and cream in a saucepan and add about half the sugar. Place the pan over medium heat and bring to a boil. Remove the pan from the heat and set aside.

In another saucepan, place the butter over low heat. When the butter is melted, increase the heat to medium. Watch the butter carefully, using a spoon to push aside any foam to check the color of the milk solids. When they turn brown and you smell a sweet, nutty aroma, remove the pan from the heat, add the lemon juice, and transfer the butter to a bowl to cool until it is no longer hot to the touch.

In a large bowl whisk the egg yolks, the remaining sugar, and the salt until light in color and thick. Whisk in the cooled browned butter, adding it slowly and whisking vigorously so that the mixture is emulsified. Once all the butter is incorporated, slowly whisk in the cream and milk mixture.

Pour the mixture into a clean pan and cook over medium heat, stirring constantly, until the mixture thickens and coats the back of a spoon. Strain the mixture into a bowl and cool quickly by placing it in a larger bowl or sink filled with cold water and ice. Stir the mixture often. When it is cool, cover and refrigerate overnight.

The next day, churn the mixture in an ice cream machine following the manufacturer's instructions.

BUTTERY NUPTIALS

Because butter represents fertility and prosperity, there is an old English wedding custom of presenting newlyweds with a pot of butter to guarantee a future blessed with many children. Across the Channel, in Brittany, butter was also a part of wedding festivities. Elaborately carved and decorated blocks of butter were presented to the happy couple and displayed during the celebrations, when guests would push coins and paper money into the butter. After the ceremony the money was collected and the blocks of butter were auctioned off, with the proceeds providing the newlyweds a nest egg for their life together.

Salted Caramel Sauce

Makes 1 1/2 cups / 375 ml

3/4 cup / 5 ounces / 150 g sugar

1/3 cup plus 2 tablespoons / 100 ml whipping (35 percent fat) cream

2/3 cup / 5 ounces / 150 g salted butter, diced

Butter tooth: either of the two middle incisors of the upper jaw

This recipe was given to me by the pastry chef at Chez Michel, a restaurant in Paris that specializes in dishes from Brittany. The salted butter is the secret to this sauce. It highlights the caramel taste and balances the sweetness, rescuing the sauce from being overly sweet. I doubt you'll be able to get Breton butter, but this sauce deserves the best lightly salted butter you can buy. At Chez Michel they serve it with their Kouign Amann (page 58), but I prefer it on ice cream, fresh fruit, or Marrow Rice Pudding (page 217).

Place the sugar in a heavy saucepan over medium-low heat. Cook the sugar until it melts and begins to turn a caramel color. Give the caramel a stir to blend in any uncooked sugar. Once all the sugar has turned into liquid caramel, remove the pan from the heat and dip the base of the pan into cold water to stop the caramel from cooking further.

Carefully stir in the cream—the mixture may splatter and foam—add the butter, and place the pan over low heat, stirring until all the caramel is dissolved.

Serve the sauce warm or at room temperature. The sauce can be kept refrigerated for up to 2 weeks or frozen.

FESTIVAL OF THE BUTTER GODS

In the pages of *Canadian Geographic Magazine* in 1948, Harrison Forman described one of the last times the Festival of the Butter Gods was held at the Kum Bum Gomba monastery in Tibet. Pilgrims came from all over Asia to join the celebrations, which lasted several days. The high point of the festival was the unveiling of giant sculptures of Buddhist gods and mythical characters on the final evening. These extremely detailed sculptures, carved in bas-relief on large panels of yak butter more than 10 feet / 3 m high, were undertaken by a large team of monks and local artists, who spent the whole winter working on them. The butter was also dyed many different colors to create subtle detail. As Forman described them, "The very texture of the silken cloth [was] so realistic in appearance that one felt impelled to reach up and touch it. Even the floral designs down to the tiniest petal, leaf and stem . . . were exquisitely fashioned." The panels were unveiled just after sundown, lit by hundreds of yak-butter lamps. Forman recounts how the massive crowds, who had been waiting hours for this moment, pushed forward to take a closer look. People lined up to view the magnificent panels all through the night. The heat of the lamps combined with the warmth of the people was too much even for the butter gods. By the end of the night the panels were reduced to a shapeless mass of colored butter, and at daybreak they were tossed over the cliff and left for the crows to finish off.

Easy Apple Tart

This easy tart is simpler to make than apple pie and way more impressive. Once you have prepared the puff pastry, all you have to do is slice your apples. When I make puff pastry, I roll out rounds for this tart and freeze them. Then, when I decide to bake an apple tart, the pastry is ready and waiting. It defrosts while I slice the apples, and I don't need to let the pastry rest in the refrigerator before baking it. The hardest part of making this tart is slicing the apples thinly; a mandoline makes this task easier. Try to time the baking so that the tart is coming out of the oven when you are ready for dessert, because it is best eaten warm. Serve it with Brown Butter Ice Cream (page 50).

Roll out pastry into a thin square about $10^{1}/2$ inches / 26 cm. Cut out a 10-inch / 25-cm circle and place it on an ungreased baking sheet. Leaving a $1/4$-inch / 6-mm rim untouched, prick the pastry with a fork; the untouched part will rise, keeping the apple slices on the pastry. Refrigerate the pastry disk for 30 minutes.

Preheat the oven to 425°F / 220°C.

Staying inside the rim, sprinkle the pastry with the ground almonds. Peel the apples, cut them into quarters, and remove the cores. Cut each apple quarter lengthwise into thin slices.

Arrange the apple slices in overlapping concentric circles on top of the almonds, leaving the rim uncovered. Drizzle the apple slices with the melted butter and sprinkle with the sugar.

Bake until the apples are cooked, the pastry is golden, and the edges have puffed up to form a rim around the apples, 25 to 30 minutes. Serve warm.

Serves 6

7 ounces / 200 g Puff Pastry (page 33)

$1/3$ cup / 1 ounce / 30 g ground almonds

2 to 3 cooking apples

3 tablespoons unsalted butter, melted

3 tablespoons sugar

WHY CAN YOU SPREAD BUTTER?

Butter is a very odd sort of solid made up of fat, water, and milk solids, all of which change state at different temperatures. Refrigerated butter is firm and difficult to spread, while room-temperature butter is still solid but soft enough to spread. A tangle of crystals keeps the butter together, making it appear solid even when it's extremely soft. Not until butter reaches a temperature of 96°F / 35°C do the crystals break apart and the butter melts. Because butter melts at just below body temperature, it creates a wonderful, luscious sensation on the tongue. For butter to resolidify, it must be cooled to 73°F / 23°C. What should you do if you forgot to take the butter out of the refrigerator? Scrape your knife over its surface. This softens the butter by separating the crystals, making it easier to spread.

Salted Butter Tart

I love the way ideas for recipes come from the oddest sources. I made the Salted Caramel Sauce (page 54) and loved the flavor. Then, a well-known Paris baker, Eric Kayser, took over one of the bakeries in my Paris neighborhood, and the following week my friend Laura dropped by with Kayser's new tart cookbook. In it was a recipe for tarte au beurre salé, or salted butter tart. I grabbed the book and made the tart. Here is my rich, sweet, and satisfying version of his recipe. When shopping for the ingredients, buy extra cream so you can serve this tart with a cloud of whipped cream to cut the sweetness—yes, another benefit of eating fat.

Roll out the pastry on a floured surface and line a 9 or 9$^{1}/_{2}$-inch / 23 or 24-cm tart pan. Prick the base of the tart with a fork and refrigerate for at least 30 minutes.

Preheat the oven to 375°F / 190°C.

Place the tart shell on a baking sheet. Line the tart with parchment paper and fill it with dried beans. Bake until the pastry is just set, about 15 minutes. Remove the paper and beans and continue to cook until the pastry is a dark golden color, 10 to 15 minutes. Transfer the tart to a wire rack and leave to cool completely.

Combine the sugar and butter in a deep, heavy saucepan over medium heat. Stir to mix and cook, stirring occasionally, until the butter and sugar caramelize, 10 to 15 minutes. The sugar and butter will go through several stages. First it will look like a flour and butter roux, then it will appear curdled, and then the butter will leak out of the sugar mixture. Don't worry: it will all come together in the end.

While the caramel is cooking, pour the cream into a saucepan and bring it to a boil over medium heat. Remove from the heat and set aside.

Keep stirring the butter and sugar mixture, watching carefully as it begins to caramelize and remembering that the heat in the pan will continue to cook the caramel once it is removed from the burner. You want a rich, dark caramel color, but you don't want to burn the mixture, which will give it a bitter taste. When the caramel reaches the right color, remove the pan from the heat and slowly and carefully pour in the cream; the mixture will bubble and spit. When the caramel stops bubbling, return it to low heat and cook for 5 minutes, stirring to dissolve the caramel in the cream. Remove the pan from the heat and let the caramel cool for 10 minutes. Slowly pour the cooled caramel into the baked pastry shell and chill the tart for at least 2 hours.

This tart is easier to cut when it is chilled. Remove the tart from the pan and, using a wet knife, cut it into wedges. Serve the tart at room temperature, however, for maximum flavor, with a dollop of whipped cream.

Serves 6 to 8

1/2 recipe Sweet Butter Pastry (page 49)

1$^{1}/_{4}$ cups / 9 ounces / 250 g superfine (caster) sugar

1/2 cup / 4 ounces / 115 g salted butter, diced

1 cup / 250 ml whipping (35 percent fat) cream

Lightly whipped cream, for serving

BUTTER-SCOTCH

Butterscotch, which originated in the nineteenth century, is a crisp toffee made from salted butter and sugar. In the United Kingdom it must contain at least 4 percent butterfat. Despite its name, its connection to Scotland is unclear.

Kouign Amann (Breton Butter Cake)

Serves 8

1 teaspoon / 4 g dry yeast

3/4 cup plus 2 tablespoons / 6 ounces / 175 g sugar

2/3 cup / 150 ml warm water

1 2/3 cups / 7 ounces / 200 g flour

3/4 cup / 6 ounces / 175 g salted butter

There are lots of good reasons to eat at Chez Michel, located near the Gare du Nord in Paris, especially in autumn, when game is featured prominently on the menu. Whatever the season, there are always specialties from Brittany, many of them unfamiliar to the foreign and Parisian diner alike. One of my favorites is the kouign amann. I first ordered it because of its name, which means "butter cake" in Breton. More pastry than cake, it is flaky and buttery, like a dense croissant with a cara-melized bottom and crisp top. Served warm, not hot, its buttery center is soft under the crisp sugar-coated exterior. Kouign amann is full of the aromas and flavors of its defining ingredient, salted butter, and it is the only dessert that has tempted my husband away from the restaurant's creamy riz au lait *(rice pudding). This recipe comes from Thierry Breton, Chez Michel's owner and chef.*

Mix the yeast with 1 teaspoon of the sugar in a small bowl. Add the warm water and stir. Leave the yeast mixture in a warm area for about 10 min-utes to proof.

Sift the flour into a bowl and stir in the yeast mixture to make a dough. Transfer the dough to a floured surface and knead gently until smooth. Form the dough into a ball, cover, and let rest for 30 minutes.

Using about 2 teaspoons of the butter, butter a 9-inch / 23-cm cake pan, and sprinkle the bottom and sides of the pan with 1 tablespoon of the sugar.

Place the remaining butter between 2 sheets of parchment paper and, using a rolling pin, beat the butter until it is pliable. The aim is to have the butter and the dough the same consistency. Form the softened butter into a 6-inch / 15-cm square about 1/4 inch / 6 mm thick.

Place the dough on a cool floured surface and roll out 4 flaps from the center. You want to make a rough 12-inch / 30-cm square to enclose the butter, with the center of the dough 4 times the thickness of the flaps. Set aside 2 tablespoons of the sugar and sprinkle the thick center of the dough with half of the remaining sugar. Place the butter on top and sprinkle the butter with the remaining sugar. Fold over the flaps to enclose the butter and sugar completely. You will have a square of pastry, with the butter in the center. Tap the pastry square firmly with a rolling pin to even it out and flatten slightly. Roll the pastry out in all directions to make a rectangle about 16 by 8 inches / 40 by 20 cm. Fold the pastry into thirds, as you would a letter, and turn the rectangle 90 degrees, so you have an open end facing you. Roll out the pastry again to the same size rectangle. Fold it in thirds again, then cover and set aside.

Preheat the oven to 425°F / 220°C.

Roll the pastry into a rough round shape about 9 inches / 23 cm in diameter. Ease the pastry into the prepared pan, pressing with the palm of your hand to flatten and fold the pastry back on itself to fit, if necessary. Let the pastry rest in the pan for 15 minutes.

Brush the top of the pastry with water and sprinkle with the remaining 2 tablespoons of sugar. Bake until golden brown and caramelized, about 25 minutes. Let it cool slightly in the pan, and then turn it out onto a plate along with any of the buttery caramel in the pan.

Serve warm or at room temperature. This pastry also keeps well in the refrigerator, but it must be served warm or at room temperature.

THE BUTTER TOWER OF ROUEN

Built in the Middle Ages from the local white stone, the cathedral of Rouen is a fine example of Flamboyant Gothic architecture. Although it originally had only one tower, in 1485 it was decided to add a second tower to the south end of the facade. When construction began, however, the ground under the cathedral subsided and the facade began to lean, making it necessary to rebuild the entire front entrance of the cathedral.

The new tower, which was finally completed in 1506, became known locally as the Butter Tower. Some speculated that the name originated with the buttery color of the stone, but there is another, more plausible explanation. During Lent it was common practice for wealthy Catholics to buy dispensations from the church. This allowed them to continue eating butter, even though it was officially prohibited. Many good citizens of Rouen were understandably unable to resist the pleasure of butter, even for the chance of eternal salvation, and willingly paid the church for the right to eat butter. Their love of butter financed the Butter Tower.

The Catholic Church is based in Rome, and southern Catholics rarely cooked with or ate butter, preferring the readily available olive oil, which was not forbidden during Lent. In the north, however, animal fat, especially butter, was an important part of the diet. The Church took the opportunity to enrich its coffers by selling butter dispensations, and enterprising southern businessmen exploited the situation, too, by exporting oil, usually of inferior quality, to the north during Lent. These practices were among the many things that enraged the outspoken priest Martin Luther. In his *An den christlichen Adel deutscher Nation*, in 1520, he wrote, "In Rome, they make a mockery of fasting, while forcing us to eat an oil they themselves would not use to grease their slippers. Then they sell us the right to eat the foods forbidden on fast days, but they have stolen that same liberty from us with their ecclesiastical laws. . . . Eating butter, they say, is a greater sin than to lie, blaspheme, or indulge in impurity."

During Lent the import of oil increased the foreign debt of northern European countries, and local agricultural production was cut back as the demand for animal products fell. I may not be able to argue that Protestantism was born out of a love of butter, but it is interesting to note that the countries that broke from the Catholic Church in the sixteenth century were those where animal fats, not olive oil, were the main cooking medium.

Shortbread

Makes 1 round (about 12 wedges)

1 cup / 8 ounces / 225 g cold unsalted butter, diced, plus 1 teaspoon softened butter

$1/2$ cup / $3^1/2$ ounces / 100 g superfine (caster) sugar

$1^1/2$ cups / $6^1/2$ ounces / 185 g flour

$1/2$ cup / 2 ounces / 65 g rice flour

Pinch of fine sea salt

$1/8$ teaspoon fleur de sel or granulated sugar (optional)

To add butter to the spinach: to add a little to the kitty (French)

My grandmother emigrated from Scotland to Australia when she was eighteen. I'd love to say that she carried this recipe with her to pass on to the future generations on the other side of the world, but, no, we bought our shortbread (it was, however, imported from Scotland). My favorite shortbread is soft and almost crumbly, and that is what this recipe gives you. I have a collection of shortbread molds, but because I bake shortbread only once or twice a year, they don't get enough use to work properly, and my shortbread always sticks. By baking the shortbread in a flan tin, however, I get a nice fluted edge, and it comes out in one piece. Instead of sprinkling the shortbread with sugar, try a little fleur de sel *instead. The salt highlights the buttery flavor.*

Using 1 teaspoon of softened butter, lightly butter the sides and bottom of a 9 or $9^1/2$-inch / 23 or 24-cm flan tin with a removable bottom.

Combine the cold butter and sugar in the bowl of a stand mixer. Using the paddle attachment, mix on low speed for 15 seconds. Add both the flours and a pinch of salt and mix again on low until the dough comes together, 3 to 5 minutes.

Form the dough into a ball and, on a floured surface, roll it into a 9-inch / 23-cm circle about $1/2$ inch / 1 cm thick. Place the dough in the flan tin, patting it so that it evenly fills the tin. Using a fork, prick the dough all over, right through to the flan tin.

Refrigerate the dough for 1 hour.

Preheat the oven to 300°F / 150°C.

Sprinkle the top of the dough with *fleur de sel* or sugar and place the flan tin on a baking sheet. Bake until the shortbread is just firm in the center and beginning to color, about 1 hour.

Transfer the shortbread to a wire rack and, using a sharp knife, score the shortbread into wedges. Let cool. When cold, remove the shortbread from the flan tin and cut into wedges, following the marks. Store the shortbread in an airtight container for up to 1 week.

BUTTER IN TIBET

In Tibet, the cool weather means that butter doesn't need to be turned into ghee to preserve it, plus the Tibetans prefer their butter rancid. Made from yak milk, butter is not simply eaten, it is also mixed into *tsocha*, a souplike mixture of tea, yak butter, and salt, which Tibetans drink several times a day. Yak butter is also mixed with toasted barley flour to make a nourishing porridge called *tsampa*, a staple food in Tibet. Butter is also used as currency, to discharge social obligations and pay off debts.

Among the largest consumers of yak butter in Tibet are the lamaseries. The monks eat the butter, burn it in their altar lamps, and use it to embalm the bodies of lamas. Large quantities of butter have also traditionally been used for religious festivals, like the Festival of the Butter Gods (see page 54).

Rhubarb King's Cake

Serves 10 to 12

7 tablespoons / $3\frac{1}{2}$ ounces / 100 g unsalted butter, softened

$\frac{1}{2}$ cup / $3\frac{1}{2}$ ounces / 100 g plus 2 tablespoons superfine (caster) sugar

Pinch of fine sea salt

$1\frac{1}{4}$ cups / $3\frac{1}{2}$ ounces / 100 g ground almonds

2 tablespoons flour

2 eggs

1 tablespoon aged rum or Cognac

1 pound / 450 g fresh rhubarb, trimmed

1 recipe Puff Pastry (page 33)

To go in with butter and sugar: to really defeat someone

The older I get, the more I value traditions. I grew up eating hot cross buns and Simmel cake on Easter Sunday, and Christmas wasn't Christmas without Traditional Christmas Pudding (page 211) and rich fruitcake, even in hot, sunny Australia. In France I discovered that there are many pastries and cakes linked to saints' days. I chose the date for my wedding because of a pastry. May 16 is Saint Honoré's day, and the Saint Honoré pastry is a wonderful combination of puff and choux pastry filled with crème chibouste, pastry cream lightened with whipping cream, and garnished with caramel. Another of my favorites is the galette des rois, *or king's cake, which is eaten to celebrate Epiphany. A bean or trinket is hidden in this puff pastry filled with an almond mixture, and the person who finds the bean in his or her slice of cake is crowned the king or queen for the day. Many cultures have this tradition of hiding tokens in desserts.*

Younger pastry chefs in France are replacing the almond filling with new flavors like pistachio, but sometimes they are a little too sweet for me. In my updated version of this dessert I add a layer of cooked, slightly tart rhubarb, which balances the sweet almond filling and reveals a colorful surprise when the pastry is cut, even if you don't get the bean.

In a food processor combine the butter with $\frac{1}{2}$ cup / $3\frac{1}{2}$ ounces / 100 g of the sugar and the salt and process until very well mixed. Add the almonds and flour and process again until the mixture is well blended. You are making a frangipane, a rich almond filling for the cake. Whisk the eggs together in a small bowl and set aside 2 tablespoons for an egg wash. Whisk the remaining eggs with the rum and pour over the almond mixture in the food processor. Process again until well mixed. Transfer the almond mixture to a bowl, cover, and refrigerate for 4 to 6 hours or overnight.

Preheat the oven to 375°F / 190°C. Place another glass baking dish in the refrigerator.

Rinse the rhubarb and cut the stalks into fingers $2\frac{3}{4}$ inches / 7 cm long. Arrange in a single layer in another glass baking dish. (If the rhubarb stalks are different thicknesses, place the thicker ones at one end of the dish and the thinner ones at the other.) The rhubarb should still be damp from rinsing; if not, sprinkle it with about 1 tablespoon of water. Sprinkle the rhubarb with the remaining 2 tablespoons of sugar.

Bake the rhubarb until the stalks are softened, 8 to 15 minutes. Watch carefully, as stems of different thicknesses will cook at different rates. Test the rhubarb by pressing the stalks with your finger; the rhubarb should yield but not be mushy. As the stalks soften, transfer them to the clean cold glass dish to cool. Transfer the cooled rhubarb pieces to a pan lined with paper towels to drain.

Line a baking sheet with parchment paper. Cut the puff pastry in half and roll the pastry out into 2 squares about 11 inches / 28 cm, then cut 2 circles, one 10 inches / 25 cm and the other $10\frac{1}{2}$ inches / 26 cm in diameter. (Save the pastry trimmings for Puff Pastry Palmiers, page 60.) Place the 10-inch / 25-cm circle on the prepared baking sheet.

Take the almond mixture from the refrigerator, place it between 2 pieces of plastic wrap, and roll it into a 9-inch / 23-cm circle. Center the almond circle on the pastry on the baking sheet, and top with the drained rhubarb pieces. Brush the edge of the pastry circle with the egg wash and then top with the larger pastry circle. Press to seal, trimming the top circle if necessary. Scallop the edges of the pastry with the back of a knife. Cut a steam vent in the top and, using a sharp knife, gently score the top of the pastry by cutting curving lines from the center to the edge. Brush the pastry with egg wash and refrigerate for at least 30 minutes.

Preheat the oven to 425°F / 220°C.

Brush the top of pastry again with egg wash and then bake until the pastry is puffed and dark golden brown, 30 to 40 minutes.

Place the baking sheet on a wire rack to cool. Serve the pastry at room temperature.

THE BUTTER SAINT

In thirteenth-century Germany, a woman named Haseka led the austere life of a religious ascetic. She inhabited a small, simple room attached to the church, helped by a devout woman named Berta, and relied on charity and gifts of food for her survival. One day Haseka received a gift of butter, which she stored in the chest in her room. Soon, however, the butter turned rancid, and its strong smell overwhelmed the tiny room. Berta told Haseka that she couldn't bear the smell and would no longer be able to help her. That night Haseka prayed to God, "Lord, this butter, regardless of what kind it is, we shall consume in your name. All things have been put in your power; in your power and strength you produce good from evil, when you will; if you will, you shall be able to make this butter good."

The next morning, when Haseka awoke, the smell of rancid butter had vanished, and when she tried the butter it tasted freshly churned. The faithful Berta returned, and Haseka lived a long, devout life eating a little of that butter every day. Miraculously, her butter remained fresh and never ran out. Although she was very old when she died, all those who saw her body remarked on her youthful looks, a result, no doubt, of eating fresh butter every day. Naturally Haseka became the patron saint of butter, and women churning butter would ask for her help to ensure that the butter would form, and they prayed to her to turn their rancid butter fresh. They also ate a little butter every day, hoping to guard their youthful good looks just like Haseka.

2 pork fat: THE KING

Juicy pork belly, smoky bacon, French fries that are crisp from a bath in hot lard, a roast leg of pork complete with crackling and flaky lard pastry: all are possible thanks to the pig. It's no wonder that pork fat is at the heart of the traditional cuisines in Europe, America, and China, and that so many recipes begin with some sort of pork fat.

With its high proportion of fat to meat, the pig is truly the king when it comes to animal fat. The pig also has more than one kind of fat. There's back fat, belly fat, caul fat, and leaf lard. Then there are the many porcine products like bacon, ham, and lardo. The pig is valued as much for his fat as for his meat . . . or at least he was.

The last one hundred years haven't been kind to the pig. At the beginning of the twentieth century, lard was the most popular fat in our kitchens. Readily available and more versatile than butter, lard was used for sautéing, frying, and baking and even as a spread. The arrival of vegetable oils and new, cheaper hydrogenated fats that could be stored without refrigeration challenged lard's place in our kitchens. Then came the campaign against animal fats. The demand for fatty pork and pure pork fat dropped precipitously, and pork producers responded by breeding leaner animals. The figures from the USDA tell a sad story: in 1950 a pig yielded about 33.2 pounds / 15 kg of fat, but by 1990 this figure had fallen to just 10.1 pounds / 4.6 kg. Today lard doesn't even register on the chart of the fats used most often in the kitchen. As the pig became leaner, our annual per capita consumption of lard fell from 12.6 pounds / 5.7 kg in 1950 to a mere 0.4 pound / 180 g in 1995. Because we have no use for their fat, pigs are slaughtered younger today, and instead of producing rosy pink flesh, pigs give us the "other white meat." Pork is now so lean it needs to be brined to give it taste. Pork has lost its fat, and with it its flavor.

Lardy cakes: a bread dough enriched with lard and flavored with sugar and dried fruits; still popular in Wiltshire, England, an area renowned for its pork

67

As for lard, the mere mention of the word strikes horror into all but the most fearless gourmet. Most of us equate lard with obesity and imagine that anything cooked in or made with lard ends up with a faintly piggy taste and loaded with bad fat. Lard, we believe, is just waiting to migrate from our food to our hips, stomachs, and, worst of all, our arteries, the moment we swallow. Even those who grew up with lard in the refrigerator have been convinced by the anti-fat forces that cooking in lard is a guilty pleasure to be indulged in only rarely. Today real lard is hard to find.

But pork fat in all its forms is not only very useful, but it is also good for us. Like all fats, it is a mixture of saturated, polyunsaturated, and monounsaturated fatty acids. While the exact percentages vary with the pig's diet and the breed of pig, pork fat is mostly monounsaturated (see page 69) in the form of oleic fatty acid, plus it contains palmitoleic fatty acid, which has antimicrobial properties. Its saturated fatty acids are stearic acid, which converts to oleic acid in the body, and palmitic acid, believed to have a neutral effect on cholesterol. Pork fat's low level of polyunsaturated fatty acids means it doesn't turn rancid easily and is very stable when heated. This makes pork fat an excellent fat for frying. Not only are foods fried in lard very crisp, but they also absorb less fat than if they were fried in oil. Lard is also great for making pastry, because its crystalline structure makes dough very flaky. So why shouldn't lard be in everyone's refrigerator?

The tide is turning for pork fat. The realization of the dangers associated with trans fats has caused many of us to reconsider the benefits of lard. In 2005, the U.S. per-capita consumption of lard rose to 1.5 pounds / 680 g—a small step, but one in the right direction. This trend, combined with cooks demanding pork with more fat and flavor, has led to an interest in heritage breeds such as Berkshire, Tamworth, and Middle White. These pigs naturally put on fat and have delicious, lightly marbled meat. The quest for lean meat is so ingrained in us, though, that butchers often meet resistance when customers see rosy meat covered with a thick layer of fat. We need to understand that this coat of fat tells us that the animal was raised slowly and that the meat underneath it will be much more flavorful. That fatty coat also means that there will be more fat to render. While some suppliers are selling rendered lard, a lot of the commercially available lard has been hydrogenated to extend its shelf life, leaving it full of trans fats, which turn this good fat bad. Rendering your own lard is simple (see page 73), and by doing so you will be able to choose the best fat for either cooking or baking. Lard keeps well in the refrigerator and can be frozen.

66They interlard their
native Drinks with choice
Of strongest Brandy, yet
scarce with these Aids
Enabl'd to prevent the
suddain Rot
Of freezing Nose, and
quick-decaying Feet.99

JOHN PHILIPS

Fat	% Saturated	% Monounsaturated	% Polyunsaturated
LARD	39	45	11
BACON FAT	39	45	11

Note: All figures are approximate and vary with the breed and diet of the animal. The numbers don't always total 100, as there is also water and connective tissue in the fat.

Types of Pork Fat

The pig yields many different types of fat, each with its own role to play in the kitchen.

Back Fat or Fatback

As the name implies, this comes from the back of the animal, but it is also found on the shoulder and rump. The layer of fat lying just below the skin, back fat is sold in pieces, usually with the skin still attached. Chilled, this fat can be thinly sliced, making it ideal for wrapping around lean cuts of meat, poultry, and game to protect them from drying out when they are roasted. Slices of back fat are used to line terrine dishes, and finely ground back fat is added to sausages, pâtés, and ground meats to keep them moist. Rendered back fat is good for sautéing and frying.

Belly

Pork belly consists of both firm and soft fat layered with meat. It is thicker and meatier at the end closer to the head, and thinner, with more fat, at the tail end. Usually sold with the skin, it can be found with or without the bones, but it is more commonly boneless, as the bones are sold as spare ribs. The primary use for this cut is in making side (slab) or streaky bacon, but it is much more versatile than that. Its combination of fat and meat makes it an ideal roast, as its thick layers of fat prevent the meat from drying out. You can cure it with a salt rub to make Salt Pork (page 91), and it is the perfect fat to add to Spanish-Style Pork Rillettes (page 79) and Faggots with Onion Gravy (page 104).

Leaf Lard

Also called flead or flare fat, leaf lard is the fat from around the pig's kidneys. Ideal for making pastry because of its brittle crystalline structure, this is the crème de la crème of pork fat.

Caul Fat

Caul fat is the membrane of fat that encloses the pig's intestines. It resembles a spidery web, sometimes studded with large pieces of fat or delicately flecked with fat. It looks more like a piece of lace than something edible and is often called lace fat. This is my favorite pork fat because it is so useful. Up to 3 feet / 1 m square, caul fat is ideal for lining terrine dishes, is easier to use and prettier than back fat, and is perfect for enclosing sausage mixtures, if casings are unavailable or you just can't be bothered with all of the rigmarole of stuffing them. Caul fat sticks to itself, eliminating any need for string or toothpicks to keep it in place, and it turns a lovely golden brown when cooked. This makes it ideal for wrapping lean cuts of meat, poultry, and game before roasting them. Usually sold fresh, caul fat needs a soak in warm water before using it to make the membrane flexible. Add a splash of vinegar if there is any smell. Gently squeeze out the water, stretch the fat out, being careful not to tear it, and then place it on a towel and pat it dry before using. Caul fat must be ordered in advance from your butcher, but it freezes well, so buy more than you need.

Frying in Lard

Deep-Frying

Although I have a soft spot for beef tallow, lard is generally easier to get and it is more neutral, imparting a crisp texture but no flavor. Like most people, I had pretty much given up deep-frying at home, not from any fear of fried foods, but because of the smell. Even though my kitchen is equipped with a commercial exhaust fan, any time I fried there was always a smell. When I was eating the crispy delights straight from the hot oil it wasn't so bad. It was the next day, when those oily molecules were still lingering in my kitchen, that put me off frying. Working on this book I have rediscovered the joys and benefits of deep-frying in lard. Now that I'm using lard again in my fryer, not only are my French fries crisp, tasting only of potato, but also my kitchen is odor-free, with no smell of fried food hanging in the air.

When deep-frying, you need enough fat to immerse the food. As soon as the food hits the hot fat it sizzles; this is the moisture being released as steam. The steam coming out of the food prevents the fat from going in, and thus stops the food from becoming greasy. This is why the temperature of the fat is so important. You must use a fat that can take the heat, and in this respect lard is ideal.

Lard is very low in polyunsaturated fatty acids, so it is very stable when heated and much slower to oxidize and turn rancid than highly polyunsaturated oils are. It also has a high smoke point, 400°F / 200°C, which is important when deep-frying. Its neutral flavor makes it ideal for everything from potatoes and fish to doughnuts, and lard can be filtered and reused several times. However, it is important not to fry your doughnuts in the same fat you cooked your fish in, unless you want fish-flavored doughnuts.

I want to strongly deter you from leaving the lard in the fryer or frying pan. If you have any English relatives you may recall the "chip pan," a battered old pot kept near the stove filled with cold fat that was used over and over again. This practice is not only bad for your health, but it's dangerous, too. All fat degrades with time, and heat makes this happen even faster. The fat should be filtered after each use, cooled, and then refrigerated. It is probably wise not to reuse the fat more than three times. When you see that the chilled fat has changed color from white to beige to brown, it's time for new fat. Also, every time fat is heated, its smoke point is lowered, making it more flammable. Never leave hot fat unattended, and immediately clean up any spilled fat. If your fat does catch on fire, turn off the heat and smother the flame by covering it with

Lard is a general term for rendered pork fat. But, because the melting point of pork fat varies, depending on which part of the animal's body it comes from, it is well worth rendering the different fats separately.

Larding, a popular technique in France, is a time-consuming way to add fat to lean meat. Long cold strips of cold pork fat are literally sewn into meat using a larding needle. A larded piece of meat has an uncanny resemblance to a hedgehog. Although I own a larding needle, I rarely use it, preferring to wrap lean cuts of meat and game in caul fat, because it's easier and quicker.

Lardo is an Italian specialty made by curing pieces of back fat. It is eaten raw, thinly sliced, and often drizzled with olive or truffle oil (see page 95).

LARD BY ANY OTHER NAME . . .

a metal lid or baking sheet. Do not use water: water and oil don't mix, and water is not effective in extinguishing a fat fire.

I admit that frying in lard is not as easy as using oil. You have to render your lard first, and lard is not liquid at room temperature, so you have to liquefy it before pouring it into your fryer. But if you store the rendered lard that is destined for the fryer in clean glass jars, you can simply pop the jars in a pan of warm water to melt the lard easily.

You can use an electric deep fryer, but I prefer using a deep heavy pan, a wire basket, and a thermometer, which is much more accurate than the temperature gauge on most fryers. Never fill the pan or fryer more than half full of fat to allow room for the food and the fat to bubble up. Heat the fat slowly, and make sure the fat is at the right temperature before adding the food. Perhaps most important, don't try to fry too much at once: the temperature of the fat will drop too low, and you will end up with greasy food.

Shallow Frying

Lard is also perfect for shallow frying or sautéing when you want a neutral flavor and a crisp texture. Lard is the best fat for making fried chicken, turning it wonderfully crisp, crunchy, and golden in dishes like Chicken Kiev (page 46).

Bacon and Ham

Wherever pork is eaten, bacon is loved. Even when pork fat fell from grace, bacon, with its great salty and often smoky flavor, remained popular. The word *bacon*, which entered the English language between the twelfth and fourteenth centuries, comes from the German word *bach*, meaning "back," so, strictly speaking, "back bacon" is a redundant term. Before the word "bacon" came into use, the piece of an animal that had been salted and cured was called a "flitch." In some regions of England, during the Middle Ages, a flitch was given to any married couple that could prove they had survived their first year of marriage without an argument. I doubt that many flitches were given away, but this custom could be the origin of the expression "bringing home the bacon."

Fear of fat made bacon a guilty pleasure that we could never quite give up. Low-fat bacon and bacon substitutes were never a match for the real thing, but it turns out that we needn't have felt guilty at all. Bacon fat, like all pork fat, is mainly monounsaturated (see page 69), and just a small amount can make a big difference in many dishes, such as pasta, dried beans and peas, and many vegetables, especially cabbage, fresh peas, pumpkin, and potatoes. A natural partner to eggs, bacon also gives fish and shellfish both taste and much-needed fat. It even goes well with sugar. Bacon is all about flavor, and the best bacon comes with a good amount of fat to carry the flavors of the cure and the smoking. Bacon from the belly, or side bacon, has lots of good fat and more flavor than does back bacon.

Not all bacon is created equal. To save money and time, bacon is often cured quickly by injecting it with a brine. It's hard to judge the quality of bacon just by looking, but good bacon should be dry, not plumped with water, and not be cut too thinly. The real proof, though, will be in the pan. If your pan fills with water the bacon has been injected; good traditionally brined or dry-cured bacon will crisp in the pan as it slowly releases its fat.

Ham, like bacon, depends on its fat for its flavor, and without a good covering of fat to protect it from bacteria, pork cannot be transformed into a quality aged ham. Every country that raises pigs produces its own distinctive ham, the flavor of which will vary with the breed, the pig's diet, and the curing method.

Perhaps the best ham in the world—certainly the best I have ever eaten—is *jamón ibérico*, which comes from Spain. Anyone who has tasted this ham loves the flavor and texture of its fat. I always serve this ham at room temperature, so the fat becomes translucent and melts on your tongue. This Spanish ham comes from a pig whose diet is rich in acorns; a single pig will eat 13 to 22 pounds / 6 to 10 kg of them a day. The acorns not only contribute to the ham's distinctive taste, but they also make the fat very high in monounsaturated fatty acids. The fat in this ham is up to 60 percent monounsaturated, and its omega-3 fatty acid levels are four times that of regular ham. So it is not only tasty, it's good for you.

> I can't tell if it's bacon or pork: I'm confused (French)

> On the pig's back: in a fortunate position (Australian)

> It was rumored that New York journalist A. J. Liebling used a piece of bacon as a bookmark.

Rendering Pork Fat

I remember my mother buying lard in waxed containers from our butcher when I was a child. While some butchers and suppliers are rendering their own lard again, it's so simple that you should really do it yourself. The big advantage of rendering at home is that you can decide which fat to render and you can control its taste. Back fat is the best for shallow and deep-frying, while leaf lard is preferred for pastry making. If you can't get leaf lard you can still make pastry with rendered back fat, but it is worth pestering your butcher for both kinds. Filtered rendered lard keeps well in the refrigerator and can be frozen.

If you are rendering just a small amount, about 1 pound / 450 g, do it on top of the stove. I usually render larger amounts, though, so I prefer to use the oven. It requires less fuss, and since the temperature stays very low, the fat doesn't color, which means it maintains its neutral taste. Some cooks prefer lard with a more roasted taste, and you can make it more strongly flavored if you wish (see page 75).

It is hard to estimate how much liquid fat will be released by a quantity of solid fat, as it depends on the moisture content and the amount of connective tissue in the fat. I always get more liquid fat from rendering in the oven than on the stove. You should average about 1 to $1^{1}/_{2}$ cups / 250 to 375 ml per 1 pound / 450 g of fat.

It goes without saying that you need the best-quality pork fat that you can lay your hands on. Find a farmer that is raising heritage breeds or a butcher that is selling them. My butcher used to throw away the fat from the heritage pork he sold. The pork was so cloaked in fat that he cut off a good 1 inch / 2.5 cm before daring to put the meat in his display case. Too much fat, he thought, would scare off his customers. Well, I gave him a tongue-lashing, and it worked, because now he gives me the fat.

To render lard, preheat the oven to 250°F / 120°C if you are using the oven instead of the stovetop. Start with the fat really cold or partially frozen, so it is easier to handle. Before rendering back fat, you can remove the skin and use it for Spiced Pork Crackling (page 76) or Crackling Brittle (page 121). If you leave the skin on when you render the fat, you will get unflavored cracklings. If you're using leaf lard, pull away the papery membrane that keeps the fat together and discard it.

Cut the fat into 1-inch / 2.5-cm pieces; the smaller the pieces, the faster they will render. Don't put the fat through a meat grinder, or you'll end with more fat in the grinder than in your pan.

Put the diced fat in a heavy flameproof casserole or Dutch oven and add about $^{1}/_{3}$ cup / 75 ml of water per 1 pound / 450 g of fat. The water keeps the fat from burning before it begins to melt. Place the pan in the oven, uncovered, or over very low heat on the stove. In the oven, stir the fat after 30 minutes, then at 45 minutes, and then every hour, watching carefully as the fat begins to color. If you are rendering on the stove, you will have to stir the fat more often and make sure you keep the heat very low. The fat will melt, the water will evaporate, and bits of firmer fat will float in the liquid fat. When you stir the fat, press the larger pieces against the side of the pan to help them melt. The process can take from 4 to 8 hours, depending on the quantity of fat and the size of the pieces. Leaf lard renders faster than back fat.

As soon as the pieces in the pan start to color, remove the pan from the oven or the stovetop and let cool slightly. Strain the fat through a cheesecloth-lined sieve into clean containers. You can return the pieces of fat remaining in the sieve to the pan and continue cooking them to extract more fat. Eventually they will turn dark golden; these bits are the unflavored cracklings. Personally, I don't find them that tasty, unless you've left the skin on the fat.

Let the fat cool completely before covering and storing it in the refrigerator for up to 2 months, or in the freezer for a year. Remember to label your fat, as it is sometimes hard to tell them apart.

FLAVORED FATS

Mexican Lard: According to Mexican cooking authority Rick Bayless, Mexicans often render their lard at a higher temperature, around 350°F / 180°C. This gives the fat a roasted pork flavor, making it a good addition to dishes like Refried Beans (page 108). I use my lard to cook, fry, and make pastry, though, so I want its flavor to be as neutral as possible. If you want the best of both worlds, once you pour off the first batch of neutral-flavored rendered fat you can continue to cook the cracklings to get a small amount of pork-flavored fat.

Bacon and Rillettes Fat: If you want to infuse your dishes with an even stronger taste, don't throw out that bacon fat. It can add a subtle smoky taste to everything from meats and vegetables to mayonnaise (see page 101) and cookies (see page 118). When you've finished cooking your bacon, simply strain the fat through cheesecloth into a container and store in the refrigerator or freezer. Don't forget to label your fats.

When making Spanish-Style Pork Rillettes (page 79), I often end up with more fat than I need. This bright-orange fat is quite highly flavored, so I use it in Refried Beans (page 108) or other dishes where the color doesn't matter and I want a spicy flavor.

Spiced Pork Crackling

Makes about 5 ounces / 150 g

1 1/2 teaspoons allspice berries

1 whole star anise, broken into pieces

1/3 small nutmeg or 1/2 teaspoon freshly grated nutmeg

1/2 teaspoon black peppercorns

10 1/2 ounces / 300 g coarse sea salt

Finely grated zest and juice of 1 lemon

10 1/2 ounces / 300 g pork skin, fat trimmed

Always eat crackling with a bit of kasha, because you sure can't spoil kasha with fat. (Ukrainian)

I've always loved homemade pork crackling. My aunt was famous in our family for always being able to get good crackling on her pork roast. You don't have to roast a joint of pork, though, to enjoy crackling; instead, you can simply cook the skin by itself. Inspired by molecular chef Heston Blumenthal, this recipe makes great crackling without any technical tricks or wizardry. The pork skin is rubbed with a spiced salt mixture, which both adds flavor and draws out the water from the skin. Plan to make this dish when you are rendering back fat for lard, as the pork fat you purchase will likely have the skin still attached. The skin on a pig's back is thicker and puffs up better than the thinner belly skin and the skin from heritage breed pigs makes the best crackling.

The pork crackling will keep for a week in an airtight container. As well as making a great snack with drinks—served plain or with a dipping sauce like plain vinegar, Fresh Tomato Salsa (page 181), or Chile Vinegar Dipping Sauce (page 78)—it can also be added to soups and salads, mixed into rice dishes, or turned into Crackling Brittle (page 121).

Combine the allspice berries, star anise, nutmeg, and peppercorns in a spice grinder or a mortar and grind until powdery. Add the salt and stir. Add the lemon zest and 2 tablespoons of lemon juice to the spice mixture and mix well.

Cut the pork skin into 4 roughly equal pieces. Sprinkle one-third of the spice mixture in the bottom of a glass dish, lay 2 pieces of pork skin on top (don't worry if you have to overlap the pieces slightly), then sprinkle with another one-third of the spice mixture. Add the remaining 2 pieces of pork skin and sprinkle with the remaining mixture. Cover and refrigerate for 24 to 36 hours, turning the pieces over after 12 hours.

Preheat the oven to 350°F / 180°C.

Remove the pork skin from the refrigerator, rinse off the spice mixture, and pat dry. Using a utility (Stanley) knife or box cutter, score the skin at 1/4-inch / 6-mm intervals, being careful not to cut all the way through the skin.

Line a rimmed baking sheet with aluminum foil and place the pork on the foil in a single layer, skin side down. Cover with a sheet of parchment paper and then another baking sheet. Place a heavy cast-iron pan or casserole lid on top to weight it down, and bake for 20 minutes.

Remove the baking sheets from the oven and lift off the pan and set aside. Pour off any fat from the bottom baking sheet and reserve for another use. Turn the pork skin side up, then cover again with the parchment paper and the second baking sheet and weight down again. Bake until the skin is golden brown, another 15 minutes. You'll hear the pork popping and crackling in the oven.

Remove the pork from the oven, pour off any rendered fat, and let cool slightly. Scrape off any excess bits of fat from the skin, if necessary.

Increase the oven temperature to 400°F / 200°C.

Return the pork skin to a single baking sheet and cook until the pieces curl and crisp up, 10 to 15 minutes. Remove them from the oven, let cool slightly, and break into pieces before serving warm or cold.

Chile Vinegar Dipping Sauce

Makes 1/4 cup / 60 ml

1 fresh red serrano chile

1/4 cup / 60 ml rice wine vinegar

Vinegar is a good match for fatty pork skin. One of my friends loves dipping pork crackling straight into malt vinegar, but I prefer this lighter, spicier vinegar.

Remove the ribs and seeds from the chile and finely chop. Stir the chile into the vinegar and let stand for 30 minutes before serving. It will keep for up to 3 days in the refrigerator.

LITERARY LARD

To lard one's prose:
to mix the solid part of a discourse with fulsome and irrelevant matter (*The Shorter Oxford English Dictionary*)

In the late ninteenth century, Émile Zola wrote wonderful descriptions of Les Halles, the huge, lively food market in central Paris that was known as the belly of Paris. Today it is hard to imagine that the modern market, now housed in huge warehouses in a distant Paris suburb, could inspire any writer. In this passage from *Le Ventre de Paris*, Zola describes his character Florent's attraction to Lisa, the charcutier's wife, and to the fat and meat that surround her:

That day she looked superbly fresh, the whiteness of her apron and sleeves reflecting that of the plates, her stout neck and pink cheeks echoing the gentle flesh tones of the hams and the pallor of the transparent fat. The more he looked at her, the more intimidated Florent became, unsettled by the four-square frankness of her bearing, resorting to surreptitious glances in the mirrors dotted around the shop. He saw reflections of her back, her front, her sides; he even found her on the ceiling, her head bowed, exposing her tight bun and her fine hair smoothed back at the temples. There was a whole crowd of Lisas, broad-shouldered, their arms powerfully jointed, the curvature of their breasts so taut and silent that they aroused no carnal thoughts in him, so much did they remind him of a paunch. He stopped to admire one particular profile, there in the mirror next to him between two sides of pork. Pork and lumps of lard, hooked over notches of a metal rail, hung from end to end of the length of the marbled, mirrored shop. And Lisa's profile, with its solid throat, its rounded lines and protruding bust, was a well-fleshed queen in effigy amid all that fat and meat.

Spanish-Style Pork Rillettes (Manteca Colorada)

When I stay with friends, I often find myself in their kitchen, leafing through their cookbook collection. I always discover new ideas and recipes to jot down in my notebook. This recipe was inspired by one in Moro: The Cookbook *by Samuel and Samantha Clark, which my friend Laura has in her collection in London.*

Rillettes can be made from any fatty meat, and the seasonings and spices you can add are infinitely variable. The most important thing is the texture: the end result should be juicy shreds of meat held together by fat. Often people suggest using two forks to pull the meat apart, but I find your fingers give a superior texture. And, because your fingers are so sensitive, you will find all the pieces of sinew while you're shredding it (you'll also condition your hands with all that fat).

I either pack the mixture into a small terrine dish, so I can cut the rillettes into slices to serve as an appetizer, or into individual soufflé dishes. Serve with baguette slices or toasts if serving with drinks, or with a sharp green salad to accompany it as a first course.

Cut the pork belly and pork fat into 1-inch / 2.5-cm pieces and place them in a large bowl. Add the sherry. Peel and halve the garlic cloves, removing the germ. Add the garlic, bay leaves, thyme, coarse salt, and fennel seeds to the bowl. Sprinkle both types of paprika over the pork and season generously with pepper. Stir to combine and marinate the pork for 6 to 8 hours or overnight in the refrigerator.

Preheat the oven to 250°F / 120°C.

Transfer the pork with all the seasonings and the sherry to a heavy pan or Dutch oven, cover, and cook in the oven, stirring occasionally, until the pork is so tender that it falls apart, about 4 hours.

Remove the pork from the oven and tip the pork with all the fat, spices, and juices into a large fine-mesh sieve suspended over a bowl. Empty the contents of the sieve onto a large platter and pour the liquid from the bowl into a measuring cup. Set aside the liquid and let the meat mixture cool slightly.

Using your fingers, pull the meat and fat apart, discarding the thyme sprigs and bay leaves as you go. Discard any pieces of membrane or sinew that don't shred. Be patient: this process takes time, and the key is to create shreds of meat and fat. Return the shredded mixture to the bowl.

The cooking liquid will have separated into fat and juices. Carefully pour off the fat and set aside. Add about 1/2 cup / 125 ml of the juices to the shredded mixture so that it is very moist. Taste and adjust the seasoning, adding salt and pepper if necessary.

Pack the mixture into ceramic dishes or a terrine, leaving a 1/4-inch / 6-mm gap at the top of each dish. As you pack the meat into the dish, you will see liquid gently oozing from the meat. Place the dishes in the

Makes about 5 cups / 1.25 l

2.2 pounds / 1 kg boneless, skinless pork belly

1/2 pound / 225 g pork back fat

1/2 cup / 125 ml dry sherry

4 cloves garlic

2 fresh bay leaves

4 sprigs thyme

1 tablespoon coarse sea salt

1 teaspoon fennel seeds, crushed

1 teaspoon hot pimentón (smoked paprika)

1 teaspoon mild paprika

Freshly ground black pepper and fine sea salt

Pumpkin and Bacon Soup

I grew up on soups based on bacon. Either the smoked bones from a side of bacon were added to the cooking liquid, or diced pieces of bacon were cooked with the vegetables, or sometimes the vegetables were sautéed in bacon fat. When you start with bacon you can make a soup simply using water rather than stock. Many vegetables balance bacon by soaking up that salty, smoky flavor and blending it with their own, and pumpkin is one of them. Whether you call this vegetable pumpkin or squash, you need one that is firm and dry, not watery. My choice for this soup is the orange hubbard or kabocha, which has a mild chestnut flavor.

Serve the soup plain or garnished with one of the following: chopped fresh sage, crumbled bacon, Spiced Pork Crackling (page 76), or slices of cooked chorizo sausage (page 107).

Remove the rind and any hard, dry skin from the bacon. Cut the bacon into 1/4-inch / 6-mm dice.

Place a large saucepan over low heat, add the bacon pieces, and cook gently so they render their fat. When most of their fat is rendered, add the onion, celery, and sage, stirring to coat with the fat. Cook until the vegetables soften slightly, about 7 minutes.

Cut the squash into quarters and remove the seeds. Peel the squash and coarsely chop into smaller, even-sized pieces. Set aside.

Pour 1 cup / 250 ml of the water into the pan with the vegetables, increase the heat to high and, using a wooden spoon, deglaze the pan, scraping up the browned bits on the bottom. Add the remaining 7 cups / 1.75 l water, the squash pieces, 1 tablespoon of salt, and some pepper. Bring the mixture to a boil, lower the heat, and simmer, covered, until the squash is very soft, 30 to 45 minutes. Remove the sage and let the soup cool slightly.

Purée the soup, in batches, in a blender and pour into a clean saucepan. Taste and adjust the seasoning, and reheat the soup to serve.

Makes 3 quarts / 3 l

1/2 pound / 225 g side (slab) bacon

1 large onion, sliced

1 stalk celery, sliced

1 large sprig sage

1 hubbard squash or other firm, dry pumpkin or winter squash (about 3 1/3 pounds / 1.5 kg)

8 cups / 2 l water

Coarse sea salt and freshly ground black pepper

Spaghetti Carbonara

Serves 2

Coarse sea salt and freshly ground black pepper

7 ounces / 200 g spaghetti

3 1/2 ounces / 100 g pancetta

2 eggs

1 egg yolk

1 cup / 30 g very finely grated Parmesan cheese

1/4 cup / 60 ml dry white wine

2 tablespoons chopped fresh flat-leaf parsley

Larder: originally called a lard house or lardy, the room where the bacon was stored; over time it was more generally applied to the place where household food provisions were stored

This was one of the first "foreign" dishes I taught myself to cook, more than thirty years ago. At the time, Italian food outside of Italy consisted mostly of lasagna and spaghetti with meatballs. The idea that a pasta sauce could be so simple was revolutionary.

As with all simple dishes, the secret is in the quality of the ingredients, in this case, pancetta, eggs, and Parmesan cheese. Pancetta, which means "little stomach," is cured (but not smoked) pig's belly that is sold either in a slab or rolled up like a jelly roll. Look for pancetta with more fat than meat, because it's the fat that is going to make this sauce flavorful. I always have some pancetta in my freezer. That way, I know I can always make myself a fast, delicious meal.

Make this for one, two, or four. Any more and you'll have too much spaghetti to handle. It's a great dish for those evenings when you're home alone. For one person, halve the recipe, using one egg and one yolk; for four people, just double everything, but use two frying pans. This dish is great with a watercress salad.

Bring a large saucepan of salted water to a boil over high heat. Add the spaghetti, stir, and return to a boil. Adjust the heat so the water boils gently and cook until the spaghetti is al dente, 10 to 12 minutes. Drain well.

While the water is coming to a boil, cut the pancetta into matchstick-sized pieces. Place a large frying pan over very low heat and add the pancetta. Cook gently so that it renders its fat and becomes crisp, about 10 minutes.

In a small bowl, whisk together the eggs and yolk, season well with pepper, and whisk in half of the cheese.

When the pancetta is cooked, pour the wine into the frying pan and stir to deglaze the pan, scraping up the browned bits from the bottom with a wooden spoon. Remove the pan from the heat.

Add the drained spaghetti to the pan. Toss the spaghetti to coat it with the pancetta and fat. Pour in the egg mixture and continue to toss until the spaghetti is coated. The heat of the spaghetti and pan will cook the eggs.

Sprinkle with parsley and serve with the remaining cheese on the side.

TIP If your spaghetti is not ready when the pancetta is finished, deglaze the pan anyway and remove it from the heat. Reheat the pancetta and wine before adding the cooked spaghetti.

Prosciutto-Wrapped Halibut with Sage Butter

Fish and seafood are often paired with bacon, which imparts both flavor and fat. In this recipe I use prosciutto because it turns very crisp and crunchy, providing a good contrast to the fish. You could simply drizzle the cooked fish with some melted butter, but I like to use a brown butter and sage sauce for another layer of flavor. This is a great dinner party dish. The fish, which can be prepped in advance, look very impressive in their prosciutto belts. Halibut, cod, or any other firm white fish works well in this recipe. Serve with a simple green vegetable and steamed potatoes.

Preheat the oven to 400°F / 200°C.

Season the fish fillets with salt and pepper. Place 2 sage leaves on top of each fillet and then wrap each with a slice of prosciutto. The prosciutto will form a belt, enclosing the leaves but leaving the fish exposed at either end. Cut 12 slices 1/4 inch / 6 mm thick from the center of the lemons, reserving the ends for their juice.

On a rimmed baking sheet, arrange pairs of the lemon slices, slightly overlapping. Place a wrapped fillet on top of each pair of lemon slices. Bake the fish until it flakes and is opaque at the thickest part, 15 to 20 minutes, depending on the thickness of the fish.

While the fish is cooking, melt the butter in a frying pan over medium-low heat. Add the remaining 24 sage leaves and cook, turning once, until the leaves are crisp and the butter begins to brown, about 7 minutes. Remove from the heat and add salt and the juice from the remaining lemon ends.

Transfer the fish and the lemon slices to warmed plates. Pour any juices released from the fish into the sage butter sauce and pour the sauce over the fish. Serve immediately.

TIP Make sure all your fish fillets are a similar size and thickness so they will all be cooked through at the same time.

Serves 6

Six 6-ounce / 175-g skinless halibut fillets

Sea salt and freshly ground black pepper

36 fresh sage leaves

6 slices prosciutto

2 large lemons

7 tablespoons / 3 1/2 ounces / 100 g unsalted butter

Bringing home the bacon: to be successful

Cheong Liew's Braised Pork Belly

Serves 4 to 6

2 pounds / 900 g pork belly, with skin

3 tablespoons light soy sauce

2 tablespoons dark soy sauce

2 tablespoons dry sherry

$1/4$ cup / $1 1/2$ ounces / 45 g firmly packed brown sugar

$1/2$ teaspoon coarse sea salt

1 tangerine

Two 3-inch / 7.5-cm cinnamon sticks, broken into pieces

One 1-inch / 2.5-cm piece fresh ginger, peeled and sliced, plus 1 teaspoon peeled, finely grated fresh ginger

1 star anise, broken into pieces

1 to 2 tablespoons lard

2 cups / 500 ml water

6 dried cayenne or serrano chiles

4 cloves garlic, peeled

3 green onions, cut into $1/2$-inch / 1-cm pieces

Born in Malaysia, Cheong Liew is a well-known Australian chef, whose restaurant, The Grange, is located in the Adelaide Hilton. Liew's original and innovative cooking blends flavors and spices from many cuisines. Unfortunately, I have yet to taste Liew's cooking, but I have shared several breakfasts and discussions about the joys of pork belly with him. He gave me this recipe for pork belly cooked in soy sauce. It uses a classic Chinese method called "red cooking" (red is a lucky color in Chinese culture) and produces rich, deeply flavorful meat. Despite the name of the cooking technique, the final dish is not red but brown. This dish produces lots of fat, so serve it with steamed rice and add a little of the fat to the rice—it's tasty and mostly monounsaturated.

Cut the pork belly into 1 by 2-inch / 2.5 by 5-cm pieces and place them in a large bowl. Mix together the soy sauces, sherry, 2 tablespoons of the brown sugar, and salt and pour over the pork. Remove a long strip of zest from the tangerine, and set the tangerine aside. Add the zest, cinnamon sticks, sliced ginger, and star anise to the pork, stir to combine, and cover and marinate for 6 hours or overnight in the refrigerator.

Drain the pork and set the marinade aside; there will only be a small amount. Pat the pork dry.

In a deep frying pan, heat 1 tablespoon of the lard over medium-high heat and brown the pork in batches, adding more lard as necessary. Transfer the browned pork to a plate. When all the pork is browned, pour off the fat and add the water to the pan. Bring to a boil and deglaze the pan, using a wooden spoon to scrape up the browned bits on the bottom.

Add the reserved marinade to the pan with the cinnamon, sliced ginger, and star anise, and add the chiles, garlic, and remaining brown sugar.

Return the browned pork to the pan and bring to a boil. Lower the heat and simmer the pork, uncovered, until it is tender and the cooking liquid thickens slightly, about 1 hour. Squeeze 2 tablespoons of juice from the tangerine and stir into the pork along with the grated ginger and green onions. Using a slotted spoon, transfer the pork to a serving dish and serve.

Miso- and Orange-Roasted Pork Belly

Serves 6

3 pounds / 1.4 kg boneless pork belly, skin removed

Sea salt and freshly ground black pepper

3 cups / 750 ml water

1/4 cup / 60 ml red miso

2 tablespoons honey

2 tablespoons brown sugar

1 tablespoon peeled, finely grated fresh ginger

3 cloves garlic, peeled and finely chopped

1 large orange

1/2 cup / 125 ml dry sherry

Once I started cooking pork belly I couldn't stop, because it is so delicious and so simple to prepare. The layers of fat in a good piece of belly outweigh the meat layers, and sometimes I have to convince my friends to eat the fat! Once they try it, though, they realize just how flavorful it is, and they are hooked like me. This recipe was born from a desire to use up some ingredients that were lingering in my refrigerator. I discover some of my best recipes this way. I serve this dish with roasted squash and steamed bok choy.

Preheat the oven to 425°F / 220°C.

Pat the pork dry and, using a utility (Stanley) knife or box cutter, score the fat without cutting the meat. Season the meat with salt and pepper. Place the pork on a rack in a roasting pan, fat side up. Add 2 cups / 500 ml of the water and roast for 30 minutes.

Meanwhile, in a bowl, mix the miso, honey, brown sugar, ginger, and garlic. Finely grate the orange zest and add to the miso mixture. Squeeze the orange to obtain 1/2 cup / 125 ml of juice, and set aside.

Remove the pork from the oven and lower the temperature to 325°F / 160°C. Brush the pork fat with half of the miso mixture, add the remaining 1 cup / 250 ml water to the roasting pan, and continue to cook for another 30 minutes. Brush the pork with the remaining miso mixture and continue to cook, making sure that there is always some liquid in the bottom of the pan and basting occasionally. Roast until the juices run clear or a kitchen thermometer inserted into the meat registers 160°F / 71°C, about 2 hours.

Transfer the pork to a plate, cover loosely with aluminum foil, and let rest for 10 minutes. Meanwhile, pour off the fat from the roasting pan and set aside for another use. Place the pan over medium heat, add the sherry, and deglaze the pan, using a wooden spoon to scrape up the browned bits on the bottom. Stir in the reserved orange juice, taste, and adjust the seasoning. Add any juices from the plate holding the cooked pork and boil until the sauce thickens slightly.

Cut the pork belly into slices and serve with the sauce.

Salt Pork

Often salt pork and side bacon are confused. Salt pork is simply salted pork belly; it looks like side or slab bacon, but it's not smoked. Salt pork used to be readily available, but it isn't today, as I discovered when I went to buy some. Frustrated, I decided to make my own. It is very easy: just rub a piece of belly with a spiced salt and leave it for several days in the refrigerator. The salt rub flavors the belly and draws out some of the moisture, making it firmer. The longer you leave it in the salt the saltier it becomes, so, by making your own, you can control the saltiness. As with making any cured meat, however, this recipe takes time, so plan to make the salt pork ahead. It can be kept, refrigerated, for up to 2 weeks. Since weighing the salt is necessary for an accurate measurement, you'll need a scale to make this recipe.

Salt pork is an essential ingredient in chowders and Boston-Style Baked Beans (page 93). It's also great to have on hand because, just like bacon and pancetta, it adds nice flavor and fat to a dish.

In a small bowl, mix the salt, sugar, juniper berries, peppercorns, bay leaves, and *quatre épices*. Rub all the surfaces of the pork belly with the mixture. Sprinkle a thin layer of the salt mixture in a glass dish and place the pork belly on top, skin side up. Sprinkle the pork with a little more of the salt mixture, setting aside any that remains. Cover the pork with plastic wrap and refrigerate for 2 days.

Remove the pork from the refrigerator and pour off and discard any liquid in the dish. Turn the pork over and rub with the remaining salt mixture. Cover and refrigerate for another 2 days.

Rinse all the salt mixture off the pork and dry well with paper towels. Wrap the pork in cheesecloth and store in the refrigerator for up to 2 weeks.

TIP You can slice the belly thinly and fry the slices like bacon, or use it for flavoring, as you would side bacon, for a salty pork taste without the flavor of smoke. Taste a slice of salt pork before using it to determine just how salty it is. If you want to reduce the salt, soak it in water for a few hours, changing the water regularly, or blanch it in boiling water for a few minutes.

Makes 2 1/2 pounds / 1.2 kg

10 1/2 ounces / 300 g coarse sea salt

1/3 cup / 2 ounces / 60 g firmly packed brown sugar

8 juniper berries, crushed

2 teaspoons black peppercorns, crushed

2 fresh bay leaves, torn

1/2 teaspoon quatre épices (see below)

2 1/2 pounds / 1.2 kg boneless pork belly, with skin

QUATRE ÉPICES

Quatre épices is a French seasoning mix that varies according to the whim of the producer. Commonly it is a mix of white pepper, nutmeg, cloves, and ginger, but cinnamon and allspice may also be included. Although it does not have the same flavor, ground allspice can be substituted.

Salt Pork and Lentils

Serves 6

1 recipe Salt Pork (page 91)

2 onions, quartered

2 carrots, peeled and thickly sliced

4 celery stalks, sliced

2 fresh bay leaves

$1/2$ teaspoon black peppercorns

$1 1/3$ cups / 240 g lentils de Puy

Dijon mustard, for serving

Salt pork usually plays a secondary role, just flavoring a dish, but here it is the star of the show. Called petit salé *in French, salt pork is often served with lentils in France; the tiny green lentils du Puy have the best flavor. If you like, you can substitute shell beans or, if you are making this dish in spring or early summer, try it with fresh peas, simmered in the salt pork cooking liquid, or with blanched shelled fava beans, popped out of their skins and stewed gently in the same way.*

Soak the salt pork in cold water for 3 to 4 hours, changing the water at least twice.

Drain the pork and place in a large saucepan with the onions, carrots, celery, bay leaves, and peppercorns. Cover with cold water and bring slowly to a boil over low heat. Simmer the salt pork, uncovered, until the skin is soft and the pork is tender, about $1 1/2$ hours. Set aside, leaving the pork in the cooking liquid.

About 30 minutes before the salt pork is cooked, rinse the lentils under cold running water. Place them in a saucepan and cover with cold water. Bring to a boil over high heat, then drain and refresh under cold running water. Discard the blanching water.

Place the refreshed lentils in a clean saucepan. Pour off 4 cups / 1 l of the salt pork cooking liquid and add to the lentils. Bring to a boil, then reduce the heat and simmer, uncovered, until the lentils are just tender, 20 to 25 minutes. Check them regularly so you don't overcook them.

When the lentils are cooked, drain and place in a warm serving dish. Transfer the salt pork from the cooking liquid to a cutting board. Strain the cooking liquid through a fine-mesh sieve. Discard the bay leaves and peppercorns, but add the cooked vegetables to the lentils.

Cut the salt pork into thick slices and serve with the lentils and Dijon mustard.

VARIATION Lentils pair well with fatty foods like pork belly, and they are delicious with duck confit. Just cook them using the method described above, substituting water for the pork cooking liquid. Season the lentils with salt and pepper when they are cooked.

Boston-Style Baked Beans

My mother often made me baked beans on toast for breakfast as part of a three-course breakfast that included cereal. The memory of those breakfasts is probably why I don't often eat breakfast today. Those baked beans came from a can, and it took me a long time to realize that I could make baked beans myself. You need Salt Pork (page 91) for this dish, so you'll need to start a week before you want to eat these beans.

I like to serve these beans with crusty bread followed by a salad, but sometimes I'll put them on toast to remind myself of those childhood breakfasts. Be warned that although this dish should serve six, four hungry people can polish it off. Once you start, it's hard to stop.

Drain the beans, discarding the soaking liquid, and place them in a large saucepan. Cover the beans with water and bring to a boil. Remove the pan from the heat, skim off any scum that has risen to the surface, and drain the beans, reserving the cooking water. Set the cooking liquid aside and transfer the beans to a heavy casserole or Dutch oven.

Preheat the oven to 275°F / 140°C.

Skewer 3 of the onions with a clove each and add them, with the remaining onions, to the beans. Cut the salt pork into 2-inch / 5-cm pieces and add to the beans. Mix the brown sugar, molasses, mustard powder, and salt with about 1 cup / 250 ml of the cooking liquid and pour over the beans and pork, stirring to mix. Add enough of the reserved cooking liquid to cover the beans and set the remaining liquid aside.

Cover the beans and cook for 4 hours, checking from time to time to make sure that the beans are always covered with liquid, and adding more of the reserved cooking liquid as necessary. After 4 hours the beans should be just tender, but the cooking time will vary depending on the age of your dried beans; older ones will take longer to cook. Uncover the pan and continue to cook them for another hour to thicken the sauce and color the salt pork pieces.

Serves 6

1 pound / 450 g dried white pea beans, soaked overnight in cold water

6 cipollini or small onions, peeled

3 whole cloves

1 pound / 450 g Salt Pork (page 91)

1/3 cup / 2 ounces / 60 g firmly packed brown sugar

1/4 cup / 60 g molasses

1 tablespoon dried mustard

1 teaspoon coarse sea salt

Baked beans are a quintessential American dish, and their origins lie in Boston, with the early pilgrims. Baked beans essentially cook themselves, so they were the ideal dish for the Sabbath: they could be put in the oven and left to cook overnight, allowing the Puritan women to avoid cooking on the holy day. Cooking beans with fatty cuts of meat is popular in many cuisines, including French, which has its beloved Cassoulet (page 156), for example. The Heinz company from Pittsburgh, Pennsylvania, introduced canned baked beans at the end of the nineteenth century. The product became so popular in the United Kingdom, using the slogan "beanz meanz Heinz," that many English people thought Heinz was a British company.

BOSTON BAKED BEANS

LARDO

In English, the word *lard* conjures up images of creamy rendered pork fat, while in French the same word denotes bacon. In Italian, though, *lardo* refers to a unique and very special food: cured pork back fat.

This centuries-old delicacy was threatened with extinction in the 1990s, but now it's on menus from Milan to London. In New York you can even order a *lardo* pizza.

The method for making *lardo* has changed little over time. It begins with back fat, usually with the skin still attached, which is cut into thick rectangular slabs. These pieces of fat are rubbed with a spiced sea salt mixture containing black pepper, fresh rosemary, and garlic. Each producer adds his own special blend of spices, which can include cloves, cinnamon, coriander, nutmeg, juniper, bay leaves, sage, oregano, thyme, and star anise. Once seasoned, the fat is packed into rectangular marble vats called *concas*. These *concas* are placed in cellars where the fat ages for six months to two years. During this time the salt draws the moisture from the fat, forming a brine that preserves it, while the combination of spices and herbs adds flavor.

Because *lardo* is high in calories, it was the perfect food for those engaged in the hard manual labor of cutting stone in the Italian quarries. *Lardo* sustained these workers and kept alive the Italian partisans who, after an unsuccessful uprising against the Austrians in 1849, fled to the Apian Alps, taking only their pigs with them. This connection with the political rebels gave *lardo* its reputation as the "food of the anarchists" and instilled an independent spirit in its producers, which is probably why *lardo* still exists today.

Like many traditional foods, *lardo* waned in popularity through most of the twentieth century. More food choices and a general movement away from animal fats, even in Italy, led to a drop in production. Then, in April 1996, the handful of remaining producers were dealt a blow. European Union health inspectors, horrified by the antiquated way in which *lardo* was made, declared it dangerous for human consumption and impounded tons of it. The bureaucrats ignored the fact that *lardo* had been eaten for centuries without endangering anyone. After a slew of onerous regulations were implemented, it appeared that small *lardo* producers would be forced out of business. However, the Slow Food movement stepped in, protecting and regulating its production. Finally, it was Slow Food's championing of *lardo* at the Salone del Gusto, its biannual food exhibition in Turin, that introduced it to the world.

The best-known *lardo* is *lardo di Colonnata*, made in Colonnata, a tiny Tuscan town perched in the hills above the marble quarries of Carrara. These famous quarries, worked since Roman times, provided the stone for sculptors such as Michelangelo and Henry Moore. *Lardo* was popular with the local stonecutters, and Michelangelo, who spent many months at a time in the area selecting his marble, was reputedly very fond of snacking on *lardo*. The quarries still provide the marble for the local *concas*, and some producers claim that it is the porous quality of this marble that is the key to the finesse of *lardo di Colonnata*. Others believe that it's the town's location high in the hills, which provides the perfect cool and humid climate for making *lardo*.

Straight from the *conca*, *lardo* can be off-putting, with its dark coating of dried herbs, but once these are brushed off they reveal a creamy white fat, occasionally streaked with a thread of meat. Despite the amount of salt added during the curing, *lardo* is not salty; on the contrary, it is soft, delicate, and almost sweet, with a hint

> " But what was *lardo*? . . . I was pretty unimpressed by my first sight of this almost deified product. It did indeed resemble a block of lard, but with a dark coating of what looked like old dry lawn cuttings. "
>
> ANNE DOLAMORE

of herbs. It is wonderfully addictive. Although the quarry workers ate their *lardo* thickly sliced in a sandwich with onions and tomato, I don't need quite as many calories as a stonecutter and prefer mine thinly sliced. Using a meat slicer is the easiest way to slice it, but if you don't have one, chill the *lardo* well before cutting it. Serve the slices at room temperature on toasted country-style bread with a good grinding of black pepper. The warmth of the toast will melt the fat slightly. If you are serving *lardo* to friends who are yet to be convinced, my advice is to call it white prosciutto. Of course, you can use it like pancetta to flavor pasta or rice or put it on a pizza, but *lardo di Colonnata* is best enjoyed simply.

While there is nothing quite like *lardo di Colonnata*, *lardo* is made in other areas of Italy as well. In the town of Arnad, high in the Alps, *lardo* is aged in vats made from chestnut wood, and the locals eat it with black bread and honey.

The term *lardo crudo* refers to a seasoned purée of pork fat, like *burro del Chianti*, made by the famous Tuscan butcher, Dario Cecchini. It is a mixture of pork fat flavored with onion, garlic, and herbs. My version is made with rendered pork fat infused with rosemary (see page 97). Try it—you might even give up butter!

Dandelion Salad with Hot Bacon Dressing

Serves 4

1 to 2 bunches young dandelions

4 ounces / 115 g pancetta or side (slab) bacon

1 tablespoon finely chopped shallot

2 tablespoons sherry vinegar

2 tablespoons dry white wine

Sea salt and freshly ground black pepper

Considered a weed by some, the dandelion is also a tasty bitter green. The name "dandelion" comes from the French expression "dents de lion," a reference to the plant's leaves, which resemble a lion's teeth. The French, however, call this plant pissenlit, *which translates as "piss in the bed," because of the dandelion's diuretic quality. The vinegar matches the dandelion's assertive quality and the fat mellows its flavor, while the hot dressing helps soften its firm leaves. Dandelions differ in size, and some bunches are more than half stems. To make this dish you'll need about 10 cups of prepared leaves. This salad, which makes a great appetizer, can be made more substantial by topping it with a poached or coddled egg.*

Trim the dandelion leaves, removing any thick stems, and rinse in plenty of cold water. Drain, spin dry, and cut the dandelions into bite-size pieces. Place the prepared dandelions in a large salad bowl.

Cut the pancetta into matchstick-sized pieces and place them in a frying pan over low heat. Cook the pancetta very gently so that it renders all of its fat before becoming crisp. Using a slotted spoon, transfer the crisp pancetta to the salad bowl, leaving the rendered fat in the pan. You should have about 1/4 cup / 60 ml of fat; add a little bacon fat or lard if necessary.

Return the pan to the heat, add the shallot, and cook over medium-low heat until it just begins to color, about 5 minutes. Add the vinegar, bring to a boil, and deglaze the pan, using a wooden spoon to scrape up any browned pieces from the bottom. Add the white wine, season with salt and pepper, and return to a boil.

Quickly pour the hot dressing over the dandelions and cooked pancetta, then toss very well. Serve immediately.

Portuguese Peas

I believe I have the whole collection of the Time Life cookbook series Foods of the World, *and while the photography is dated, the books contain some fascinating recipes. I used to frequently make a dish of peas, eggs, and sausage that was described in the volume on Spain and Portugal. Then a friend living in Portugal sent me his version of the recipe. This recipe is somewhere between the two. It could serve four for lunch, but it's the perfect dinner for two.*

Cut the sausages into $1/4$-inch / 6-mm slices.

In a 10-inch / 25-cm heavy frying pan, melt the lard over medium heat. Add the onion and cook, stirring occasionally, until it is translucent and just beginning to color. Add the peas, half of the cilantro, and the sugar and season with salt and pepper. Stir in the water and arrange the chorizo slices around the edge of the pan on top of the peas, overlapping the slices. Bring to a boil, then lower the heat, cover, and simmer gently until the peas are barely cooked, about 5 minutes.

Break the eggs, one by one, into a small dish, and then slide them on top of the peas, inside the ring of sliced sausage. Season the eggs well with pepper and cover again. Simmer very gently until the whites are just set, about 4 minutes.

Uncover the pan, sprinkle with the remaining cilantro, and serve directly from the pan.

Serves 2 to 4

2 Brenda's Chorizo sausages (page 107), cooked

2 tablespoons lard or bacon fat

1 onion, chopped

3 cups / 400 g frozen peas, defrosted

1 cup / 15 g cilantro (coriander) leaves, chopped

$1/2$ teaspoon sugar

Sea salt and freshly ground black pepper

$1/2$ cup / 125 ml water

4 eggs

Rosemary-Flavored Pork Fat

Once, at a special dinner in a Toronto restaurant, I was served a charcuterie platter as a first course. It was filled with wonderful house-cured sausages and meats, but my favorite part was a small bowl filled with a soft white spread that turned out to be flavored pork fat. This is my version of that "white butter." Perfect on dark rye bread and in cold roast pork sandwiches, it's also good enough to place on the dinner table, exactly as you would that yellow fat—butter. Make your guests taste it before you tell them what it is.

Combine the lard, rosemary, and salt in a small saucepan. Bring slowly to a simmer over low heat and then let the fat gently sizzle, stirring occasionally to dissolve the salt, for 15 minutes.

Remove the pan from the heat and let the fat cool slightly. Remove the rosemary sprigs and pour the lard into a bowl. Chill until it begins to set and turn white.

Using a wooden spoon, beat the fat until it is creamy and light. Taste and adjust the seasoning and transfer to a serving dish. Keep the fat refrigerated until it is ready to serve. It will soften much more quickly at room temperature than butter will.

Makes about $1/2$ cup / 100 g

$1/2$ cup / $3^1/2$ ounces / 100 g lard

2 sprigs rosemary

$1/8$ teaspoon fine sea salt

Chinese-Style Green Onion Pancakes

Makes twelve 4-inch / 10-cm pancakes

2 cups / 8³/4 ounces / 250 g flour

1 teaspoon fine sea salt

1/2 cup / 3¹/2 ounces / 100 g lard, melted (see page 73)

12 to 20 green onions

To lard: to enrich

Lard stone: a soft stone, like soapstone (agalmato-lite), found in China and often used for carving

I love going out for dim sum. I know I can always get my quota of pork fat for the week by going to a Chinese restaurant on Sunday morning. One of my favorite dim sum choices is green onion pancakes, which my Chinese-Canadian friends call Chinese pizza. I guessed it was lard giving these pancakes their flaky texture, and I was right. The dough is rolled out very thinly in a series of steps, and allowed to rest between rolling. These pancakes are best straight out of the pan, but you can keep them warm in the oven until you finish cooking them. The number of green onions you need will vary with the season. When I made these in winter I needed twenty, but when I used big, fat summer green onions, twelve were enough.

Combine the flour and salt in a food processor and pulse to mix. Pour 1 tablespoon of the melted lard into a measuring cup and add enough boiling water to make 1 cup / 250 ml.

With the machine running, pour the lard and boiling water over the flour mixture. Process until the dough forms a ball, about 40 seconds. Transfer the dough to a floured surface and knead gently until the dough forms a smooth ball. Dust with flour, cover with a clean cloth, and leave the dough to cool slightly, about 15 minutes.

Trim the green onions, removing the white root ends. Thinly slice the green part of the onions; you should have about 2 cups. Set aside.

On a floured surface, roll the dough into a log 12 inches / 30 cm long. Cut the log into 12 equal pieces and cover the pieces with a cloth. Working with 1 piece of dough at a time, use your fingers to flatten it into a circle about 3 inches / 7.5 cm in diameter. Repeat with the remaining pieces, keeping the pieces and the circles of dough covered with the cloth at all times.

Take 1 dough circle and roll it out to twice its original size, about 6 inches / 15 cm in diameter. Place it back under the cloth and repeat with the remaining circles.

Repeat the process once more, this time rolling each circle even thinner, into an oval about 10 by 6 inches / 25 by 15 cm. The ovals don't have to be perfect, but at this point the dough should be very thin (you will be able to see newspaper print through it, but not be able to read anything).

Brush 1 oval with some of the melted lard and sprinkle it with 2 tablespoons of chopped green onions. Starting at the long side of the oval, roll the dough up as tightly as possible, pinching the ends to seal it. Coil the dough like a snake, tucking in the ends and then flattening it slightly with the palm of your hand. Roll the flattened coil into a 4-inch / 10-cm pancake and place it on a baking sheet lined with waxed paper. Cover with a cloth. Repeat with the remaining dough ovals, layering with waxed paper as necessary. The pancakes can be made up to a day in advance and refrigerated, well covered, until ready to cook.

Preheat the oven to 200°F / 100°C.

Place a large, heavy frying pan over medium heat and add enough of the lard to lightly coat the bottom of the pan. When the pan is hot, cook the pancakes in batches until crisp and golden brown on the first side, about 4 minutes. Brush the uncooked surface with some melted lard, turn the pancakes, and cook on the second side for another 4 minutes. You want the pancake to cook through before it browns too much, so adjust the heat as necessary. Transfer the cooked pancakes to a baking sheet lined with paper towels and serve immediately, or keep warm in the oven.

A FRIED BREAD BREAKFAST

Somerset Maugham once said that to eat well in England you must eat breakfast three times a day. Although that is no longer necessary, a good English breakfast is a great meal. I don't know why we restrict bacon and eggs to breakfast; I like them for lunch, or even for dinner.

The best time for a breakfast like this is the weekend, when you have time to prepare it and, more important, time to enjoy it at a leisurely pace. Everybody makes bacon and eggs, but fried bread has all but disappeared from breakfast, and it is time to bring it back. Properly cooked, it's crisp, not greasy, with a soft center infused with the smoky taste of bacon.

You probably don't need a recipe for breakfast, but here are a few pointers. You must begin with quality bacon that oozes fat, not water. It must be side (slab) bacon, with a good amount of fat and not cut too thickly. Cook it gently so that it releases all its fat, and then keep it warm in the oven. Two to three slices per person should be enough. Now cook your eggs, but not in the bacon fat. Use butter and another pan. Heat the butter until it begins to foam and just starts to color, slide in the eggs, lower the heat, and cook until they are done to your liking. Basting the whites with butter will help them set. The bacon fat is for cooking the bread. One slice per person is probably enough, but I can eat two. Use good white bread that is a couple of days old; if it's too fresh, it will soak up the bacon fat before it gets crisp. Cook the bread in the hot bacon fat for 2 to 3 minutes a side, or until it's crisp and golden. Depending on the type of bacon you're using and how many slices of bread you are cooking, you might run out of bacon fat. If you do, just add a little lard or, in a pinch, butter.

A Perfect Bacon, Lettuce, and Tomato Sandwich

Is it possible to improve upon this classic sandwich? I think so, by adding another layer of flavor with my Bacon Mayonnaise. It's not mayonnaise with crumbled bacon, but mayonnaise made with bacon fat. The recipe makes only a small amount, about enough for 4 sandwiches. It's best to use it all up at once because any leftover mayonnaise must be refrigerated, and the bacon fat will turn it solid.

This mayonnaise is good in any sandwich, especially those made with eggs, grilled vegetables, cooked shrimp, or lobster. It is also good stirred into a warm potato salad, and I'm sure you can find other uses as well. You can use the fat from cooking the bacon for your sandwich, but since you can never be sure just how much fat your bacon will render, it's a good idea to have some extra bacon fat on hand. In a pinch you could add a tablespoon or two of lard, but no more, or you'll lose that special bacon flavor. In addition to the mayonnaise and good bacon, you'll need ripe, juicy tomatoes, so this is a mid- to late summer treat.

Spread 1 tablespoon of mayonnaise on each slice of bread. Arrange the lettuce and tomato slices on 1 slice of bread and season well with pepper. Top the tomato with the bacon slices and then the second slice of bread. Press together gently and serve.

TIP I am sure everyone has his or her own special flourish for this classic sandwich. I like to replace the lettuce leaf with several large fresh basil leaves and substitute pancetta for the bacon.

Makes 1 sandwich

2 tablespoons Bacon Mayonnaise (recipe follows)

2 slices of your favorite bread

1 lettuce leaf

2 or 3 slices tomato

Freshly ground black pepper

3 or 4 slices cooked bacon

BACON MAYONNAISE

Combine the egg yolk, mustard, and lemon juice in the small bowl of a food processor or in a blender and process to mix. Season with salt and pepper.

Have the bacon fat liquid, but not hot. With the machine running, gradually add the bacon fat until the mixture starts to stiffen and emulsify, about 2 minutes. Once it starts to emulsify, you can add the fat more quickly. If the mayonnaise is too thick, just blend in 1 teaspoon of boiling water to thin it. Taste and adjust the seasoning.

Makes about 1/2 cup / 125 ml

1 egg yolk

3/4 teaspoon Dijon mustard

1 teaspoon freshly squeezed lemon juice

Sea salt and freshly ground black pepper

1/2 cup / 125 ml liquid bacon fat

BACON BEDAT

This sandwich is a variation on the one found in the book *A Pike in the Basement: Tales of a Hungry Traveller*, by Simon Loftus. I am sure if Simon had known about my Bacon Mayonnaise he would have spread that on the toast before topping it with the salmon. Try it.

Start with thinly sliced top-quality white bread that has been lightly toasted. Spread some mango chutney on one toast slice and top with a couple of slices of smoked salmon and cooked bacon. Spread the other slice of toast with Bacon Mayonnaise (page 101) and use it to top the other slice. Eat at once.

French Fries in Lard

Serves 2

1 pound / 450 g large baking (floury) potatoes

4 cups / $1^3/4$ pounds / 800 g lard, melted (see page 73)

Sea salt

“To say that this is a good bacon sandwich is only to say that by the criteria applied to like-minded lovers of bacon sandwiches, this one is worthy of approbation . . . all statements implying goodness or badness, whether in conduct or in bacon sandwiches, are not statements of *fact* but merely expressions of feeling, taste or vested interest.”

TOM STOPPARD, *Jumpers*

I love frying in lard: it leaves no smell and results in wonderfully crisp food. Even so, I don't like to spend a long time over a deep fryer, so I only make French fries in small batches. You can make a larger batch of fries and keep them warm in a low oven, but a French fry is best straight from the hot fat. French fries must be cooked twice, first at a lower temperature to cook the potatoes through, and then at a higher temperature to crisp and color them. The first round of frying can be done several hours ahead. A frying basket is a necessity when cooking fries, as is reading the instructions for deep-frying (see page 70).

Peel the potatoes and cut them lengthwise into $1/2$-inch / 1-cm slices. Cut these slices lengthwise again to make fries approximately $1/2$ by $1/2$ inch / 1 by 1 cm thick. Rinse the cut potatoes under cold running water and place them in a large bowl. Cover them with cold water and leave to soak for 30 minutes.

Drain the potatoes and dry them well. Wrap them in a clean towel and set aside for 30 minutes.

Pour the melted lard into a heavy, deep pan and insert a kitchen thermometer. Place the pan over medium-low heat and heat the lard to 325°F / 160°C. When the lard reaches temperature, add the potatoes in batches and cook until the potatoes are soft and just starting to color, 5 to 7 minutes. Drain the potatoes on paper towels and leave them uncovered until the final frying.

Heat the lard to 375°F / 190°C and fry the potatoes in batches, until crisp and golden brown, about 4 minutes. Drain the fries on paper towels, sprinkle with salt, and serve immediately.

TIP When you have finished frying, carefully remove the pan of hot fat from the stove and leave it to cool on a trivet. Strain the cooled fat through cheesecloth back into its container, discarding any debris in the cloth.

For the German artist Joseph Beuys, fat was a medium just like clay. Beuys's interest in fat had two sources: an encounter with Tatars, and his theory of sculpture.

Born in northern Germany in 1921, Beuys was a wartime pilot who survived a horrific plane crash in 1943. According to Beuys's own account of the accident, Crimean Tatars rescued him from his wrecked plane, saving his life by coating him in fat and wrapping him in felt. He wrote, "I remember voices saying water, then the felt of their tents, and the dense pungent smell of cheese, fat and milk. They covered my body in fat to help it regenerate warmth, and wrapped it in felt as an insulator to keep the warmth in."

Although Beuys later downplayed this incident, it became part of the mythology surrounding his sculpture, in which he often employed felt and fat. Always radical in his approach to art and life, Beuys was fascinated by natural, everyday materials and loved to incorporate them into his work. Fat, in Beuys's thinking, was an even better medium than clay, as it was lighter and easier to work with, and could be used in liquid or solid form. For Beuys, sculpting was a dynamic process and working in fat gave him the flexibility that he desired and conformed to his theory of sculpture: that "in human physiology, everything that is ultimately hard has begun its existence in a fluid process; this can be clearly traced back to embryology. . . ."

Beuys was fascinated by fat's transformation over time and its dependence on the ambient temperature. His first "fat" work was the installation piece *Fat Corners*, completed in the early 1960s. It was a cardboard box with one corner filled with fat. In 1964 he created the sculpture *Fat Chair*, a simple wooden kitchen chair with a large wedge of fat on the seat. In 1966 *A Chair with Fat* followed. This time the seat was entirely coated with animal fat.

Beuys's biggest fat piece was his 1977 work *Tallow*. To create it he melted 20 tons of mutton fat mixed with some beef fat and then poured the liquid fat into a 16-foot / 5-m high plywood mold. Before beginning this project Beuys consulted several scientists to find out how long the fat would take to set. None of them could give him a definite answer, and their predictions ranged from 3 days to 3 months. This didn't upset Beuys; it proved fat's dynamism. After $1\frac{1}{2}$ months the sculpture was still liquid in the center, and after 3 months it was barely cool.

Beuys did not stop at fat. Sausages, chocolate, and gelatin all made it into his artwork.

Following in Beuys's footsteps, the New York performance artist Janine Antoni created her work *Gnaw* in 1992. Antoni gnawed—yes, chewed away—at two 600-pound / 272-kg blocks, one made of lard and the other of chocolate. From the gnawed and chewed pieces of lard she fashioned 130 lipsticks, and she turned the chocolate pieces into 127 heart shapes to complete the installation. It is now housed in the MoMA in New York City.

FAT AND THE ARTIST

Faggots with Onion Gravy

Serves 6

1 pound / 450 g pork liver

$10^{1/2}$ ounces / 300 g pork belly, skin removed

5 onions

2 cloves garlic, peeled

$1^{1/2}$ cups / 4 ounces / 120 g fine fresh bread crumbs

1 cup / 15 g flat-leaf parsley leaves, chopped

12 fresh sage leaves, chopped

1 teaspoon chopped fresh thyme leaves

Coarse sea salt and freshly ground black pepper

2 large sheets of caul fat (about 12 by 18 inches / 30 by 45 cm)

2 tablespoons lard, plus more for greasing the pan

2 cups / 500 ml pork or chicken stock

2 tablespoons port

1 tablespoon sugar

Variations of this recipe are made all over Europe, as it was a common way to use up the offal when a pig was slaughtered. Traditionally, the heart, liver, and spleen are ground up with pork fat, then spiced and made into patties that are wrapped in caul fat (see page 70). These little packages are called "faggots" in the British Isles, from an old English term for a bundle. When the term faggot *entered American slang as a derogatory term for a homosexual, faggots became something of a joke even in England. John Ayto, in* A Diner's Dictionary, *describes a 1970s advertising campaign aimed at British housewives that employed the tag line "Surprise your husband with a faggot!" It wasn't a big success.*

Whatever you call them, these savory little bundles are a delicious change from meatballs. Liver, the only offal I include in them, gives them flavor and texture. You must use a meat grinder, as a food processor will not yield the right texture. Once cooked, faggots keep well refrigerated. I like to make them ahead, so the flavors have time to blend, and then reheat them in the onion gravy.

Serve these with mashed potatoes and an assertive green vegetable like kale or rapini. Or, since faggots are really just individual pâtés, you could eat them cold with some cornichons and pickled onions or sliced in a sandwich.

Place the bowl from your stand mixer and the meat grinder in the refrigerator about 2 hours before starting.

Cut the liver and pork belly into small pieces that will fit into your meat grinder, removing any sinew from the meat as you go. Chop 2 of the onions. Using the finest die of your grinder, grind the liver, pork belly, chopped onions, and garlic into the chilled bowl. Add the bread crumbs, parsley, sage, and thyme to the ground meat mixture and season with 2 teaspoons salt and lots of pepper.

Using the paddle attachment on your stand mixer, mix the ground meat on low speed for 1 minute. Form about 1 tablespoon of the mixture into a patty, and cook it in a frying pan. Taste and adjust the seasoning. Refrigerate the ground meat mixture until well chilled, about 2 hours.

Meanwhile, place the caul fat in a bowl of warm water to cover and leave to soak for 1 hour.

Preheat the oven to 350°F / 180°C and lightly grease a 9 by 13-inch / 23 by 33-cm baking dish with a little of the lard.

Remove the caul fat from the soaking water and gently squeeze out the water. Place the caul fat on a towel and pat dry. Cut it into 12 pieces about 6 inches / 15 cm square. Place about $1/3$ cup / 90 g of the pork mixture on each square and double wrap in the fat, trimming off any excess. Place the wrapped faggots in the baking dish, seam side down. Pour enough stock into the dish to come halfway up the faggots, reserving any remaining stock. Bake until the faggots are browned and cooked in the center, about 1 hour. Insert a metal skewer into the center of a faggot; it should be warm to the touch and the juices should run clear.

While the faggots are cooking, cut the 3 remaining onions in half lengthwise and then cut into 1/8-inch / 3-mm slices. Melt the lard in a large frying pan with a lid over medium heat. Add the onions, stir well to coat with the lard, and season with salt and pepper. Lower the heat, cover the pan, and cook the onions, stirring occasionally, until very soft, 35 to 40 minutes. If the onions begin to stick, add a spoonful of the reserved stock or water. When the onions are very soft, uncover, add the port and sugar, and increase the heat to medium-high. Cook the onions, stirring constantly, until they begin to caramelize. Set aside.

Transfer the faggots to a dish and keep warm. Pour the cooking liquid into a measuring cup and let stand for several minutes. Skim off the fat and set aside for another use. Pour about 1 cup / 250 ml of the cooking liquid (add any remaining stock if necessary) into the onion-port mixture to make a thick sauce. Reheat over medium heat, deglazing the pan by using a wooden spoon to scrape up the browned bits from the bottom. Taste, adjust the seasoning, and serve the sauce with the faggots.

Fennel and Orange Sausages

Fat is essential for good sausages: without it, they are dry and tasteless. Making sausage might seem like a lot of trouble, but a good sausage is hard to find. Besides, making them from scratch is very satisfying, and it ensures that you know exactly what is in your sausages. Once you've mastered the technique, you'll be making up your own recipes. You will need a meat grinder, a sausage stuffer, and a supplier who can provide you with sausage casings. I can't emphasize enough the importance of owning an accurate scale, not only for weighing the meat, but also for the salt. This mixture of fennel and oranges complements pork. If blood oranges are not in season, use a regular one.

Cut the pork and fat into small pieces that will easily fit into your meat grinder, removing any sinew from the meat as you go.

In a large bowl, combine the meat and fat with the salt, fennel fronds, fennel seeds, and pepper. Finely grate the zest from the orange. Add the zest to the meat and stir to mix. Cover and refrigerate for 4 to 6 hours or overnight.

Pour the Pernod into a measuring cup and squeeze 1/4 cup / 60 ml of juice from the orange. Refrigerate the Pernod mixture along with the bowl from your stand mixer and the meat grinder for about 2 hours.

Remove the meat mixture, grinder, mixer bowl, and Pernod and orange juice mixture from the refrigerator. Using the finest die for your grinder, grind the meat mixture into the chilled bowl. Alternate pushing the pieces of fat and meat through the grinder to ensure that the fat doesn't stick inside.

Using the paddle attachment on your stand mixer, mix the ground meat on low speed, adding the cold orange juice and Pernod. When the

Makes ten to twelve 6-inch / 15-cm sausage links

2 1/4 pounds / 1 kg fatty pork shoulder

1/2 pound / 225 g pork fat

0.8 ounce / 25 g coarse sea salt

2 tablespoons chopped fennel fronds

1 tablespoon fennel seeds, crushed

1 teaspoon freshly ground black pepper

1 blood orange

1/4 cup / 60 ml Pernod

6 feet / 2 m sausage casing

COOKING SAUSAGES

There are several ways to cook sausages; my favorites are to fry or grill them. Remember: it is important to cook sausages over medium-low heat so they have time to cook thoroughly, without bursting. They will take 10 to 15 minutes; cut one sausage open to check that it is cooked all the way through.

mixture is homogenous and sticky, after about 2 minutes, form about 1 tablespoon of the mixture into a patty, cook it in a frying pan, and taste to check the seasoning, adding more salt if necessary. Refrigerate the ground meat mixture until well chilled, about 2 hours.

While the meat mixture is chilling, soak the sausage casings in warm water for 1 hour. Rinse the casings in cold water, then run water through the casings. I slip one end of the casing over the tap and gently turn on the water to let it flow through the casing. Place the casings in a fine-mesh sieve to drain; you want them to be moist when you fill them, as they will be easier to work with.

Attach the sausage stuffer to the grinder and push the damp sausage casing over the tube until about 4 inches / 10 cm is hanging from the end and tie a knot in this piece. At this point it is a good idea to rope in a friend to help you, especially if it is your first time making sausage.

Add the chilled mixture to the grinder on low speed and slowly stuff the sausages, trying to minimize the air pockets in the casings. As filling enters the casing, it should slowly slide off the tube.

If there are two of you, one can concentrate on putting the mixture in the grinder while the other can devote his or her attention to easing the meat into the casings. Once all the mixture is used up, ease any remaining casing off the tube.

Roll the sausage on a damp surface to distribute the filling as evenly as possible, and then form the sausage into links by twisting the casing at 6-inch / 15-cm intervals. Twist each link in the opposite direction to prevent them from unwinding.

Cover the sausages and refrigerate for up to 3 days. They can also be frozen.

SAUSAGE CASINGS

Sausage casings, which are usually the cleaned membrane from a pig's intestine, can be purchased from a good butcher. About 1 1/2 inches / 4 cm in diameter, they are preserved in salt and will keep for at least 6 months refrigerated. They must be soaked and rinsed before use to remove the salt. If they have any odor, add a squeeze of lemon juice to the soaking water. You can also use sheep or beef casings to make sausage (sheep will be smaller and beef will be larger in diameter), but pork are the easiest to find.

Although sausages are usually formed into links, the stuffed casing can also be shaped into a coil, skewered to hold it together, and cooked. Or the sausage mixture can be shaped into patties and wrapped in squares of caul fat (see page 70), or it can be cooked without any wrapping at all.

Brenda's Chorizo

Chorizo is a sausage popular in the Iberian Peninsula and in Mexico. In my Toronto neighborhood there are lots of Portuguese immigrants, and smoked chorizo—both sweet and hot—is widely available. I wanted to make a fresh pork chorizo, so I asked my friend Brenda, who lives in northern Mexico, for a recipe. This is a spicy sausage that gets its depth of flavor from a mix of chiles. I use this sausage when I make Portuguese Peas (page 97). As with all sausage recipes in this book, it's essential that you weigh the salt to get an accurate measure.

Cut the pork and fat into small pieces that will easily fit into your meat grinder, removing any sinew from the meat as you go. In a large bowl, combine the meat and fat with the salt, cumin, oregano, garlic, black pepper, chile powder, and allspice. Toss to mix, cover, and refrigerate for 4 to 6 hours or overnight.

Break the ancho chiles into pieces, discarding the stems and seeds. Place them in a bowl and cover with the boiling water. Leave the chiles to soak for 1 hour.

Remove the chile pieces from the liquid and place in a blender or food processor. Strain the soaking liquid through cheesecloth, discarding any debris or dirt. Add 1/4 cup / 60 ml of the soaking liquid and the vinegar to the chiles and purée the mixture until smooth. Refrigerate the chile purée along with the bowl from your stand mixer and the meat grinder for about 2 hours.

Remove the meat mixture, grinder, mixer bowl, and chile purée from the refrigerator. Using the finest die for your grinder, grind the meat mixture into the chilled bowl. Alternate pushing the pieces of fat and meat through the grinder to ensure that the fat doesn't stick inside.

Using the paddle attachment on your stand mixer, mix the ground meat on low speed, adding the chile purée. When the mixture is homogenous and sticky, after about 2 minutes, form about 1 tablespoon of the mixture into a patty, cook it in a frying pan, and taste to check the seasoning, adding more salt if necessary. Refrigerate the ground meat mixture until well chilled, about 2 hours.

Follow the instructions for stuffing the casings provided in the recipe for Fennel and Orange Sausages (page 105). Cover the sausages and refrigerate for up to 3 days. They can also be frozen for up to 3 months. To cook the sausages, see page 106.

Makes ten to twelve 6-inch / 15-cm sausage links

2 1/4 pounds / 1 kg fatty pork shoulder

1/2 pound / 225 g pork fat

0.8 ounce / 25 g coarse sea salt

1 tablespoon cumin seeds, crushed

2 teaspoons dried Greek oregano

2 cloves garlic, peeled and finely chopped

1 teaspoon freshly ground black pepper

1 teaspoon chipotle chile powder

1/2 teaspoon ground allspice

3 ancho chiles

1 cup / 250 ml boiling water

1 tablespoon white wine vinegar

6 feet / 2 m sausage casings

Kugelhopf au Lard

Makes one 9-inch / 23-cm cake

1 cup / 250 ml milk

1 tablespoon sugar

1 package (8 g) dry yeast

4 cups / 17$\frac{1}{2}$ ounces / 500 g flour

1 teaspoon fine sea salt

$\frac{2}{3}$ cup / 5 ounces / 150 g plus 1 tablespoon unsalted butter, softened

3 eggs, lightly whisked

$\frac{1}{2}$ pound / 225 g side (slab) bacon, skin removed

2 shallots, finely chopped

1 tablespoon finely chopped fresh sage

To trim a ball or piece of fat: to talk with friends or chew the fat (French)

To save a person's bacon: to rescue someone

Kugelhopf is popular with German bakers from Alsace to Austria. Usually it is a sweet yeast cake filled with raisins, candied fruits, and nuts, baked in a turban-shaped tube pan with swirled sides. I spent a week in Alsace with friends chasing a savory version of this cake flavored with bacon, kugelhopf au lard. In every town we visited, our first stop was at the bakery, where we asked for one. Each time we were greeted with smiles and apologies. The kugelhopf au lard, it appeared, was baked only once a week, and each town baked it on a different day. We kept missing that kugelhopf au lard by twenty-four hours. Finally, on our last day in Alsace, we were in the right town on the right day. We celebrated by buying two kugelhopfs au lard and enjoying then with a glass or two of Riesling.

In a small saucepan over low heat, warm the milk until it is just warm to the touch. Pour $\frac{1}{2}$ cup / 125 ml of the milk into a bowl, add the sugar, and sprinkle over the yeast. Stir and leave to proof. The mixture should start to bubble in 5 to 10 minutes. If it doesn't, discard the yeast and start over with new yeast.

Combine the flour and salt in the bowl of a stand mixer and add the yeast mixture and the remaining milk. Using a dough hook, mix the ingredients on low speed. Cut the $\frac{2}{3}$ cup / 150 g butter into cubes and slowly add them to dough, 1 cube at a time. When all the butter is incorporated, add the eggs 1 at a time, beating well after each addition. Increase the speed to medium and knead the dough until it is smooth, very soft, and sticky, about 5 minutes.

Using some of the remaining 1 tablespoon of butter, butter a large bowl. Tip the dough into the bowl, cover with a towel, and leave in a warm place until the dough is doubled in size, 1 to 1$\frac{1}{2}$ hours. Use the remaining butter to butter a 9-inch / 23-cm (8-cup / 2-l) tube pan.

Cut the bacon into $\frac{1}{8}$-inch / 3-mm dice. In a frying pan over medium-low heat, cook the diced bacon until the fat is rendered and the bacon is crisp and begins to pop, about 10 minutes. Add the shallots and continue cooking until the shallots soften slightly, about another 5 minutes. Stir in the sage and remove the pan from the heat. Leave to cool.

Punch down the dough in the bowl and then tip onto a floured work surface. Scatter the dough with the cooled bacon mixture and knead it into the dough. Shape the dough into a sausage 18 inches / 45 cm long and place in the prepared pan.

Cover the pan with a towel and leave in a warm place until it has risen to within $\frac{3}{4}$ inch / 2 cm from the top of the pan, about 1 hour.

Preheat the oven to 400°F / 200°C.

Place the pan on a baking sheet and bake until golden and the cake sounds hollow when tapped, 35 to 40 minutes. Transfer the cake to a wire rack and let cool for 5 minutes before turning it out of the pan. Serve the cake warm or at room temperature; it will keep for about 3 days.

Choux Paste Beignets

Makes about 20 beignets

3 tablespoons sugar

1 tablespoon fennel seeds

$1/2$ cup / 125 ml water

$1/4$ cup / 2 ounces / 60 g
unsalted butter, diced

$1/2$ teaspoon fine sea salt

$1/2$ cup / 2 ounces / 60 g flour

2 eggs

1 tablespoon pastis

4 cups / $1^{3}/4$ pounds / 800 g
lard, melted (see page 73)

**" He wears a short
Italian hooded cloake,
larded with pearls. "**

CHRISTOPHER MARLOWE

I couldn't write a book about fat and leave out doughnuts. I remember when a shop selling hot doughnuts rolled in sugar opened near our home in the suburbs of Melbourne, Australia. You could stand right next to the window and follow the doughnuts' progress, from the mixing of the ingredients to the machine squeezing out perfect rings of dough to the cooking of the doughnuts in the hot fat. At the end the doughnuts were deposited on a bed of powdered sugar and then scooped into a bag. Only moments passed between them hitting the bag and our stuffing them into our eager mouths. When I arrived in North America I couldn't understand why everyone was happy to eat cold doughnuts. These simple beignets are best straight out of the fat, not bad warm, and still good a couple of hours later.

Combine the sugar and fennel seeds in a spice grinder and grind them until powdery. Place the mixture in a shallow dish and set aside.

Pour the water into a small saucepan and add the butter and salt. Place the pan over medium-low heat and stir to melt the butter. As soon as the butter is melted, increase the heat and bring to a boil. When the mixture boils, remove the pan from the heat, add the flour all at once, and stir until well mixed.

Return the pan to low heat and cook, stirring, until the mixture is very smooth and comes away cleanly from the sides of the pan, about 2 minutes. Let the mixture cool slightly.

In a small bowl, whisk the eggs with the pastis. Add about half the egg mixture to the pan. Stir until it is completely incorporated and the mixture is smooth. Add the remaining egg mixture and stir until you have a smooth, shiny mixture again.

Place the lard in a deep saucepan and clip a kitchen thermometer to the side. Heat the lard over medium-low heat until it reaches 375°F / 190°C. Carefully drop a few small teaspoonfuls of the beignet mixture into the fat; they will double in size, so don't crowd the pan. Cook, turning occasionally, until they are a dark golden color, 6 to 7 minutes. Drain the beignets on paper towels and then roll them in the fennel sugar.

Continue cooking until all the dough is used up. When you have cooked and coated all the beignets, place any remaining sugar in a fine-mesh sieve and dust the beignets again. Cool, strain, and reuse the fat (see page 71).

Spanish-Style Lard Cookies

Makes about 22 cookies

1 cup / $4^{1}/_{2}$ ounces / 125 g flour

$3/_{4}$ cup / 2 ounces / 60 g ground almonds

$1/_{2}$ cup / $3^{1}/_{2}$ ounces / 100 g sugar

2 teaspoons ground cinnamon

Pinch of fine sea salt

$1/_{2}$ cup / $3^{1}/_{2}$ ounces / 100 g lard, diced, at room temperature

1 egg

Finely grated zest of 1 orange

1 tablespoon brandy

Confectioners' (icing) sugar, for dusting

Lard is a popular fat for making cookies in lots of cuisines, because it makes the cookies very delicate and tender. In Spain they make cookies called polvorones, *but today butter often replaces the lard, completely changing the texture and flavor of the cookie. For this recipe it's important to use a neutral-flavored lard, which will add texture but allow the cinnamon and orange to shine through. The flour and nuts are lightly toasted to give the cookie a slightly nutty flavor.*

Preheat the oven to 350°F / 180°C.

Spread the flour and ground almonds on a baking sheet. Place them in the oven until the flour and almonds smell toasty and have just begun to color slightly, about 10 minutes. Let cool.

Lower the oven temperature to 300°F / 150°C.

When the flour and almond mixture is cool, tip it into a large bowl. Add the sugar, cinnamon, and salt and stir to mix. Add the lard and, using a wooden spoon, work it into the flour mixture.

Whisk together the egg, orange zest, and brandy and pour over the flour and lard, stirring to make a soft dough.

Take level tablespoons of the dough and form them into balls. Place the balls on parchment-lined baking sheets about $1^{1}/_{2}$ inches / 4 cm apart. Bake the cookies until firm to the touch and lightly browned on the bottom, about 30 minutes.

Transfer the cookies to a wire rack. When the cookies are cool, using a fine-mesh sieve, dust them with the confectioners' sugar. Store the cookies in an airtight container for up to 1 week.

SALO

The Italians are not the only ones to appreciate pork fat. Throughout central Europe, pork fat is very popular. In Ukraine, pork fat, called *salo*, commands such a special place in the national psyche that poems and songs have been written about it. While *salo* can be preserved in salt, spiced with paprika, or smoked, the most popular way to eat it is raw, with black bread, gherkins, and garlic, and washed down with—what else?—vodka.

Every October *salo* festivals are held across Ukraine, giving everyone a chance to celebrate the pig and its fat. These festivals often feature giant *salo* sandwiches; in Simferopol, the capital of the Crimea, the *salo* sandwich measured 30 feet / 9 m square and required a police guard to prevent enthusiastic attendees from grabbing pieces of it before the appointed time. As at all good festivals, there is also an all-you-can-eat *salo* competition. At the 2006 festival in Lutsk, in northwestern Ukraine, the competition winner swallowed 2.2 pounds / 1 kg of *salo* in just 20 minutes, without the aid of bread or vodka. After his winning performance, he told reporters he could have eaten more!

Crackling Brittle

Sugar and fat is everybody's favorite combination, and when you add salt, it's perfection. Salted Caramel Sauce (page 54) and Bacon Baklava (page 119) are good, but there is nothing more delicious than caramel and pork crackling. This recipe takes the Spiced Pork Crackling (page 76) and changes it from a savory snack to a sweet one. It can also be crushed up like praline to top a savory dish like roasted pork belly, or even added to ice cream.

Lightly butter a small rimmed baking sheet.

Place the sugar in a sauté pan over medium-low heat. Cook the sugar until it melts and begins to turn a caramel color. Stir the caramel to blend in any uncooked sugar. Once all the sugar has turned into liquid caramel, remove the pan from the heat.

Add the pork crackling pieces to the caramel and stir to coat. Pour the mixture onto the baking sheet, and spread out to cool. Once the brittle is cool, break it into pieces and store in an airtight container. It will keep for up to a week.

Makes more than enough

Unsalted butter, for greasing

2 cups / 14 ounces / 400 g sugar

1/2 recipe Spiced Pork Crackling (page 76), broken into small pieces

THE BUN THAT KILLED THE KING

In Sweden, Fettisdagen, or Fat Tuesday, is the day to eat *semlas*. The *semla*, which first appeared in 1541, is a bun made from white flour (*semilia* is the Latin word for white wheat flour), and only the king and the aristocracy ate them.

On Fettisdagen, February 12, 1771, King Adolf Frederick of Sweden sat down to his pre-Lenten meal. A large man with a prodigious appetite, he ate a huge meal to prepare himself for the upcoming rigors of Lent. He devoured lobster, Russian caviar, fish, sauerkraut, boiled meats, and turnips and washed it all down with large amounts of Champagne. To complete his feast he gobbled up fourteen helpings of his favorite dessert, *semlas*. Now, the hungry king didn't eat just the buns; each of the fourteen *semlas* came floating in a bowl of hot milk flavored with cinnamon and raisins. Alas, it was a case of one bun too many, and King Adolf died that night. He had, however, enjoyed his last meal, and he died without having to face the privations of Lent.

Still popular in Sweden, the *semla* has undergone various transformations since King Adolf's day. Originally wedge-shaped, boiled, and eaten hot, the bun is now round, flavored with cardamom, filled with marzipan and whipped cream, and dusted with confectioners' (icing) sugar before it is eaten cold. I doubt even King Adolf could have eaten fourteen modern-day *semlas*. Although some traditionalists still like to wash the buns down with hot milk, most *semlas* are enjoyed with a cup of coffee. The bun has also lost its close ties to Fettisdagen and appears in the pastry shops in early January. The Swedes still, however, stick to the tradition of eating them on Tuesdays, and most will consume four or five *semlas* between the New Year and Lent.

3 poultry fat:
VERSATILE AND GOOD FOR YOU

A bowl of steaming chicken soup with golden droplets of chicken fat floating on its surface; a fragrant roast chicken, its sauce enriched with the chicken's fat and juices; crisp-skinned duck confit, accompanied by potatoes sautéed in duck fat: this is poultry fat at its best. Readily available, multipurpose poultry fats can be used for frying, baking, and preserving, and they have enough of their own flavor to enjoy simply spread on bread.

Unlike pork and beef fats, poultry fat doesn't marble birds' flesh. Instead, most of it is found just under the skin and in lumps in the bird's cavity. As with meat, it's the fat that gives the bird its flavor. Traditionally, a plump bird has always been chosen first for the pot, but with the current demand for lean meat and poultry, birds are losing their fat. Why should we care? Poultry fat is not only important for a bird's taste, but it is good for us, too. Many cultures believe in the restorative quality of a bowl of hot chicken soup, and we all know it's the perfect food when you're under the weather. It's not simply its warmth, aroma, or digestibility that makes you feel better. Chicken soup really is good for you, but only if it has those pools of golden fat floating on top. All poultry fats contain the monounsaturated fatty acid palmitoleic acid, which is believed to boost our immune system. Chicken fat has more palmitoleic acid than other types of poultry fat. So what has been instinctively understood for hundreds of years, science has now validated: chicken soup, with a layer of fat, will cure what ails you.

That's not all that is good about poultry fat. While the bird's diet and breed influence the composition of its fat, all poultry fats are mainly monounsaturated, which is why they are fairly soft at room temperature and melt easily. The chief monounsaturated fatty acid in poultry fat is oleic acid, well known for its beneficial effects on cholesterol.

The Germans believe if you cannot see *fettauge*, blobs or circles of fat, floating on top of your soup, then the soup is no good.

This set of facts helps explain what is often called the French Paradox. In the 1990s it was realized that despite consuming large amounts of animal fats, the French had lower rates of heart disease than North Americans did. Within France, the rates were lowest in the southwest, where the food is awash in goose and duck fat. Many postulated that it was the calcium from all the cheese the locals ate that protected their hearts, while others claimed it was the daily quaffing of red wine. The media ran with the wine theory, and sales of red wine doubled in the United States. It turns out it probably wasn't the cheese or the wine. The real reasons are complex, but part of the answer lies in the fat. Like all poultry fat, duck and goose fats are mainly monounsaturated, and they are even more unsaturated than chicken and turkey fats. Even the saturated fatty acids in poultry fats are good for us, with their high percentage of palmitic fatty acid, which is believed to have no effect on or even lower cholesterol levels. So those canny French cook in fat that is not only tasty, but also good for them. And if the birds eat grass and weeds, their fat has a good dose of omega-3 fatty acids, too.

Poultry fats are also low in polyunsaturated fatty acids, which makes them great fats for cooking and frying, as they are very stable at high heat. Duck fat is especially useful, as its fatty acid profile is similar to that of lard, making it an excellent substitute for pork fat where that fat is forbidden by religion.

With all this going for poultry fats, why aren't we cooking everything in them? The problem is that the low-fat mentality has robbed birds of their fat.

Eating chicken was once a luxury, with the expensive bird reserved for special occasions, like the Sunday roast. Wily politicians from Henry IV of France to President Herbert Hoover won the hearts and votes of their nation with the promise of a chicken for every citizen—a symbol of prosperity. Today, however, modern breeding methods have made chicken (and turkey) cheap to produce, turning it into an inexpensive protein gobbled up by the fast- and processed-food industries. Quickly raised, these birds don't have time to put on fat, so they perfectly fulfill the demand for low-fat meat. Any fat that they might have developed is often removed along with their skin, leaving them lean but tasteless. Turkeys, naturally very lean, are so difficult to keep moist during roasting that producers inject them with mixtures of fake fats to stop them from drying out.

As these birds get leaner and leaner, we keep adding spices, rubs, and marinades—anything to give them some taste. Chicken and turkey are proudly marketed as "low-fat" or "90 percent fat free." Perhaps if the labels read "low-taste" or "90 percent taste free" we'd reconsider our choice. They are tasteless and less satisfying, and they have none of the healthy benefits found in their fat. For taste and our health, it is time to eat real chicken and turkey again.

I once stayed on a farm in France where they raised an odd-looking breed of chicken called *cou-pelé*, or peeled neck chicken. The name is apt, since from the base of their heads to the top of their breastbones these chickens are featherless. They happily wandered around the farm foraging for bugs, eating grubs, and munching on weeds and grass. I roasted one of them, leaving all the golden fat under the skin and in the cavity and adding some butter for good measure. The flesh was firm and succulent. I knew it was full of good fat that was boosting my immune system and lowering my cholesterol but, more important, it tasted like chicken. That single chicken easily fed six of us, for its fat not only gave it flavor, but it made the bird more satisfying as well. A similar sized mass-produced bird on this side of the Atlantic would barely stretch to feed four, but it would cost a third of the French one. You don't have to live on a farm in France to eat good chicken, but you must be prepared to pay for it. Perhaps chicken should become a special occasion bird again.

Unlike chicken, duck and geese are born with more fat, and this has protected them from the low-fat obsession. As migratory birds, they are genetically programmed to store fat, especially in the autumn, as it provides them with the energy to fly south. This is why ducks and geese can produce foie gras (see page 128). While the birds we buy don't fly anywhere, they fatten up nonetheless. Both ducks and geese are waterfowl, so they also have an extra layer of fat to protect them from the cold water. The low-fat message is so pervasive that we often feel guilty when we enjoy a crisp, fatty duck or see the amount of fat in the pan when we roast a goose, but there is no reason to feel guilty. Remember how much eating duck and goose has helped the French.

Fat	% Saturated	% Monounsaturated	% Polyunsaturated
DUCK	33	50	13
CHICKEN	30	45	21
TURKEY	29	43	23
GOOSE	28	57	11

Note: all figures are approximate and vary with the breed and diet of the animal. The numbers don't always total 100, as there is water and connective tissue in the fat.

Schmaltz

Poultry fats have a long history in the Jewish kitchen, where pork fat is forbidden by religious dietary laws. It was an especially important fat for Jews living in northern Europe, where oil was rare and expensive. The word *schmaltz* makes most of us think of Jewish cooking and chicken fat. However, the word is German in origin. *Schmalz* denotes an animal fat that has been rendered for cooking, and in Germany it is often pork fat. Yiddish appropriated the German word, and "schmaltz" in the Jewish kitchen refers to rendered poultry fat, originally goose but now more commonly chicken. Unlike other rendered fats, schmaltz is often flavored. Sliced onions are the most popular addition, and often apples are included to give the fat a slight sweetness. This tradition was probably borrowed from the Germans, who flavor their *Schmalz* with herbs, bacon, onion, and apple. Once the fat is rendered, it is strained, leaving behind crispy bits of chicken skin and onion or cracklings called *gribenes* (see page 133) in Yiddish. Schmaltz is not simply for cooking, though; it's also a popular spread for bread, especially dark rye.

One of my school friends now lives in Frankfurt, and each Christmas she embraces the German tradition of making cookies using butter and *Schweineschmalz*, the equivalent of our lard. This unflavored *Schmalz* made from rendered pork fat is used for everything from cookies to sauerkraut. It is also preferred for frying fish, meat, and sausages. In Germany you can buy the following different varieties and flavors of *Schmalz*:

Schweineschmalz	pork fat
Flomenschmalz	pork belly fat (lighter and smoother than *Schweineschmalz*)
Griebenschmalz	pork fat with cooked pieces of bacon, onions, and apples, plus herbs like marjoram or thyme
Gänseschmalz	goose fat, yellow in color and almost liquid at room temperature

SCHMALTZY

The word *schmalz* has traveled far from Germany, and the meaning of the word has morphed. The word arrived in New York with the Yiddish-speaking Jewish immigrants. In the 1930s it was picked up by jazz musicians, who used it to describe mainstream and sentimental music. The word caught on, spreading beyond the world of jazz, and now "schmaltzy," an American English innovation, refers to anything cloying or excessively sentimental, from music to novels and movies. The word *schmalz* is employed in English as an adjective meaning "full of fat," as in a schmaltz herring, a mature, often pickled, herring.

Confit

I think of confit as fast food. My French friends always have several cans of duck leg confit or, even better, duck neck stuffed with foie gras in the back of their cupboard. Add a can opener and a frying pan, and in thirty minutes you have a great meal. The stuffed neck is really just a tasty sausage packaged in the skin of the neck, filled with a mixture of duck, pork, and foie gras, and then preserved in fat. It is wonderful hot, but even better straight from the can, sliced and served at room temperature with a salad.

Confire is a French verb meaning "to preserve." Southwestern France is famous for its foie gras and confit. Once the liver is removed from a duck or goose, the rest of the fatty bird is cut into pieces and cooked slowly in its own fat, which adds a wonderful flavor and texture to the meat. The cooked meat is then stored submerged in the strained rendered fat. Covering the pieces totally in fat preserves them by preventing contact with the air and light. Even though modern refrigeration means that this method of keeping poultry and meat is no longer necessary, it still remains popular.

The popularity of duck breast means that duck legs are readily available for confit, although other fatty meats, like pork, can also be preserved in this way. It is also a good method for cooking other poultry, pheasant, squab, and lean turkey: all gain flavor and succulence from a long, warm bath in fat. Often today foods are simply cooked slowly in a bath of fat and then eaten immediately, rather than stored and allowed to age like a traditional confit. Simple to make, confit provides the cook with the beginnings of many other dishes: duck confit is an essential ingredient for Cassoulet (page 156), but it also makes a savory filling for ravioli and can be added to risotto, soup, salad, or a sandwich. Rillettes are really a type of confit in which the meat is cooked until it falls apart and then preserved with the cooking fat.

The best thing about making confit is it requires no special skill, only time. Since the birds available at the market do not contain large amounts of fat, like foie gras birds, fat must be added when making confit. You can render your own duck fat, or simply buy it from a specialty supplier. You can also make confit using lard, but the flavor won't be as good.

When making confit, first rub the poultry or meat with a spiced salt mix. This can be any combination of spices and herbs you choose, as long as you use enough salt: about $1/3$ ounce / 8 g salt for each 1 pound / 450 g of meat. After the pieces of meat or fowl marinate in the salt rub for up to 48 hours, they are cooked very slowly in the fat in the oven. Confit can be eaten straight away, but the flavor improves if you let it mature for at least a week in the refrigerator. It can be stored for a short time in the pan it was cooked in, or smeared with some of the cooking fat and wrapped in plastic wrap. To store confit for a longer period, place the pieces in clean glass, ceramic, or even plastic containers and cover them carefully with the strained cooking fat. Leave behind the cooking juices and set this aside as confit jelly (see page 142).

Foie Gras

Imagine a slice of terrine with a crown of melting, golden fat accompanied by warm toast, or a hot caramelized escalope of foie gras, its crisp exterior masking a soft, melting center. Eating foie gras is not simply about taste; it is also, importantly, about texture.

Foie gras is a food enveloped in myth, romance, and misconception. It conjures up images of luxury and even cruelty. "Foie gras" translates as "fat liver," and refers to the liver of a duck or goose that has been enlarged by feeding the birds a controlled diet at regular intervals. This technique is closely associated with the French, but its origins lie elsewhere.

Many Roman historians claimed the discovery of foie gras for their civilization, and while it is true that the Romans produced foie gras by feeding geese figs, the practice is much older than ancient Rome. The origins of foie gras lie in the Nile River delta sometime around 3000 B.C. The delta is a wintering ground for migrating water birds, and the ancient Egyptians noticed that before the birds returned to northern climes, they gorged themselves. They trapped the birds just before migration and discovered they were delicious to eat.

Migrating waterbirds naturally store large amounts of fat, especially in their livers, to prepare for a long flight without food. The Egyptians decided to exploit this process by force-feeding the birds. This task was performed by the Egyptians' Hebrew slaves, who, after fleeing Egypt, passed the techniques on to the Greeks and Romans.

Although the Egyptians discovered the benefits of force-feeding birds, historians are not sure if they actually consumed foie gras by itself. All we know is that they ate the fattened birds. The same is true of the ancient Greeks and Romans. It is not until the first century A.D. that we have evidence of foie gras presented as a unique dish: in his *Satires*, Horace records a Roman banquet that included dishes of eel, blackbird, pigeon, and the liver of a female goose fattened with figs.

With the fall of the Roman empire and the arrival of the barbarians, the recorded history of foie gras disappears until the sixteenth century. It is not known for certain who guarded the practice of making foie gras during these gastronomic dark ages, though a good case could be made for the Jewish communities who originally spread the knowledge from Egypt. The goose was a major source of dietary fat in kosher diets, especially for people living in northern Europe.

In 1564, foie gras reappears in the French text *L'Agriculture et la maison rustique*, which describes the method for fattening geese. Around the same time, in Italy, Bartolomeo Scappi, who was chef to Pope Pius V, wrote about large goose livers supplied to him by Jewish butchers in Rome.

Today, France is not only the biggest producer of foie gras, but it also consumes almost four-fifths of all foie gras produced in the world. Many French foie gras products, in fact, use imported livers, especially from Hungary and Bulgaria. Among the other countries producing foie gras are Poland, Spain, China, Japan, the United States, and Canada. In the United States, foie gras comes exclusively from ducks, as they are easier to raise. Geese tend to be more fragile and prone to disease and so require special handling (though two producers in Quebec do raise geese).

To produce an enlarged goose liver—weighing between $1^{1/4}$ and $1^{3/4}$ pounds / 570 and 800 g—for foie gras, the birds are fed three times a day for up to twenty-five days. For duck foie gras the birds are fed just twice a day for about two weeks, resulting in livers ranging from 1 to $1^{1/2}$ pounds / 450 to 700 g. It is this feeding, or *gavage*, that is commonly misunderstood, bringing cries of protest from animal rights groups and even some chefs. The outcry against foie gras has led to its being banned in several U.S. cities and states. During *gavage*, the birds are fed a mixture containing cooked corn via a funnel placed down their necks. While people love to anthropomorphize animals, geese and ducks are not human. Unlike us, they do not have a gagging mechanism—they don't even chew their food, preferring to swallow it whole—so they don't find this feeding process unpleasant at all, nor does it do them any harm if correctly done. Dr. Daniel Guémené, an expert on the physiological effects of foie gras production on geese and ducks, states, "A careful study of the nervous system of ducks and geese reveals that these animals do not feel either stress or suffering when they are being force fed." This of course refers to birds fed by the traditional hand-feeding method.

No foie gras producer wants his birds under stress, as stressed birds do not produce good foie gras. Therefore, they have a vested interest in keeping their birds healthy and happy. My own experience during a stay with a foie gras producer in the Dordogne echoes Dr. Guémené's findings. As soon as the farmer appeared, the birds went running toward him, happy to be fed, and it was obvious from the way he handled his birds that he cared about their well-being. It is also important to note that foie gras is not a diseased liver, as some people believe. Rather, it is simply an enlarged liver, which returns to normal size in several days if the intensive feeding stops. When the liver is sufficiently fattened, the bird is slaughtered and its liver is removed and vacuum packed, allowing it to be kept for up to two weeks. The rest of the bird is either sold fresh in pieces or turned into confit.

Foie gras is available all year, but the best season for this delicacy is from autumn to spring, when the birds' livers are generally bigger. Foie gras is graded from A to C. Grade A, the highest, is sold by good butchers and is suited for making most dishes. Grade B livers are smaller, with more veins and blemishes, but can be used for sautéing. Grade C livers are used for commercial pâtés and mousses.

Choose livers that are a uniform pale creamy color, and avoid any with bruises or blood spots. Those who believe foie gras is an overindulgence should consider Raymond Blanc's opinion. The respected Michelin-starred chef refers to foie gras as a superfood, pointing out that it is rich in B vitamins and a source of copper, iron, and iodine.

Ultimately, foie gras is a sensual pleasure to enjoy and appreciate while remembering its history and the skill involved in its preparation. The fact that it may be good for us is a comforting side benefit.

Foie Gras Fat

Whenever you cook foie gras, it always gives off fat. Save this fat and use it. The fat from sautéing is likely to be caramelized and have a strong flavor, so use it for flavoring, stirring it into mashed potatoes, topping a baked potato with it, or adding it to rice. The fat that results from steaming or poaching foie gras is great for pan-frying, and it can be used just like butter. Whatever cooking method you use, remember to strain the fat carefully and keep it refrigerated or frozen.

Preparing Foie Gras

FOR A TERRINE

To prepare foie gras for a terrine, clean it carefully. For this task, temperature is your greatest aid. When cold, the liver can be quite brittle, but, like butter, it softens as it warms up to room temperature, making it easier to remove the veins. If the liver gets too warm, however, it will be difficult to handle. If this happens, refrigerate the liver for a short time.

Place the liver on a plate, loosely cover with a towel, and leave at room temperature for about 30 minutes. Gently separate the liver into two lobes by pulling them apart, and use a knife to sever the connecting vein. Cut off any fat pieces between the lobes and keep any small pieces of liver that break off. Cut away any patches of green discoloration.

From the larger lobe, cut a 3/4-inch / 2-cm wide strip down the tapered outside edge, slicing down the length of the lobe. This will help the salt penetrate the liver. Place all the pieces of liver in a large non-reactive bowl and add 1 tablespoon of coarse sea salt and enough ice-cold water to submerge the liver. Cover with plastic wrap and refrigerate for 8 hours or overnight, to draw the blood out of the liver.

Remove the liver from the water and pat dry. Transfer the strip and any small pieces of liver to a large, clean, dry bowl, cover with plastic wrap, and refrigerate.

To devein the lobes, place them on a clean towel and cover with another towel. Leave them at room temperature for about 30 minutes.

Begin with the smaller lobe. Starting where the vein was cut, make an incision the length of the liver to expose the main vein. A scalpel is the best tool for this job, if you have one, or a small sharp paring knife. Use tweezers to gently pull out the main vein and its branches; if the liver is at the right temperature, the veins will come right out. Try to remove as many veins as possible without breaking up the liver too much. Leaving behind some veins will not alter the taste or texture of the final dish, only its appearance. Reform the lobe and place it in the bowl in the refrigerator. Repeat the process with the remaining lobe.

FOR SAUTÉING

Remove the foie gras from its packaging and place it on a plate loosely covered with plastic wrap. Leave it at room temperature for about 30 minutes.

Gently separate the livers into their two lobes by pulling them apart and cutting the vein where they join. Using a pair of tweezers, gently pull on the vein. If it comes out, great, but don't worry if it doesn't: since you're sautéing the liver, the blood spots won't be visible. Pull the vein from the second lobe. Set aside any small pieces of liver that break off and keep refrigerated. Cut off any pieces of fat where the livers were joined and any patches of green discoloration.

> **66** My idea of heaven is eating *pâté de foie gras* to the sound of trumpets. **99**
> SYDNEY SMITH

DUCK PRIMER

It can be confusing buying a duck. Long Island, Pekin, Muscovy, Moulard . . . which one to choose?

The first tip is that Pekin and Long Island are two names for the same duck, which is tender and has a good amount of fat. The males and females are similar weights, so you are more likely to get legs of equal size. They are a good choice for confit and rillettes.

Muscovy ducks are up to 40 percent leaner than Pekin; they produce a well-flavored meat but are not the best choice for confit.

The Moulard duck, my favorite, is a cross between Muscovy and Pekin and is raised primarily for foie gras. It yields a large breast with a good layer of fat, making it ideal for *magret de canard*.

Rendering Poultry Fats

Depending on where you live, you may be able to buy rendered duck or chicken fat. I usually render small amounts of chicken fat and I buy my duck fat. At Christmas I add goose and foie gras fats to my collection. If you can't buy rendered poultry fats, making them is easy. You will need the skin and fat from several birds, and the fatty tail is a good addition. Backs and necks also yield a good amount of fat. There is really no need to have every type of poultry fat in your refrigerator; I find duck fat the most useful.

Chop the skin and fat into small pieces and place them in a heavy, deep saucepan with about $1/3$ cup / 75 ml water per 1 pound / 450 g. Place the pan over very low heat and let the fat melt very gently, stirring from time to time. The fat will liquefy, the water will evaporate, and the skin will slowly turn golden and crisp. This can take anywhere from 2 to 4 hours. When the skin starts to color, strain off the fat through a double layer of cheesecloth into a clean container. Return the skin to the pan and continue to cook until very crisp. You will obtain a little more fat from this second cooking. Strain the additional fat through the cheesecloth. To end up with $3/4$ to 1 cup / 175 to 250 ml of rendered fat you will need about 1 pound / 450 g of poultry pieces. If you want to render a large amount, then it is easier to do it in the oven. Put the pieces in a heavy flameproof casserole or Dutch oven and place in a 250°F / 120°C oven. Rendering fat this way requires less supervision, but it will take up to 4 hours.

Rendered and carefully strained, poultry fat can be stored in the refrigerator for up to 2 months and can be frozen for a year. Poultry fat is very stable but, like all fat, it will eventually turn rancid.

FAT HEN

Fat hen or *grasse poulette* are the English and French names for a type of weed belonging to the Chenopodiaceae family. A very old plant, it thrives in manure and has been discovered in Neolithic middens. Its name comes from the fact that chickens love to eat it. In North America it must be more popular with pigs, because its common name on this side of the Atlantic is pigweed.

POULTRY CRACKLINGS

Poultry cracklings are the crisp pieces of skin left in the pan after rendering the poultry fat. Sprinkle them with a little salt while they are hot and use them in salads, in soups, or in Duck Fat Biscuits with Cracklings (page 141).

You can make them anytime, even if you don't want to render fat. Pull the skin off the back of a carcass or use the skin from the Butter Chicken (page 44) and cut it into small strips. Put the strips in a heavy frying pan over very low heat and cook until crisp—you will get a little fat.

You can make cracklings with the skin from duck confit the same way, or flavored poultry cracklings (see below).

Gribenes

Gribenes, sometimes written grivenes, are the Jewish answer to pork cracklings. They are the result of making a poultry alternative to Griebenschmalz (see page 126). This recipe comes from my friend Nancy. You can use necks or backs, but I prefer backs, as there is more skin on them, and it's the skin that makes the tasty cracklings. The quantity of backs used here is just a suggestion; using a few more or a few less won't make a difference. I guarantee that the first time you make them, you'll be snacking on them hot out of the pan. If you manage to keep some, sprinkle them on a salad or mashed potatoes or spread a thick piece of German rye with schmaltz and top it with gribenes. That should cure just about any illness. The fat, which has a strong chicken flavor with onion overtones, is great in the Chicken Liver Spread (page 145) or spread on bread.

Makes about 1 cup / 250 ml

About 3 pounds / 1.4 kg chicken backs

1 large onion, chopped

Sea salt

Remove the fat and skin from the chicken backs and cut it into small pieces. Reserve the backs for making stock.

Combine the chicken fat, skin, and onion in a heavy frying pan over low heat. Cook gently, stirring occasionally, until the fat renders. Once there is a good layer of fat in the pan, after about 30 minutes, increase the heat to medium and cook, stirring often, until the skin and onion turn dark golden brown, about another 30 minutes.

Tip the *gribenes* into a fine-mesh sieve set over a bowl to catch the fat. Drain the *gribenes* on paper towels and sprinkle them with salt while they are still warm. Let the fat stand so any sediment sinks to the bottom, and then strain the chicken fat through cheesecloth. Let cool and refrigerate.

Duck Rillettes

Makes about 2 cups / 500 ml

1 1/2 pounds / 700 g duck legs, neck, wings, skin, and fat

10 1/2 ounces / 300 g pork belly, skin removed

1/4 cup / 60 ml dry white wine

1 orange

2 cloves garlic

1 fresh bay leaf

1 1/2 teaspoons coarse sea salt

1 teaspoon coriander seeds, crushed

Freshly ground black pepper and fine sea salt

Once you have made the Spanish-Style Pork Rillettes (page 79), you can make any sort of rillettes. The technique is always the same, and you can vary the flavorings to suit your taste. I like to buy a whole duck, use the breasts for Duck Breast with Blackberries (page 147), then use up the rest of the duck to make rillettes, adding some pork belly to make sure there is enough fat in the mixture and to make the legs go a little further. Leave the duck legs on the bone, add the wings to the mix, and don't forget to include the neck, too, as there is a lot of meat on it. Keep the duck carcass and wing tips for stock. Serve the rillettes with baguette slices or toasts, or with a salad as a starter.

Cut the duck legs, neck, and wings in half. Cut the skin and fat into small pieces and the pork belly into 3/4-inch / 2-cm pieces. Place all the duck and pork in a large bowl and add the wine. Remove a large strip of zest from the orange and set the orange aside. Peel and halve the garlic cloves, removing the germ (see page 85). Add the orange zest, garlic, bay leaf, coarse salt, and coriander seeds to the duck mixture. Season generously with freshly ground pepper and toss to mix. Marinate 6 to 8 hours or overnight in the refrigerator.

Preheat the oven to 250°F / 120°C.

Tip the duck mixture with all the seasonings and wine into a heavy casserole or Dutch oven, cover, and cook, stirring occasionally, until the meat is falling off the bone, about 3 hours.

Remove the duck mixture from the oven, and tip it with all the fat and juices into a large fine-mesh sieve suspended over a bowl. Empty the contents of the sieve onto a large platter, then pour the liquid from the bowl into a measuring cup and set aside. Let the meat mixture cool slightly.

Using your fingers, pull the meat and fat apart, discarding the bones, orange zest, and bay leaf as you go. As you work, discard any pieces of membrane that don't shred. This takes time, so be patient. The key is to create shreds of meat and fat. Return the shredded meat mixture to the bowl.

The cooking liquid will have separated into fat and juices. Carefully pour off the fat and set aside. Add about 1/4 cup / 60 ml of the juices to the shredded meat mixture so that it is very moist. Taste and adjust the seasoning, adding more pepper and fine sea salt if necessary. Finely grate 1 tablespoon of zest from the orange and then squeeze 2 tablespoons of juice. Stir the zest and juice into the mixture.

Pack the mixture into ceramic dishes (I use individual soufflé dishes) or a terrine, leaving a 1/4-inch / 6-mm gap at the top of each dish. As you pack the meat into the dishes, you will see the liquid gently oozing from the meat. Place the dishes in the refrigerator for a few minutes to firm up. Once the surface is firm, seal the dishes with a layer of the liquid fat and refrigerate. Leave the rillettes for 2 to 3 days to allow the flavors to

meld. Sealed with fat, the rillettes will keep in the refrigerator for up to 2 months. Once the seal is broken, eat the rillettes within a week.

TIP If you do not have enough fat from cooking the rillettes to seal the dishes, you can use clarified butter instead.

VARIATIONS There is no need to stop at using duck. It goes without saying that you can use goose, and rabbit also makes good rillettes. For rabbit use about 1 pound / 450 g of pork belly for every $1^{1}/_{2}$ pounds / 700 g of rabbit, add thyme and marjoram for flavoring, and omit the orange.

POTTED MEATS

The French, awash in duck and goose fat, may be the undisputed masters of confit and rillettes, but many other cultures use fat to preserve meat. In England there is a long tradition of potted meats, cooked meat pounded with seasonings into a paste and packed into an earthenware pot then sealed with fat or clarified butter, similar to rillettes. Potted meats used to be a popular breakfast food in England, and they provided nourishment for travelers on long sea voyages. I think I might take one on my next trans-Atlantic flight.

Today, with the help of a food processor, you can make these potted delights easily. They are a perfect way to use up leftovers, when you just don't want another slice of roast turkey, or you've had enough of cold chicken.

To make potted meat, weigh the cooked meat, dice it, and combine it in a food processor with about $^{1}/_{2}$ to $^{3}/_{4}$ of its weight in duck fat, lard, or softened butter. Season well with salt and pepper and add some chopped herbs and a teaspoon or two of brandy, port, or wine before processing until well blended. Taste and adjust the seasonings and add more fat if you want a softer consistency. Pack the mixture into small dishes and seal with a layer of fat. They will keep for about two weeks refrigerated. Bring to room temperature before serving with toast or crackers.

Here are some additions to try:

Chicken: marsala, sherry, tarragon, thyme, paprika
Duck: orange liqueur, brandy, orange zest, ground cumin, star anise
Beef: port, horseradish, mustard, nutmeg, mace, cinnamon, Worcestershire sauce
Pork: Pernod, ground fennel seeds, chile, sage, ginger
Lamb: red wine, anchovy, oregano, rosemary, garlic

Potatoes Sarladaises

Curnonsky, the celebrated twentieth-century French food writer, described the cuisine of southwestern France as "without butter and without reproach," and he was right. In this part of France the cooking medium of choice is goose or duck fat.

These potatoes are named after the town of Sarlat in Périgord, a region renowned for its foie gras and black truffles. There are several variations of this potato dish. I like them with just a dusting of sea salt, but often the recipe includes finely chopped shallot or garlic, added right at the end of cooking, and a sprinkling of chopped parsley, as it does here. For a subtler taste of garlic, omit the garlic and cook the potatoes in the fat from the Garlic Confit (page 144). Serve these potatoes with confit or grilled meats and a green salad to make you feel virtuous.

Peel the potatoes, cut into 3/4-inch / 2-cm dice, and place in a large bowl. Rinse the potatoes well with cold water. Drain and pat dry with a clean kitchen towel.

Place the duck fat in a large frying pan over medium-high heat. When the duck fat is very hot and just starting to smoke, add the potatoes. Cook without stirring until the potatoes are golden on one side. Give the pan a shake and turn the potatoes, but do not attempt to turn any potatoes that are still sticking to the pan. Leave them until they detach themselves from the pan.

Continue to cook the potatoes until they are golden on all sides. Lower the heat and cook until soft in the center, about 15 minutes more.

When the potatoes are cooked, add the shallot and stir to mix. Season the potatoes well with salt and pepper, sprinkle with parsley, and serve immediately.

Serves 2

2 potatoes

2 tablespoons duck fat

1/2 shallot or 2 cloves peeled garlic, finely chopped (optional)

Sea salt and freshly ground black pepper

2 tablespoons chopped fresh flat-leaf parsley

FAT MAN

Fat Man was the code name for the second atomic bomb dropped on Japan in August 1945. The first bomb, Little Boy, was made of uranium, but Fat Man contained plutonium. The plutonium was too dangerous to detonate using Little Boy's gun type method, so an implosion method was developed. Although Fat Man was bigger and heavier than Little Boy, that was not the reason for its moniker. The name is a reference to the shape of these early bombs. The fact that the two bombs had different detonation methods was kept highly secret and was not revealed until the Rosenberg trial in 1951, and no photographs of either bomb appeared until the 1960s.

Simple Roast Chicken

Serves 4

One 3-pound / 1.4-kg free-range chicken

A large handful of mixed fresh herbs, such as parsley, chives, tarragon, and marjoram

1 large clove garlic, peeled and finely chopped

7 tablespoons / $3^1/2$ ounces / 100 g unsalted butter, softened

Coarse sea salt and freshly ground black pepper

1 lemon

The hardest part of this recipe is finding a chicken with a good amount of fat. Once you have accomplished this, the rest is simple. If you baste the chicken as it roasts, its juices and fat will mix with the lemon and butter to make a sauce—there's no need to fuss over making gravy. If I have four hearty eaters or more I prefer to roast two chickens rather than a single larger one. It leads to fewer arguments over who gets a piece of leg or breast, and I might even have leftovers. Make your life simple and serve this dish with crusty bread for mopping up those delicious juices and a salad or green vegetable.

Preheat the oven to 450°F / 230°C.

Pat the chicken dry, fold the neck flap under the bird, and secure it in place using the wings.

Set aside a few herb sprigs and chop the remainder; you should have about $1/2$ cup / 7 g. Using your hands, mix the chopped herbs and garlic into the butter until blended. Smear the herb butter all over the bird, placing a little inside the bird, too.

Season the bird well with salt and pepper. Place the bird in a roasting pan and squeeze the lemon juice over the top. Put the lemon halves in the bird's cavity with the reserved herb sprigs.

Roast the chicken for 15 minutes. Remove from the oven and baste the chicken with its own juices. Reduce the heat to 375°F / 190°C and continue to roast, basting occasionally, until the thigh juices run clear when pierced with a skewer or the temperature of the thigh registers 165°F / 73°C on a kitchen thermometer, 45 minutes to 55 minutes. Turn off the oven, open the oven door, and leave the chicken in the pan in the oven to rest for at least 15 minutes.

Transfer the chicken to a cutting board and cut into serving pieces. Add any juices from the chicken to the pan and place the pan over medium heat. Bring to a boil, deglaze the pan, using a wooden spoon to scrape up the browned bits from the bottom, then strain through a fine-mesh sieve, and serve the pan sauce with the chicken.

FATTY SOAP

I find it fascinating that we use fat to wash ourselves, our clothes, and those greasy dishes . . . or at least we did.

The origins of soap are lost in the past, but there are some wonderful myths surrounding soap's discovery. One from ancient Rome describes how the rain would wash away the fat left from animal sacrifices on the altar at Mount Sapo. The fat mixed with wood ashes and ran down into the clay banks of the Tiber River. The women washing their clothes at this spot on the river soon realized that their clothes were cleaner than when they washed them upstream. And so this is how, the legend continues, we get the name for this magical cleaning mix: the word *soap* comes from Mount Sapo. It's wonderful to think that animal sacrifices both appeased the gods and kept the Romans in clean togas, but, alas, it's not true. First, there was no Mount Sapo on the Tiber River, and it's unlikely there would have been enough tallow left over from the sacrifices to make soap. The Romans probably learned about soap from the Celts or Germanic tribes. Pliny the Elder mentions a soap made from tallow and ashes, but he adds, rather disapprovingly, that the Gauls and Germanic tribes used it as a hair pomade.

The earliest traces of a soaplike mixture have been found in Babylonian clay containers dating from 2800 B.C. This soap was probably not used for bathing, as at that time it was customary to coat the body with a mixture of oils and unguents, often fat-based, which mixed with the dirt, dust, and dead skin on the body. The mixture was then scraped off with a curved blade called a strigil. This early soap was used for washing clothes but also for treating wounds, dressing hair, and preparing wool and cotton fibers for weaving.

Soap is a combination of fat and a strong alkali, originally lye, which is a mixture of water and wood ash. Its discovery was probably a lucky accident. If you cook, you probably know that fat and water usually don't mix. This is why it's easy to skim the fat that floats on top of a sauce or stock, but it is difficult to clean that greasy stockpot with just plain water. When lye is mixed with fat and heated, though, a chemical reaction called "saponification" occurs, emulsifying the water and fat. Today the lye is commercially produced as either caustic soda or potash. Caustic soda or sodium hydroxide contains salt, and when added to fat makes a hard soap, while potash, potassium hydroxide, produces a soft soap.

Soap works because the soap molecule has a split personality: one half loves water, while the other half hates it. Grease molecules, which also hate water—that's why oil floats on water—join forces with soap's water-hating half, while the water combines with soap's water-loving side. For the soap to work well, energy must be added with heat, agitation, or, preferably, both. When we wash dishes the hot water melts the grease, while the agitation helps the soap pull the grease and dirt away from the dishes into the larger pool of water. But the dishes are not clean until they are rinsed with more water to wash the grease and soap away. While soap is a good cleaning agent, the minerals in hard water reduce its effectiveness, and soap scum often remains on dishes or as a ring around the bathtub. So, if you decide to take a cleaning job, take one in Melbourne, Australia, where the water is soft, rather than in Paris, France, where it is very hard.

Detergents based on petrochemicals have largely replaced fat-based soaps today. They work by lowering the surface tension of the water so they can attack the oil and grease. Detergents have added perfumes, enzymes, bleach, and blue dyes that counter yellowing, making them very effective. Soap is also added to detergents, not for its ability to clean, but to reduce the amount of suds produced. Detergents are not affected by hard water and are less likely to leave that ring around the tub, but they are not environmentally friendly. Soap made from animal fat, however, is biodegradable, and tallow-based cleaning products that work in both hard and cold water have now been developed.

Duck Fat Biscuits with Cracklings

Duck fat makes a very tasty, tender tea biscuit or scone, which is even better if you add some poultry cracklings (see page 133). These are great to serve with soup, salad, or Duck Rillettes (page 134). If you like to fuss more than I do, you could make smaller biscuits and serve them warm, split and filled with duck confit, a perfect accompaniment with drinks. There is no need to stick to duck fat: goose or chicken fat will work just as well.

Preheat the oven to 425°F / 220°C.

Combine the flour, baking powder, and salt in a food processor. Pulse to mix, add the cracklings and chives, and pulse again. Add the cold duck fat and pulse until the mixture has coarse lumps of fat about the size of small peas. Transfer the mixture to a bowl and stir in the $2/3$ cup / 150 ml of milk to make a soft, slightly sticky dough. Turn the dough onto a floured surface and knead gently.

Pat the dough into a disk $1/2$ inch / 1 cm thick and, using a floured $2^1/2$-inch / 6-cm biscuit cutter, cut out rounds. Knead any leftover dough together, pat into a disk, and cut out additional biscuits until all the dough is used up. Arrange the biscuits on a baking sheet and brush the tops with the remaining 1 tablespoon of milk. Bake until the biscuits are puffed and golden, about 15 minutes. Allow to cool slightly before serving.

Makes 9 or 10 biscuits

2 cups / 8$3/4$ ounces / 250 g flour

1 tablespoon baking powder

$1/2$ teaspoon fine sea salt

4 tablespoons poultry cracklings, chopped (see page 133)

2 tablespoons chopped chives

3 ounces / 90 g duck fat, cubed and well chilled or frozen

$2/3$ cup / 150 ml plus 1 tablespoon milk

Duck Confit

This is the classic confit recipe, pieces of duck slowly cooked in their own fat until meltingly tender, then stored in the same fat. I prefer to make confit from legs, but there is no reason not to use the breasts as well. Although it is simple to make, confit does require some advance preparation, as the legs are marinated in a spice-salt mixture for 2 days before they are cooked. Confit is best cooked slowly at a very low temperature, so I cook it in the oven. Don't worry if your legs are a bit bigger or smaller; just cook them until they are very tender but not falling off the bone. Keep the confit for at least a week before eating to allow the flavor to mature.

If you do not have quite enough duck fat, you can make up the difference with lard. Once made, confit is a quick meal just waiting in your refrigerator. You can heat it up and serve it with lentils or potatoes cooked in duck fat, or serve it at room temperature with a salad.

Combine the coarse salt, bay and thyme leaves, peppercorns, and nutmeg in a spice grinder and grind until powdery.

Rub the duck legs with the garlic cloves and place both the duck and the garlic in a glass dish. Sprinkle the legs with the salt mixture, turning to coat. Cover and refrigerate for 2 days.

Preheat the oven to 200°F / 100°C.

Makes 6 whole legs

$1^1/2$ ounces / 40 g coarse sea salt

2 fresh bay leaves, torn

3 sprigs thyme, stemmed

2 teaspoons black peppercorns

$1/4$ teaspoon freshly ground nutmeg

6 whole duck legs (about 4.5 to 5 pounds / 2 to 2.25 kg)

3 cloves garlic, peeled and halved

$6^1/2$ cups / 3 pounds / 1.4 kg duck fat, melted

Rinse the legs to remove the excess seasoning mixture and pat dry. Place the legs in a heavy flameproof casserole or Dutch oven, putting the biggest legs on the bottom, skin side down, and the smaller legs on top, skin side up. Add the garlic cloves and enough fat to just cover the legs and place the pan over medium heat. When you see the first bubble in the fat, remove the pan from the heat and place on a rimmed baking sheet in the oven. Cook, uncovered, until the meat is very tender and has shrunk away from the bone, 4 to 5 hours. The juices should run clear when a leg is pierced with a skewer. If any part of the legs is not quite covered, just turn the legs after 2 hours of cooking.

While the confit is cooking, place three wooden skewers in a saucepan and cover with water. Bring to a boil over high heat and boil for 5 minutes. Let cool, remove the skewers from the water, and set aside.

CONFIT BASICS

To Extract and Reheat Confit

Remove the container of confit from the refrigerator and place it in a pan of barely simmering water. After 20 to 30 minutes the fat will be soft enough for you to pull the legs out in one piece.

Preheat the oven to 350°F / 180°C.

Place the duck legs, still with a very light coating of fat, skin side down in a heavy frying pan, preferably cast-iron. Cook the legs in the oven until the duck is heated through, 15 to 20 minutes. (Turkey pieces will take longer.) Insert a metal skewer into the center of the meat; it should be hot to the touch when you remove it.

Preheat the broiler to high.

Remove the duck from the oven, remembering that the handle of the pan will be very hot. Turn the legs skin side up and place under the broiler to crisp the skin.

Confit Jelly

When you cook confit, juices are released from the legs and they settle in the bottom of the pan. Make sure you separate these juices from the fat before covering the cooked confit with the fat. These juices can cause the cooked confit to spoil, but that doesn't mean you should throw them away. They will solidify in the refrigerator, making a strongly flavored jelly. Think of it as a salty demi-glace that can be added to sauces, stews, vegetables, and beans for extra flavor, but use it judiciously because of the high salt content. The jelly can also be stored in the freezer; it will keep for about 3 months frozen and 2 weeks refrigerated.

Confit Jars

I like to store my confit in wide-mouthed glass preserving jars, but you could also store it in earthenware dishes or plastic tubs. The containers, however, should have an opening wide enough so that you can remove the legs easily. I usually store my legs in pairs. Before marinating the legs, check that they will fit into the container with enough space to allow them to be completely covered with the fat. The containers should be impeccably clean.

Let the legs cool slightly in the fat. Break the wooden skewers into pieces and place them in the bottom of the sterilized jars or containers you are using to store the confit. This is to prevent the confit from touching the bottom of the container. Place the legs on top of the skewer pieces and ladle over the warm fat to cover the legs completely and fill the containers to the brim. Leave the confit on a wire rack to cool. The fat will contract as it cools, so once it is set, ladle a little more fat into the containers to seal them completely, then cover. The confit will keep, refrigerated, for up to 6 months.

TIP When ladling the hot fat, be careful not to disturb any of the juices at the bottom of the pan. You do not want any of these juices to go into the storage containers. Strain the remaining fat through cheesecloth, leaving behind the juices. Pour the juices into a bowl and refrigerate the strained fat and juices separately. The fat can be reused several times until it becomes too salty. The confit juices will set into a jelly (see page 142).

The short-tailed shearwater lives in large colonies along the eastern coast of Australia and the shores of New Zealand. These migratory seabirds, which contain a good amount of fat, were an important source of food for early European settlers, who thought they tasted like mutton and named them "mutton birds." These birds were also important to the New Zealand Maoris, who preserved them by cooking them in their own fat, making a southern hemisphere confit.

MUTTON BIRD CONFIT

Turkey Confit

Although duck legs are the most popular ingredient for making confit, any piece or type of poultry, including lean birds like squab, pheasant, and turkey, benefits from a bath in warm fat. My local market had large turkey wings, which were about the same size as the duck legs I'd been using, so I decided to confit them. This recipe shows you that you can confit any piece of poultry. All you have to do is adjust the cooking time, since it depends on the size of the pieces.

Combine the salt, sage leaves, peppercorns, cardamom seeds, and mace in a spice grinder and grind until powdery.

Remove the tips from the turkey wings and set aside for stock. Cut the wings into two pieces.

Rub the turkey wing pieces with the garlic cloves and place both the turkey and the garlic in a glass dish. Sprinkle the turkey pieces with the salt mixture, turning to coat. Cover and refrigerate for 2 days.

To finish the confit, follow the directions for Duck Confit (page 141).

Makes 12 pieces

$1^1/2$ ounces / 40 g coarse sea salt

20 fresh sage leaves

2 teaspoons black peppercorns

Seeds from 6 cardamom pods

$1/4$ teaspoon ground mace

6 whole turkey wings (4.5 to 5 pounds / 2 to 2.25 kg)

3 cloves garlic, peeled and halved

$6^1/2$ cups / 3 pounds / 1.4 kg duck fat, melted

Duck Breast with Blackberries

Think of a duck breast (in French, magret de canard*) as a good steak with a crisp crust of fat. Like a good steak, it is best served medium-rare. As the duck breast cooks, it renders its fat, which bastes the lean breast meat. You need a good layer of fat between the skin and the meat to achieve the perfect combination of crisp skin and juicy meat. The duck breasts will spit and sputter, so I recommend using a splatter screen, which will minimize cleanup and keep all the fat in the pan.*

Duck is often paired with fruit, and although this combination is often too sweet, the acidity of blackberries strikes a perfect balance with the rich duck meat. Fat Fat-Cooked Fries (page 152) and a green vegetable would go well with this dish.

Remove the duck breasts from the refrigerator 30 minutes before cooking. Score the skin in a crosshatch pattern, cutting through the skin and fat but not cutting the meat. Season both sides with salt and pepper and set aside.

Finely grate the zest of the orange and set aside. Squeeze enough juice to measure $1/4$ cup / 60 ml.

Place a heavy frying pan over high heat. When it is hot, add the breasts, skin side down. Reduce the heat to medium, cover the pan with a splatter screen, and cook for 5 minutes. Pour off the fat, set aside, and continue to cook the breasts, skin side down, for another 5 minutes.

Pour off any excess fat, turn the breasts over, and cook for another 2 to 5 minutes, depending on the thickness of the breasts. To test doneness, press the meat side of the breast with your finger; it should feel soft and spongy. Transfer the cooked breasts to a plate, cover loosely with aluminum foil, and leave to rest for 5 minutes.

Pour off all but about 2 tablespoons of the fat in the pan. Add the shallot and cook over medium heat, stirring, until softened. Add the port and bring to a boil. Deglaze the pan, using a wooden spoon to scrape up the browned bits from the bottom. Add the orange zest, juice, and blackberries, lower the heat, and simmer until the liquid is slightly reduced and the berries are warm and softened. Season with salt and pepper.

Cut the duck breasts into thick slices and serve with the sauce.

VARIATION To serve the duck breast as a warm salad, replace half the orange juice with 2 tablespoons of wine vinegar. Toss together some frisée and watercress, top with the sliced duck breast, and pour over the warm sauce.

Serves 4

2 boneless duck breast halves, about 8 to 10 ounces / 225 to 285 g each

Sea salt and freshly ground black pepper

1 large orange

1 shallot, finely chopped

$1/2$ cup / 125 ml port

$1 1/3$ cups / 6 ounces / 175 g blackberries

Fat Fat-Cooked Fries

Serves 4

4 Yukon gold potatoes (about 1 3/4 pounds / 800 g total)

1/4 cup / 1 3/4 ounces / 50 g duck fat

1 clove garlic, unpeeled

2 tablespoons chopped fresh flat-leaf parsley

Fleur de sel

This is a recipe for big, fat wedges of potato cooked in duck fat. Unlike the Potatoes Sarladaises (page 137), these potatoes are soft, not crisp, but they are equally satisfyingly, imbued with the flavor of the duck fat. I love that the source of this recipe is Michel Guérard, the author of Cuisine Minceur (Diet Food). *It is reassuring to know that the chef who gave us French lean cuisine also appreciates the power of duck fat. Yukon gold potatoes are a good all-purpose potato, but this dish is also good with a floury baking potato like russets. Oval potatoes make the best-shaped fries. This is a good dish to make when you want to use up the fat from making confit, especially Garlic Confit (page 144). Serve these potatoes with confit or grilled meats.*

Peel the potatoes and cut lengthwise into quarters. Rinse them under cold water and place in a bowl. Cover with cold water and leave to soak for 30 minutes.

Drain the potatoes and dry them well. In a heavy flameproof casserole large enough to hold the potatoes in a single layer, heat the duck fat over medium-high heat. When it begins to smoke, add the potatoes and the garlic clove. Reduce the heat to medium and cook the potatoes, turning them so that they color evenly, until golden on all sides, 15 to 20 minutes.

Remove the garlic and discard. Transfer the potatoes to a large plate and pour off all but 1 tablespoon of the fat. Return the potatoes to the pan, cover, and cook over low heat until they are cooked through, about 15 minutes. Check the potatoes regularly, turning if necessary, and if you hear the fat spitting, lift the lid and wipe off the excess moisture on the inside of it.

When the potatoes are soft in the center, transfer them to a warmed dish and sprinkle with the chopped parsley and *fleur de sel*, turning so they are well coated.

JAZZY FAT

Fats Waller's real name was Thomas Wright Waller. A son of a preacher man, he played the organ at his father's services. He moved from the church to playing the music behind silent movies at the Lincoln Theatre in Harlem. Although his father hoped his son would follow him into the church, show business had captured Thomas's attention and in the 1920s he was performing live and on radio. By the time the movies had sound, he was not only singing and writing songs but was acting, too. One of his best-known roles was in the 1943 movie *Stormy Weather* alongside Lena Horne, Cab Calloway, and Bill Robinson. He played himself and sang his own composition, "Ain't Misbehavin'." Unfortunately, Waller's real life was stormy, too. He was a prodigious eater and drinker and had protracted legal problems over alimony payments. The stress, his lifestyle, plus a punishing touring schedule took its toll on his health and Waller, at only 39 years old, died of pneumonia just several months after *Stormy Weather* was released.

Sautéed Foie Gras with Gingered Vanilla Quince

Serves 6 as an appetizer

2 ripe yellow quinces (about 1 pound / 450 g total)

2 tablespoons duck or foie gras fat

Sea salt and freshly ground black pepper

$1/4$ cup / 60 ml vin santo or dry sherry

2 tablespoons honey

2 teaspoons peeled, finely chopped fresh ginger

$1/2$ cup / 125 ml water

$1/2$ cup / 125 ml freshly squeezed orange juice

3 tablespoons sugar

$1/2$ teaspoon pure vanilla extract

1 duck foie gras (about $1 1/2$ pounds / 675 g prepared) (see page 130)

2 tablespoons flour

Although you can substitute apples for the quince in this recipe, they have none of the perfume and power of my favorite fruit. Quince also stays whole even when cooked for a long time, so there is no risk of it turning to mush, like apples can. Autumn is the season for quince, and it's also the perfect time to eat foie gras. The secret to serving hot foie gras is having everything prepared ahead, so all you have to do is cook the foie gras and plate it. Sautéing foie gras gives off smoke and fat—there is no way to avoid it. Also be prepared for those slices to shrink in the pan.

Peel the quinces and cut into quarters. Remove the core and cut the quarters crosswise into $1/4$-inch / 6-mm slices.

In a frying pan with a lid, heat the fat over medium-high heat. When hot, add the quince slices and season with salt and pepper. Cook, stirring, until the quince slices are lightly colored. Add the wine and deglaze the pan, scraping up the browned bits from the bottom. Add the honey, 1 teaspoon of the ginger, and the water. Lower the heat so the quince slices just simmer, cover, and cook until the quinces slices are tender, about 30 minutes.

Transfer the quince slices to a fine-mesh sieve suspended over a bowl. Set the quince slices aside. Pour the strained liquid into a measuring cup and add the orange juice. You should have about 1 cup / 250 ml; if not, add some water or wine. Pour the liquid into a small saucepan and add the sugar and remaining ginger. Bring to a boil over high heat, boiling until it is reduced to about $1/3$ cup / 75 ml. Strain the liquid into a measuring cup, add the vanilla extract, and set aside. The recipe can be prepared to this point up to a day in advance.

Using a hot, dry knife, and starting from the center of each lobe and working out in each direction, cut the foie gras into slices $1/2$ inch / 1 cm thick. By starting in the center you will end up with slices that are more uniform in size. The diameter of the slices will vary, but keep the thickness the same. As you cut, small pieces of the liver may break off; set them aside. You will be left with small, rounded pieces from each end and the inside of the liver. Add these to any liver pieces that broke off and use them for Foie Gras Butter (page 159). You have should at least 12 slices; you might end up with a couple of extra slices.

Place the foie gras slices on a parchment-lined baking sheet, cover with plastic wrap, and refrigerate. This can be done up to 6 hours before cooking the foie gras.

Remove the foie gras from the refrigerator 15 minutes before cooking. Preheat the oven to 200°F / 100°C.

Put the serving plates in the oven to warm and reheat the quinces and sauce separately in saucepans over low heat. Divide the quince slices among the warm plates and return the plates to the oven. Turn off the oven.

Line a baking sheet with paper towels. Lightly dust the foie gras slices on both sides with the flour and season with salt and pepper.

Heat a large frying pan over medium-high heat. When it is hot, cook the foie gras in 2 batches, until it is nicely browned and gives a little when pressed with your finger, about 1 minute per side. Transfer the cooked slices to the baking sheet, pouring off the fat between batches. Reserve the fat for another use.

Divide the foie gras slices among the plates of quince slices and drizzle with the sauce. Serve immediately.

Without salt and fat: boring and wishy-washy (German)

Quinces are large, lumpy, greenish-yellow fruit that are often covered with gray fuzz. On first glance you might mistake them for large, ugly, misshapen apples. Although there is a rare variety that can be eaten raw, most quinces are dry, sour, and astringent and must be cooked before eating. This member of the rose family turns a rosy red when slowly cooked and has an amazing fragrance that will turn your head, reminiscent of vanilla, musk, lemon blossom, and pineapple.

Quinces are like avocados: you have to buy them well before you want to use them. Try to buy green quinces, free of any marks, as they are less likely to be bruised than the yellow ones that have been knocking against each other at the store. Quince blemishes hide under the skin, only to be discovered when you peel them.

Once you get them home, place the quinces in their own bowl and allow them to ripen at room temperature. As they turn yellow they will perfume your kitchen. If you only have green quinces you can still use them, but they will be harder to peel and cut and will take longer to cook. Once quinces are yellow and ripe, they can be stored in the vegetable drawer of your refrigerator. If you can't get quinces, substitute cooking apples, such as Rome, Spy, or Mutsu, but remember that they'll cook much more quickly than quinces will.

HANDLING QUINCE

Cassoulet

Serves 6 to 8

$4^1/2$ cups / $1^3/4$ pounds / 800 g dried white (navy or Great Northern) beans, soaked overnight in cold water

2 onions

2 cloves

3 cloves garlic, peeled

6 sprigs thyme

4 sprigs flat-leaf parsley

1 fresh bay leaf

$1/2$ pound / 225 g pork belly, skin on

$1/2$ pound / 225 g boneless lamb shoulder

Sea salt and freshly ground black pepper

$1/4$ cup / $1^3/4$ ounces / 50 g duck fat

2 garlic pork sausages (about $10^1/2$ ounces / 300 g total)

$1/2$ cup / 125 ml dry white wine

4 plum tomatoes, cored, seeded, and chopped

1 teaspoon tomato paste

2 legs Duck Confit (page 141)

$1^1/4$ cups / $3^1/2$ ounces / 100 g fine fresh bread crumbs

This classic from southwestern France is a very contentious dish, and almost every town in the region has its own "genuine" cassoulet recipe. Some add lamb, others tomatoes. Some add both, and some believe that neither should be included. Then there are endless discussions on how to make the crust. As long as you begin with white beans and add fatty meats you'll end up with a great-tasting dish. After all, it is just a bean stew.

Most cassoulet recipes serve 10 to 12 people. Maybe I am short of friends, but I think the best dinners are for 6 or 8. So I don't have to eat leftover cassoulet all week, I've pared the recipe down. If you have more friends than me, or a big family, you can double it.

This is a rich dish, so I like to follow it with a spinach or watercress and orange salad topped with duck cracklings. You can, of course, sprinkle those cracklings over the cassoulet, too.

Drain the beans, discarding the soaking water. Place the beans in a large saucepan and cover with cold water. Cut 1 of the onions in half and skewer each half with a clove. Add to the pan with 2 of the garlic cloves, the thyme and parsley sprigs, and bay leaf. Bring to a boil over medium heat, then lower the heat, skim any foam from the surface, and discard. Simmer the beans, uncovered, until they are just tender, about 1 hour.

While the beans are cooking, remove the skin from the pork belly, cut into $1/2$-inch / 1-cm squares, and set aside. Cut the pork belly into 1-inch / 2.5-cm pieces and the lamb into $1^1/2$-inch / 4-cm pieces. Season the pork belly and lamb pieces with salt and pepper.

Heat 2 tablespoons of the duck fat in a frying pan over medium heat. When hot, add the pork belly and lamb and brown on all sides. Transfer to a plate. Prick the sausages several times with a fork and add them to the pan. Lower the heat to medium and brown the sausages on all sides. Transfer the sausages to a plate and cut each sausage into 4 pieces.

Chop the remaining onion, add to the pan, and cook over low heat until softened. Add the remaining garlic and the wine and bring to a boil. Deglaze the pan, using a wooden spoon to scrape up the browned bits from the bottom. Stir in the tomatoes and tomato paste and simmer until reduced slightly, about 10 minutes.

Remove the skin from the duck legs and set aside, then remove the meat from the bones in large pieces. Set the meat aside and discard the bones.

When the beans are cooked, drain them, reserving the cooking liquid. Transfer the beans to a large bowl, discarding the onion halves and herbs.

Preheat the oven to 300°F / 150°C.

Stir the reduced tomato and onion mixture into the beans and season with salt and pepper, remembering that the confit will add some salt to the finished dish. Put about half the bean mixture in a large Dutch oven

or casserole. Now place the pieces of pork skin, pork belly, lamb, and duck confit on top, making sure the different meats are well distributed.

Cover the meats with the remaining bean mixture and push the sausage pieces into the top bean layer so they almost disappear into the beans. Pour in enough of the reserved cooking liquid to come up almost to the top of the beans. Cover the surface of the cassoulet with about half of the bread crumbs and dot with pieces of the remaining duck fat.

Bake, uncovered, for 3 hours or until a golden crust has formed over the creamy textured beans. Three or four times during the cooking time, break the bread crumb crust with the back of a spoon and sprinkle the cassoulet with a few more tablespoons of bread crumbs. Also make sure the cassoulet is not becoming dry, adding more of the bean cooking liquid if necessary.

While the cassoulet is cooking, use the reserved duck skin to make poultry cracklings (see page 133).

Serve the cassoulet straight from the dish, making sure that everyone gets a little crust and beans and some of each of the meats.

FAT FUEL

Since humans began eating animals, animal fat has been used for more than just food. Tallow was once used for heat and lighting, but today it has been replaced by petroleum products. The meat and poultry processing industry, however, still uses a small amount of the tons of animal fat it produces every year to heat the water that cleans and sterilizes the processing equipment. Much of that fat, though, is dumped. I am hoping that this book will increase the demand for fat, but I doubt the demand will ever exceed the supply.

As the price of oil increases, everyone is talking about alternative fuels, and biodiesel is the new buzzword. There are now cars that run on French fry oil, despite complaints that their exhaust fumes rival the odor of fast-food outlets, and crops like corn, sugarcane, and soy are being turned into fuel, despite the fact that many of these alternatives use more energy to produce than they yield. Animal fat could be the fuel of the future. Tyson, the world's largest meat producer, and the oil giant ConocoPhillips have joined forces to produce a fuel from animal fat. They claim that their animal diesel is more efficient than ethanol, plus it gives better engine performance and can be distributed by existing pipelines. Tyson generates some 2.3 billon pounds of animal fat a year from processing beef, pork, and chicken, and they believe they can convert it into about 300 million gallons of fuel. Experts in the field believe that by 2012 about 1 billon gallons of biodiesel will be produced in the United States, half of it coming from animal fat.

Foie Gras Butter

If you have any leftover raw foie gras, you can simply dice and quickly sauté it and use it to garnish a steak or roasted game bird or add it to a salad. Or you can make this butter. Even a few tiny bits of foie gras are worth using up, because adding the butter doubles the amount. Use foie gras butter to make great crostini, sandwiches, or pasta sauce, or add it at the last minute to enrich a pan sauce for any sautéed meat.

Place the foie gras trimmings in a bowl and leave at room temperature to soften. When they are soft, mash them together with a fork. Place the mashed foie gras on a piece of plastic wrap and shape into a roll about $1/2$ inch / 1 cm in diameter. Wrap tightly, twisting the ends of the plastic wrap to enclose the foie gras, and refrigerate until firm.

Bring a saucepan of salted water to a boil. Reduce the heat to a bare simmer, drop in the foie gras roll, and poach until the foie gras is very soft and the fat is beginning to melt, 1 to 2 minutes. Remove the foie gras from the water and leave to cool.

Weigh the cooked foie gras, remove it from the plastic wrap, and place it in the small bowl of a food processor. Add the same weight of diced softened butter. Season the mixture with salt and pepper and add the *quatre épices*. Process until the mixture is well blended. Taste, adjust the seasoning, and transfer to a dish. The foie gras butter can be kept in the refrigerator for 1 week, or frozen for up to 3 months.

Makes about $1/2$ cup / 120 g

2 ounces / 60 g foie gras trimmings

About $1/4$ cup / 2 ounces / 60 g unsalted butter, softened

Fine sea salt and freshly ground black pepper

Pinch of quatre épices (see page 91)

Among the more than 20,000 anatomical and pathological specimens at the Mütter Museum, a medical museum in Philadelphia, Pennsylvania, is the Soap Lady. No, she wasn't an early washerwoman or an exceptionally clean person, but she is actually made of soap. When she died, sometime in the nineteenth century, a unique combination of factors transformed her body fat into adipocere. This grayish-white fatty, soaplike substance can occur in corpses when there is a high percentage of body fat and an alkali present. The decomposition of the body stops as the fatty tissues are converted into adipocere, preserving the form of the body and keeping the facial features intact. This transformation, which is related to the process of making soap, is most likely to take place in a humid environment.

THE SOAP LADY

Terrine of Foie Gras

Serves 12

2 fresh duck foie gras (about 2 to 3 pounds / 1 to 1.5 kg total)

4 teaspoons fine sea salt

3/4 teaspoon freshly ground white pepper

$1\frac{1}{2}$ teaspoons superfine (caster) sugar

$1\frac{1}{2}$ teaspoons quatre épices (see page 91)

1/2 teaspoon freshly grated nutmeg

Although it is more fashionable to serve foie gras hot, my favorite way to eat foie gras is in a terrine, because you can take your time and enjoy the texture and the taste. You may look at this recipe and think that it is too long and complicated to tackle. It also requires planning: the cooked terrine needs a good 5 days in the refrigerator to mature, and you must start preparing the livers 24 hours before you cook them. This is certainly not fast food, but making your own terrine is very satisfying. The inspiration for this recipe comes from one of my culinary heroes, French chef Joël Robuchon. Accompany the terrine with toasted brioche or country-style bread and fleur de sel.

On the morning of the day before you plan to cook the terrine, remove the foie gras from the packaging and carefully note the combined weight of the livers. Prepare the livers for cooking according to the instructions on page 130.

In a small bowl, combine the salt, pepper, sugar, *quatre épices*, and nutmeg. Sprinkle this mixture over the deveined liver lobes and pieces, turning to evenly distribute the spices. Return the pieces to the bowl, cover, and refrigerate overnight.

Remove the livers from the refrigerator and discard any liquid that has seeped from them. Let them rest at room temperature for about 15 minutes.

Cut a heavy piece of cardboard to fit inside the bottom of a 6-cup / 1.5-l earthenware or enameled cast-iron terrine dish with a lid. Wrap the cardboard in plastic wrap and set aside. Place the terrine dish in an ovenproof pan deep enough to allow the water to come within 1 inch / 2 cm of the top of the terrine dish. Estimate the amount of water required for this water bath and pour it into a large stockpot. Set the pan and the pot aside.

Put one of the large lobes, flat side down, in the bottom of the terrine dish, pressing firmly so it molds to the bottom of the dish. Place the strips and smaller pieces of liver around to fill in the gaps. Add the two smaller lobes and finish with the second large lobe. Arrange the livers so they fit as snugly as possible, pressing down firmly.

Don't worry if the livers rise above the top of the terrine; they will sink during cooking. If your livers are small, they may not reach the top, but this is fine; it will simply result in a thinner finished terrine. Cover the terrine with its lid or aluminum foil and refrigerate for 30 minutes.

Preheat the oven to 250°F / 120°C.

Clip a kitchen thermometer to the side of the pot with the measured water. Bring the water to exactly 176°F / 80°C over medium-high heat. Put some ice cubes in a bowl and remove the terrine from the refrigerator.

Place the covered terrine in the ovenproof pan and carefully add the hot water to the pan. Using the kitchen thermometer, check the temperature of the water again; it should drop to 158°F / 70°C. Add a couple of ice cubes if it has not dropped enough. When the temperature is correct, place the pan with the covered terrine in the oven and cook for exactly 25 minutes per 1 pound / 450 g. The cooking time and temperature is crucial. Too hot or too long and the liver will melt; too cold or short and it will not be cooked. The internal temperature of the cooked terrine should be 120°F / 48°C.

Remove the cooked terrine from the pan, uncover, and let cool slightly. The livers will be floating in a bath of golden fat. Place the plastic-wrapped cardboard template on top of the terrine and, using it to hold the livers in place, carefully pour off the fat that has been released from the livers into a large measuring cup. Let the fat stand for about 10 minutes so the cooking juices sink to the bottom, then pour enough of the fat back over the livers so that they are barely covered. Discard any cooking juices at the bottom of the measuring cup, but reserve any extra fat for another use (see page 71).

Let the terrine cool on a wire rack until cool, 2 to 3 hours, and refrigerate until the fat is just firm, 1 hour. Place the plastic-wrapped cardboard on top of the terrine and weight it down with 2 cans of beans or something of a similar size and weight. Refrigerate the weighted terrine for 24 hours.

Remove the weights and the cardboard and cover the terrine with the lid or aluminum foil. Leave to mature in the refrigerator for at least 2 days, and preferably 4 days.

You can slice the terrine directly in the dish, but you will get better slices if you turn it out. To unmold the terrine, dip the dish in hot water for about 30 seconds and then loosen the edges with a small, hot palette knife. Turn the terrine out onto a cutting board and then invert it so that the fat is on top. Using a hot knife, cut the terrine into slices. As you slice, have a pair of tweezers handy to pull out any missed veins.

Lay each slice on a plate, covering each slice with a square of plastic wrap and pressing it firmly onto the surface. Leave the slices at room temperature and serve just when the layer of fat is beginning to melt.

Once the terrine is cut, it should be eaten within 10 days. Keep it wrapped in plastic wrap in the refrigerator.

"The Gascons understand—truly, fundamentally understand—the velvety, seductive, opalescent brilliance of that most misunderstood and maligned of ingredients: fat. Fat is venerated and adored."

A. A. GILL

Vegetable Cake

This is not really a cake at all, but a variation on the French classic Pommes Anna, thinly sliced potatoes layered with butter, cooked in a pan, and then turned out and cut into wedges. Although the dish is good with just potatoes, it's even better made with a mixture of vegetables and duck fat. The choice of vegetables is up to you: any combination of thinly sliced vegetables will work. I like using potatoes, sweet potato, and squash, and sometimes parsnip for flavor. I always add an apple, too. Yes, I know it isn't a vegetable, but it adds sweetness and disappears into the cake. The bottom layer becomes the top of the cake, so it's the only layer you have to be careful with when arranging the vegetable slices. Use the potato for this layer, because it turns golden and shows off the thyme. This is a great dish for entertaining because it can be prepared in advance and reheated in the oven. It goes with any roasted poultry, like the Roast Goose (page 150), and roasted meats.

Preheat the oven to 375°F / 190°C.

Brush an 8½-inch / 22-cm cake pan about 1½ inches / 4 cm deep with a little of the melted duck fat and line the bottom with a round of parchment paper.

Peel the potatoes, sweet potato, and squash (remove seeds from the squash) and slice them all into rounds ¼ inch / 6 mm thick. Peel and core the apple and slice it the same thickness as the vegetables. This is an easy job if you have a mandoline. If you don't have one, your slices might be thicker, which is fine, but the cake will take a little longer to cook.

Place a sprig of thyme on the parchment paper and layer half the potato slices in concentric circles in the pan. Sprinkle the potato slices with some thyme leaves, season with salt and pepper, and drizzle with a little duck fat. Now layer half the sweet potato slices, sprinkling the top with thyme leaves, seasoning with salt and pepper, and drizzling with a little duck fat. Repeat the process with half the squash. Layer all the apple slices on top of the squash, sprinkle with thyme leaves, season with salt and pepper, and drizzle with duck fat. Continue layering the vegetables and seasonings, ending with the remaining potato slices. The layers will reach above the top of the pan.

Transfer the pan to a baking sheet and cover the top of the cake with a piece of parchment paper. Place a cast-iron frying pan or heavy casserole lid on top of the parchment to weight down the vegetables. Bake for 15 minutes and then carefully remove the weight from the top of the cake. Continue to cook the cake until the vegetables can be easily pierced with a skewer, another 30 to 40 minutes.

Remove the cake from the oven and let stand for 10 minutes. Invert the cake onto a warm plate, remove the parchment paper, and cut into wedges to serve.

Serves 6

⅓ cup / 2¼ ounces / 65 g duck fat, melted

3 potatoes

1 large sweet potato

½ medium-size butternut squash

1 cooking apple

1 bunch thyme

Fine sea salt and freshly ground black pepper

CHICKEN FAT FACT

Most chicken fat is under the skin and in the body of the bird, not found throughout the meat. There is, however, a strip of fat on the leg. This line of fat runs exactly across the joint between the chicken's thigh and its leg. To cut a chicken leg in two, just cut along the line of fat.

Lentil Soup with Foie Gras

Serves 4

1 cup / $6^{1}/_{2}$ ounces / 180 g lentils du Puy

1 fresh bay leaf

1 small onion, halved

1 clove

1 small carrot, peeled and trimmed

2 celery stalks with leaves, halved

2 cloves garlic, unpeeled

$3^{1}/_{2}$ cups / 875 ml water

Fine sea salt and freshly ground black pepper

4 slices foie gras, each $^{1}/_{2}$ inch / 1 cm thick

$1^{1}/_{2}$ cups / 375 ml duck or chicken stock

$^{1}/_{2}$ cup / 125 ml whipping (35 percent fat) cream

$2^{1}/_{2}$ ounces / 75 g pancetta, skin removed

Chervil or small flat-leaf parsley leaves, for garnish

Lentils are called "poor man's caviar" in France, where they are considered a perfect match for fatty foods like duck, foie gras, and confit. Do try to use the small green lentils du Puy from France, as they have a superior flavor.

This is another recipe inspired by the French chef Joël Robuchon. I doubt he would approve of my addition of pancetta, but I prefer it to side (slab) bacon because it isn't smoked. Make sure your pancetta isn't spicy and has lots of fat, and, if possible, it should be unrolled. This is a good way to use up small pieces of foie gras left over from slicing a liver, but it's important that the pieces all be the same thickness.

Rinse the lentils well and place them in a saucepan. Cover with cold water and bring to a boil over high heat, then strain through a fine-mesh sieve and refresh under cold running water. Discard the blanching water.

Place the refreshed lentils in a clean saucepan. Skewer the bay leaf to 1 onion half using the clove and put both halves in the pan with the lentils along with the carrot, celery, and garlic cloves. Add the water and 1 teaspoon salt and season with pepper.

Bring the lentils to a boil, then reduce the heat and simmer, uncovered, until the lentils are very soft, 30 to 40 minutes.

While the lentils are cooking, place each slice of foie gras on a piece of plastic wrap and season with salt and pepper. Wrap and refrigerate.

Using a fine-mesh sieve suspended over a bowl, drain the cooked lentils. Remove the onion, carrot, celery, and garlic and then pass the lentils through the fine grill of a food mill, using the cooking liquid to help. You should have about 2 cups / 500 ml of lentil purée and about $^{1}/_{4}$ cup / 60 ml of lentil debris. Discard the debris and place the lentil purée in a saucepan. Add the stock and cream.

Preheat the oven to 200°F / 100°C.

Cut the pancetta into batons $^{1}/_{2}$ by $^{1}/_{4}$ inch / 1 cm by 6 mm. Place them in a heavy frying pan and cook over low heat until the pancetta renders its fat and the pieces become golden. Drain the pancetta on paper towels and reserve the fat for another use. Transfer the pancetta to the oven to keep warm.

Remove the foie gras from the refrigerator 15 minutes before cooking. Put 4 shallow soup bowls in the oven and turn the oven off. Reheat the lentil mixture and taste, adjusting the seasoning. Bring some water to a boil in a steamer. Place the plastic-wrapped foie gras slices in the steamer, lower the heat so the water simmers, and steam the slices until soft and the fat is just beginning to melt, about 6 minutes. Remove the foie gras slices from the steamer and place them on paper towels. Unwrap the slices and slide them into the 4 warmed soup bowls.

Ladle over the hot lentil soup and garnish with the pancetta and some chervil leaves.

Duck Fat and Grapefruit Salad Dressing

This is my friend Colin's recipe. One evening when he came over for dinner he brought his own salad and dressing. I was a bit miffed, until I tasted it. The combination of grapefruit and hot duck fat sharpened with vinegar was wonderful. Colin poured it over a bowl of shredded napa cabbage, and I've since made this dressing with foie gras and goose fat and poured it over everything from spinach to dandelion greens. If you have any duck cracklings (see page 133), they make an excellent addition to this salad.

Finely grate 2 teaspoons of zest from 1 grapefruit and set aside. Cut a thick slice off the top and bottom of both grapefruit to expose the flesh. Stand the fruit on a cutting board and cut away both the skin and the pith. Holding the fruit over a bowl, cut along either side of each segment to the center to free it from the membranes. Squeeze the juice from the spent membranes. Measure 1/4 cup / 60 ml of the juice, pour into a bowl, add the grapefruit zest and segments, and set aside.

Place the shredded cabbage in a serving bowl.

Heat 1 tablespoon of the duck fat in a small frying pan over medium heat. Add the shallot and cook until softened and just beginning to color. Add the remaining duck fat and the grapefruit zest, segments, and juice to the pan and stir until hot. Add the vinegar and season well with salt and pepper.

Pour the hot dressing over the shredded cabbage and toss to mix. Serve immediately.

Serves 4

2 grapefruit

6 cups / 300 g shredded napa cabbage

1/4 cup / 1 3/4 ounces / 50 g duck fat

1 tablespoon finely chopped shallot

1 tablespoon sherry vinegar

Sea salt and freshly ground black pepper

EXPLOSIVE FAT

Glycerin is a by-product of soap making. When left in the soap, it makes it softer and better for your skin, but most soap today contains very little glycerin because it is too valuable. This syrupy substance is the base for many medical and pharmaceutical preparations, such as cough syrups and laxatives, and it is also added to food products to keep them moist.

When combined with nitric and sulfuric acids, glycerin turns deadly, creating the highly explosive nitroglycerin. Ascanio Sobrero, an Italian chemist, discovered nitroglycerin in 1846, but it is highly unstable and was too dangerous to use at the time. It was the Swedish scientist Alfred Nobel who combined nitroglycerin with an inert solid and created dynamite. It takes 4 pounds / 2.2 kg of animal fat to make 1 pound / 450 g of explosives.

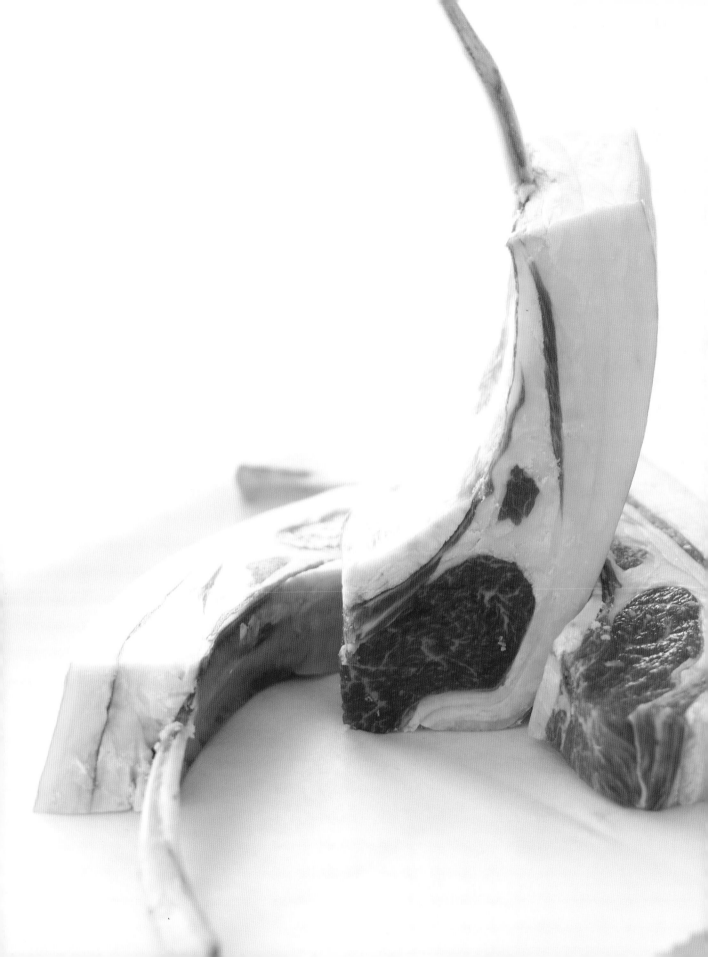

4 beef and lamb fats:
OVERLOOKED BUT TASTY

A large rib roast with a cap of crisp, brown fat, or a leg of lamb wrapped in a golden cloak of garlic-impregnated fat, resting on a bed of potatoes flavored with its drippings: these are two delicious examples of how tasty the fat on these meats can be. There is no mistaking which roast is which; you could never confuse a piece of beef with a slice of lamb . . . or could you? If I cut a slice from each roast, carefully removed all the fat, and made you eat them with your eyes closed, I doubt that you could tell them apart. Studies have shown that we can't tell the difference between lean beef and lean lamb. Why? Because there is no fat. It is the beef fat that makes our beef "beefy" and lamb fat that gives lamb its distinctive taste. Their flavor lies not in their meat, but in their fat.

Beef and lamb contain two types of fat: the external fat found just below the skin, and internal fat, found throughout the meat and in the animal's body. A good layer of external fat reveals that the meat came from a healthy animal. This external fat is also important because it protects the meat from bacteria and allows it to be hung and aged, which greatly improves the meat's taste and texture. This fat also keeps the meat moist and juicy when it's cooked in the dry heat of an oven or on a grill. Marbling, or the streaks of fat found running through the meat, is minimal in young animals like veal and lamb, but it adds a succulence to beef. These threads of fat baste the meat as it cooks, making it moist and giving the meat its juicy mouthfeel. Unfortunately, meat, and beef in particular, has been getting leaner in recent years.

In the United States, the USDA grades beef according to its degree of marbling. The original grading scale, created in 1927, listed twelve levels of marbling, but today only six are left. The three lowest levels have been axed—no great loss—but the top three have been dropped, too. The USDA and the fat police would argue that this reduction in

Jack Sprat would eat no fat,
His wife would eat no lean
And so betwixt the two
of them
They licked the platter clean.

167

beef's marbling is primarily for our health, and the fear of fat is one reason for the dearth of good, fatty beef on the market. Another reason is economic. Marbled beef takes more time and more feed to produce than lean beef does. Animals are usually finished with grain, often corn, and corn prices are on the rise with the promotion of corn-based biofuels. With the amount of money we spend on food falling every year, well-marbled (and thus more expensive) meat is doubly hard to sell to a fat-phobic public used to paying less, not more, for their groceries.

Unlike beef, most of the lamb we eat is less than a year old, so it has little marbling. Although many people argue that the best-tasting meat comes from older animals, whose marbled meat gives them more flavor, the market for older lamb and mutton is very limited in North America. Lamb's lack of marbling makes its external fat even more important; without it, the meat is dry, flavorless, and tough. If you find the taste of too much lamb fat off-putting, cut away the fat once the meat is cooked and the fat has done its job, but not before. Cook fatty cuts like breast ribs or shoulder with potatoes or dried beans, which will absorb the fat, or add an acidic ingredient, like lemon or tamarind, to the dish to balance the fat. The tastiest lamb fat is found on the racks and loins. Softer and more palatable than internal lamb fat, it can be used like pork back fat; add it to lamb sausages and lamb burgers to keep them juicy and boost their flavor.

There is more to beef and lamb fat than what we see on a cut of meat, however. There is suet, or kidney fat, found in the animal's cavity. Firm and brittle, suet has a high melting point. There is also marrow, found in the animals' bones, and dripping, the fat released when the meat is roasted. All of them are very useful for cooking.

Beef and lamb fat have a high saturated fatty acid content, and so are very firm at room temperature, but this doesn't mean we shouldn't use them. More than half their saturated fatty acid is stearic acid, which behaves like a monounsaturated fat in our bodies, rapidly converting to oleic acid. The other main fatty acid in beef and lamb fat is palmitic acid. Both stearic and palmitic acid are believed to lower LDL cholesterol. The rest of lamb and beef fat is mostly the monounsaturated oleic fatty acid. Beef tallow and suet have a very low quantity of polyunsaturated fatty acids, making them very good fats for frying. There is no reason, then, to fear beef and lamb fat. Remember, however, that cattle and sheep are ruminants, and the main component of their diet should be pasture. Grass-fed beef and lamb develop higher ratios of the essential omega-3 fatty acids and CLA (conjugated linoleic acid), which are deposited in their fat and are beneficial to our health.

Killing the fatted calf

To make a fat morning: to sleep late (French)

Wool fat is another name for lanolin. Closer to wax than fat, lanolin is found in the sheep's wool and is extracted for use in lubricants and cosmetics.

Fat chance

Fat	% Saturated	% Monounsaturated	% Polyunsaturated
BEEF TALLOW AND SUET	50	42	4
LAMB TALLOW	47	40	9
CALF BONE MARROW	31	63	6
DRIPPING	45	42	8

Note: all figures are approximate and vary with breed and diet of the animal. The numbers don't always total 100, as there is water and connective tissue in the fat.

Suet

Suet is an ingredient seldom seen in recipes today. For many people it conjures up images of bird feeders rather than culinary delights. Suet is the fat that surrounds an animal's kidneys, and although all animals have it in varying amounts, in the kitchen the term usually means beef suet, which is the most readily available. Suet is a very hard fat with a high melting point, making it excellent for deep-frying and pastry. Rich, but with no strong beefy flavor, suet is good for both savory and sweet dishes. While it is best known for enriching mincemeat, suet is essential for steamed puddings and makes light, fluffy dumplings. Unlike other animal fats, suet doesn't need to be rendered before use; it can simply be grated, making it a great fat to have on hand. So get that suet out of the birdfeeder and put it back in your kitchen.

To kill a fat calf: to make a special celebration (French)

A miser and a fatted calf are useful only after death. (Yiddish)

Bone Marrow

Although both sheep and cattle produce marrow, veal and beef marrow are more popular in the kitchen than lamb marrow is, in part because their leg bones provide a higher ratio of marrow to bone. Although I have done my bit to spread the word about the delights of bone marrow, it is still only a small minority who appreciate it. People are willing to throw marrow bones into their stockpot, but not to extract the marrow from the bone at the dinner table. This is a shame, because eating marrow is a tasty, textural experience similar to eating foie gras, plus it's good for you.

Unlike all other beef fats, marrow is mainly monounsaturated and contains iron, phosphorous, vitamin A, and trace amounts of thiamin and niacin. In the nineteenth century, it was regarded as a health food and given to invalids and sickly children to improve their strength. And Queen Victoria, who died at the ripe old age of eighty-one, was a lover of bone marrow, reputedly eating it every day.

Marrow may have helped keep Queen Victoria alive, but it played an even more important role in the survival of early explorers in northern Canada, the Arctic, and Antarctica. Marrow is an ingredient in pemmican (see page 195), a high-calorie, long-lasting food that helped keep these adventurers and many northern Native American populations alive. The Inuit also made a dish called *akutuk*, sometimes called "Eskimo ice cream," a mixture of bone marrow, snow, caribou back fat, and berries.

Unless you're planning a trek across Antarctica, you'll probably never make pemmican or whip up a batch of bone marrow ice cream, but bone marrow nevertheless deserves a place in our kitchens. You can add this mainly monounsaturated fat to hamburgers and beef sausages to keep them juicy, and it's great for enriching everything from savory sauces to sweet dishes like Marrow Rice Pudding (page 217). And, of course, bone marrow can simply be melted to make an excellent fat for frying.

When you are tossing marrow bones into a stockpot, they need no special handling, but to use the marrow from the bone you need to prepare it in advance (see page 172).

Tallow

Tallow is the general term for fat rendered from cattle and sheep. In the past, tallow, and especially sheep tallow, was used for making candles and soap. Today, however, candles and soaps are manufactured from petroleum by-products (see page 138), and tallow is a source of biodiesel fuels (see page 158). The high saturation of tallow makes it very stable when heated and slow to break down or turn rancid, so tallow is a perfect fat for frying. Some of us are old enough to remember the taste and texture of French fries cooked in beef fat. In the 1990s, beef tallow was at the center of another controversy in the fast-food industry, and as a result it was replaced by vegetable oils—often hydrogenated ones. Not only did the fries lose their taste, but they also became greasier. Even the FDA admits that a potato cooked in beef tallow absorbs half as much fat as one fried in vegetable oil. Unfortunately, tallow is not commercially

> "We should pay more attention to this fundamentally correct idea, to the extent of cooking any meat joint with its own particular fat. This applies not only to the obvious basting fat, but also throughout the recipe. The crust for mutton pies should be made with mutton dripping; the pork-pie crust is always made with lard—and this use of the appropriate fat should be carried out through all forms of meat cooking."

DOROTHY HARTLEY

available for the kitchen, but if you fry at home you can render suet and use it for both deep-frying and sautéing.

Dripping

Dripping is just what it sounds like: the fat that drips from meat as it cooks. It can be from any type of meat, but it generally refers to beef dripping. We're all familiar with dripping, but often we don't give it a second thought. We know that dripping makes the best gravy, but how many of us throw away all but the tablespoon we use to cook the onions or flour before adding stock or wine?

Dripping is more than just fat; it also has the essence of the meat. Pour the dripping from your roast, add back what you need to make your sauce, and let the rest cool. Once cold, it forms two layers, with a flavorful jelly at the bottom and the fat on top. Use the fat as is for maximum taste, but if you want to keep it for any length of time, you should clarify it (see page 173). The jelly is an excellent addition to stews or sauces.

Similar to dripping, stocks and slow-cooked braises are other sources of fat. When they are chilled, the fat in them sets, at which point it can be lifted off and clarified. It will have the intense, meaty taste of roast drippings, but it will have some of the flavors of the stock or braise, and it's good for sautéing meat and vegetables.

I always have dripping and rendered beef and lamb fat in my refrigerator and use them when I am cooking lamb or beef. By browning beef in beef fat or lamb in lamb fat, you add another layer of flavor to the finished dish.

Although these fats may take a little more work, because you will have to render and clarify them yourself, they are cheap. Today, when everyone is talking about sustainability and the importance of using every part of the animals that we eat, I think it makes sense to extend this approach to using all types of animal fat.

Handling Beef and Lamb Fat

Preparing Suet

To prepare suet, the fat that protects an animal's kidneys, you must cut off any traces of kidney or blood and any discolored pieces of fat. As you do this, you will realize that there is a papery membrane holding

"Let me have men
about me that are fat;
Sleek-headed men and such
as sleep o'nights:
Yond Cassius has a lean and
hungry look;
He thinks too much: such
men are dangerous."

WILLIAM SHAKESPEARE

this hard, brittle fat together. Pull it off as you cut the suet into chunks. Although many recipes suggest chopping suet with a knife or grating it on a box grater, I prefer grating it in a food processor. Cut the suet into pieces that will fit easily through the tube of your food processor, and put them in a bowl in the freezer for several hours or overnight. Also chill the fine grating disk of your food processor. Dust the grating disk with flour before grating the chunks of frozen suet. There is no denying that this is a messy job, and you'll have to stop and clean the blade and dust it with flour again at frequent intervals. Prepare a large batch and store it in the freezer. Suet can be used straight from the freezer.

Don't be tempted by packaged suet; it is dehydrated and inferior. Vegetarian suet, made from hydrogenated oil, should also be avoided.

Preparing Marrow

Ask your butcher to cut marrow bones from the center of the leg, where the ratio of marrow to bone is highest. Marrow bones must be soaked for 12 to 24 hours in salted water to remove the blood. Place the bones in a large dish of ice water to cover, add 2 tablespoons of coarse sea salt, and refrigerate for 12 to 24 hours, changing the water 4 to 6 times and adding 2 more tablespoons of salt to the water each time. Use the bones immediately after soaking, or freeze them for up to 2 months.

To extract raw marrow from presoaked bones, you have two choices, depending on how you plan to use the marrow:

You can let the marrow warm up and then dig it out with a small knife, making sure you scrape the inside of each bone. This will give you small pieces of marrow that are perfect for dumplings and sausage mixtures.

Or, if you want a whole piece of marrow to slice, place the soaked marrow bones in a saucepan of simmering salted water. Simmer the bones, uncovered, until the marrow shrinks slightly from the ends of the bone, 5 to 7 minutes. You don't want to fully cook the marrow, but just loosen it from the bone. Run a knife between the marrow and the bone and gently push the marrow out of the bone into a bowl of ice water. Refrigerate until you are ready to poach the marrow. The amount of marrow varies widely depending on the bone. A 3-inch / 7.5-cm bone will yield anywhere from 3/4 to 3 ounces / 20 to 90 g.

Clarifying Dripping

After removing the fat from the meat jelly, stock, or braise, melt it in a saucepan over low heat and then strain it through a piece of cheesecloth.

Rendering Suet and Lamb Fat

Beef and lamb fat are rendered in exactly the same way as pork and poultry fat.

To render suet, cut it into 1-inch / 2.5-cm pieces, removing any traces of kidney or blood and the papery membrane. Grating the suet instead of cutting it into chunks will help it render faster.

Put the diced fat in a heavy flameproof casserole or Dutch oven and add about $^1/_3$ cup / 75 ml water per 1 pound / 450 g of fat. The water keeps the fat from burning before it begins to melt. Place the pan, uncovered, over very low heat on the stove or in a 250°F / 120°C oven. If you are rendering on the stove, you will have to stir the fat often. In the oven, stir the fat after 30 minutes, then at 45 minutes, and then every hour, watching carefully as the fat begins to color.

BREAD AND DRIPPING

"You'll have nothing but bread and dripping for supper" was the threat my mother uttered whenever I misbehaved as a child. This was a serious threat when I was young, because I much preferred my bread buttered and sprinkled with the tiny multicolored sugary balls we called hundreds and thousands. Now I'd be quite happy to go to bed with a slice of bread spread with dripping, which to my mind is the best part of a roast. Dripping is fundamental to making good gravy and Yorkshire Pudding (page 177), and every time I roast beef I always hope there will be enough dripping for me to enjoy cold. This tasty mixture of the fat and juices from the roast is delicious thickly spread on bread, and is the ideal starting point for a cold roast beef sandwich. Dripping usually needs a little salt, and you can further enhance it by whipping it with Dijon mustard, finely grated fresh horseradish, or Worcestershire sauce.

For a cold roast beef sandwich, you'll need:

Beef dripping with the jelly, at room temperature
2 thick slices of country-style bread
Maldon salt (see page 174) and freshly ground black pepper
Thinly sliced cold roast beef
Prepared horseradish

Spread the dripping with the meat jelly on both slices of bread and season well with salt and pepper. Add the sliced beef to one slice of bread and horseradish to the other, and press the sandwich together. You could add lettuce and tomato, but it does rather detract from the beefy experience.

As you stir the fat, press the pieces against the side of the pan to help them melt. The rendering can take from 4 to 8 hours, depending on the quantity of fat and the size of the pieces. Not all the fat will liquefy; some pieces of connective tissue will remain solid. As soon as the pieces in the pan start to color, remove the pan from the oven and let cool slightly. Strain the liquid fat through cheesecloth into clean containers. Let the fat cool completely, then cover and store in the refrigerator for up to 2 months or in the freezer for a year. Beef fat is generally very stable, but, like all fats, it will eventually turn rancid. Remember to label the fat, since it is hard to tell different types of fat apart.

I render only small amounts of lamb fat for frying the Lamb Fat and Spinach Chapati (page 204). Ask your butcher for the soft fat he trims from the lamb loins and racks, as it renders more easily and has the mildest flavor.

MALDON SALT

This salt comes from the coastal town of Maldon in eastern England, one of the driest places in the United Kingdom. Like *fleur de sel*, it is a totally natural product, but unlike the French salt, it requires a final drying in heated saltpans before being harvested by hand. This final drying gives Maldon salt its distinctive hollow, pyramid-shaped crystals and very flaky texture.

Roast Beef with All the Trimmings

The classic way to serve standing rib roast of beef is with roast potatoes and York-shire pudding, both, of course, made with dripping. If you want to make this meal, read through all three recipes; you'll need to plan ahead so that you can cook all the dishes in one oven. To round out the meal, add a green vegetable. Brussels sprouts would be very English, but I prefer peas, green beans, or even some braised kale.

ROAST BEEF

There are lots of reasons to cook a standing rib roast of beef: it is the perfect dish for entertaining, simple but impressive; the leftovers are delicious; and a well-marbled joint with a good covering of fat will yield plenty of dripping.

Remove the roast from the refrigerator $1\frac{1}{2}$ hours before you plan to cook it.

Preheat the oven to 450°F / 230°C.

Pat the beef dry and rub the fat side and two ends with 2 tablespoons of the beef dripping. Sprinkle the mustard over the fat side of the roast and season well with salt and pepper. Put the remaining beef dripping in a roasting pan and place in the oven. When the dripping is spitting hot, about 5 minutes, add the beef, bone side down, and roast for 30 minutes. Reduce the oven temperature to 325°F / 160°C and continue to cook until a kitchen thermometer inserted into the meat away from the bone registers 125°F / 51°C, about $1\frac{1}{4}$ hours.

Transfer the beef to a warm platter, cover it loosely with aluminum foil, and allow it to rest for 30 minutes before carving. During this time, the internal temperature of the roast will rise to 130°F / 54°C for medium-rare.

While the beef rests, pour all but 2 tablespoons of the dripping from the pan into a bowl. Place the pan over medium heat, add the shallot, and cook, stirring, until softened, about 2 minutes. Add the wine and bring to a boil. Deglaze the pan, using a wooden spoon to scrape up the browned bits from the bottom. Continue to boil until the wine reduces by half, then add the stock and boil for another 5 minutes. Taste and adjust the seasoning.

Carve the beef into thick slices and add any juices from the platter to the sauce. Reheat the sauce and serve with the beef.

Serves 6 to 8

One 3-rib standing rib roast (about 6 pounds / 2.75 kg)

3 tablespoons beef dripping or rendered beef fat

$1\frac{1}{2}$ teaspoons dried mustard

Sea salt and freshly ground black pepper

1 shallot, finely chopped

1 cup / 250 ml red wine

2 cups / 500 ml beef stock

BREAD AND POINT

While bread and dripping was the threatened punishment for my childhood misdemeanors, it would not have been as bad as "bread and point," which was a common expression in our family. My grandfather, undoubtedly exaggerating for dramatic effect and to make us understand how well off we grandchildren were, used to tell us that all he had as a child was "bread and point." And just what was that? It was a slice of bread at which you pointed your knife because you didn't have either butter or dripping to spread on it.

ROAST POTATOES

Serves 6 to 8

2.2 pounds / 1 kg baking (floury) potatoes

1 fresh bay leaf

Sea salt

3 tablespoons dripping or rendered beef fat

To ensure that the potatoes are crisp on the outside and fluffy in the center, you must do two things. First, choose the right potato: you need a floury potato, like a russet. Second, you must parboil them just enough to slightly soften them and scrape their surface with a fork to roughen them up. This will give you potatoes with a crisp outer shell and a cooked center. If you are serving these with the Roast Beef (page 175), start them with the roast, at a lower temperature, and then crisp them up at a higher temperature, along with the Yorkshire Pudding (page 177).

Peel the potatoes and cut them into 2-inch / 5-cm chunks. Place them in a large saucepan of cold salted water, add the bay leaf, cover, and bring to a boil over medium heat. Uncover, lower the heat so the potatoes boil gently, and cook until the outside edges are soft, about 8 minutes. Drain well, let cool slightly, and then scrape all the surfaces of the potatoes with a fork. Season with salt.

Preheat the oven to 400°F / 200°C.

Put the dripping in a roasting pan and place it in the oven to heat up, about 7 minutes. When the fat is very hot, add the potatoes and turn to coat them in the dripping. Roast them, turning once or twice, until they are golden, crisp, and soft in the center, about 45 minutes. Season with a little more salt and serve.

TIP If you are making these potatoes with the Roast Beef and Yorkshire Pudding, place the pan for the potatoes in the oven about 40 minutes before the roast is done being cooked. Taking into consideration the time it takes for the fat to get hot, about 15 minutes at this lower temperature; this will give the potatoes about 25 minutes in the oven with the roast. Finish cooking them with the pudding. If you are serving these potatoes with a roast chicken, use chicken or duck fat instead of beef dripping.

Golden crisp and lighter than air, Yorkshire pudding is the perfect food for sopping up the juices from the roast beef. It needs a hot oven to puff up, so mix the batter while your roast is in the oven and slip it into the oven while the roast is resting. The dripping from the roast will give the pudding the best flavor, but beef fat will also do. Make sure the fat is very hot; it should just begin to smoke before you pour in the batter. If you really like Yorkshire pudding you can double the recipe, but you must make it in two pans.

Preheat the oven to 425°F / 220°C.

Sift the flour and salt into a bowl. Add the water to the milk. Make a well in the flour and add the eggs. Whisk the eggs into the flour and then whisk in enough of the milk and water mixture to make a very smooth batter thick enough to coat the back of a spoon. Cover and let the batter rest for 1 hour at room temperature.

Place the beef dripping into a 9-inch / 23-cm square metal pan and put it in the oven. Check the consistency of the pudding batter, adding a little more of the milk and water mixture or just cold water, if necessary, so that it's the thickness of thin cream. When the fat in the pan starts to smoke, pour in the pudding batter; it should sizzle immediately. Bake the pudding until it is puffed and golden, about 25 minutes.

Remove the pudding from the pan and cut into squares to serve.

Serves 6

1 cup / 4$^{1}/_{2}$ ounces / 125 g flour

$^{1}/_{2}$ teaspoon fine sea salt

$^{1}/_{3}$ cup / 75 ml water

$^{1}/_{3}$ cup / 75 ml milk

2 eggs, beaten

2 tablespoons beef dripping or rendered beef fat

Yorkshire pudding is not really a pudding at all, but rather a pancake batter that is cooked in a very hot oven, which causes it to puff up. Originally, when beef was roasted on a spit, Yorkshire pudding was baked in the pan set underneath the roast to catch the dripping and the meat juices. The earliest recipe for a dripping pudding, as it was called, appeared in the mid-eighteenth century and was cooked under a roast of mutton. Hannah Glasse, a northerner herself, was the first to call it Yorkshire pudding in her cookbook *The Art of Cookery Made Plain and Easy*. Although Mrs. Glasse was not a professional cook and large sections of her book were plagiarized from other writers, a combination of timing and marketing savvy made it the best-selling cookbook in eighteenth-century Britain, with more than twenty editions in fifty years. In Yorkshire, the pudding was traditionally served before the roast, to dampen people's appetite for the meat. Any leftover pudding reappeared at the end of the meal sweetened with golden syrup, jam, or sugar.

YORKSHIRE PUDDING

Puchero

Serves 6

$2^{1/2}$ pounds / 1.1 kg beef shank (see headnote)

$2^{1/4}$ pounds / 1 kg beef short ribs, in 2 or 3 pieces

3 quarts / 3 l cold water

2 onions, halved

2 quinces or cooking apples, halved

$1/4$ teaspoon whole black peppercorns

8 large sprigs cilantro (coriander), with the root attached if possible

2 serrano chiles

Coarse sea salt

3 turnips, peeled

3 carrots, peeled

7 large sprigs mint

2 corn cobs, husked and trimmed

3 green zucchini, trimmed

Fat kitchen, thin inheritance: if you live too lavishly, you will not have much to leave your children (German)

A fat job

This recipe comes from my friend Brenda, who knows a lot more about Mexican cooking than I do. She sent me her grandmother's recipe, so I hope she isn't too upset with the changes I've made. Puchero is a Spanish word meaning either the pot the stew is cooked in or the stew itself, and the dish is basically a Mexican pot-au-feu. This type of dish, made with meat and vegetables cooked in water along with the local herbs and spices, is made by cooks the world over. Brenda's family recipe mixes the flavors of the Old World with those of the New World. Ask your butcher to bone out the beef shank and keep the bone for you. This bone, a marrow bone, will be used for the bone marrow tacos. This is a two-day project, so read this recipe and the recipe for Bone Marrow Tacos (page 180) through before starting. Serve with Bone Marrow Tacos (page 180) and Fresh Tomato Salsa (page 181).

Eating pot-au-feu has its own special etiquette. First, the marrow tacos or marrow bones are served with the salsa and fleur de sel or fine sea salt. Then comes the clear broth, and finally the meat and vegetables are presented on a large platter with an extra jug of hot broth and the remaining salsa so everyone can help themselves. Part of the fun of eating this dish is its communal nature.

Prepare the shank by tying the meat together with a piece of string so it keeps the same form. In a large (about 8-quart / 8-l) stockpot, place the beef shank and the ribs bone side down. Add the water; the meat should be almost covered. Place the pot over medium-low heat and slowly bring to a simmer. This will take a good 45 minutes. It is important to bring the pot slowly to a boil, as this will result in a clearer broth.

Using a soup ladle, skim off any scum that rises to the surface (rotate the bowl of the ladle on the surface of the broth to make ripples: these will carry the scum to the edges of the pot, and you can then use the ladle to lift it off). Add the onions, quinces, peppercorns, 2 of the cilantro sprigs, the whole chiles, and 1 teaspoon of salt. Simmer very gently, uncovered, skimming occasionally, for $1^{1/2}$ hours. Add the turnips and whole carrots and continue to simmer until the meat and vegetables are tender, about another hour.

Transfer the meat, carrots, and turnips to an ovenproof dish and set aside to cool. Strain the broth into a large bowl, discarding the onions, quinces, peppercorns, cilantro sprigs, and chiles. Cut the turnips into quarters and the carrots in half. Cut the shank and short ribs into large serving-size pieces. Cover and refrigerate the vegetables, meat, and broth overnight.

Remove the meat, vegetables, and broth from the refrigerator. Preheat the oven to 300°F / 150°C.

Skim the fat from the broth and set aside for another use. Pour the broth into a large stockpot, leaving behind any of the debris in the bottom of the bowl; you should have about 7 cups / 1.75 l. Tie the remaining cilantro and mint sprigs together with some string and add them to the broth. Taste and adjust the seasoning of the broth, adding more salt if necessary.

Place the pot over medium heat and bring to a boil, then reduce the heat to low. Spoon some of the hot broth over the meat and vegetables in the dish, then cover the dish with aluminum foil and place in the oven to reheat for about 45 minutes. Cover the pot and simmer the broth and herbs for 20 minutes.

Meanwhile, cut each corn cob and zucchini crosswise into 3 pieces. Add them to the broth, cover, and simmer until cooked, 10 to 15 minutes. Transfer the cooked vegetables to the oven to keep warm, and remove and discard the herbs from the broth.

BOILED BEEF

Lots of cuisines have their own variation of pot-au-feu, or boiled beef. The Italians make *bollito misto*, a dish combining meat, poultry, and offal, while the English like to cook salted or corned beef with carrots, cabbage, and potatoes. So if this recipe is too spicy for you, or you prefer a more traditional take on pot-au-feu, you can change the recipe to suit your taste, the season, or what's in your refrigerator.

For English boiled beef, cook the meat in water flavored with leeks, carrots, celery, peppercorns, thyme, and bay leaves. Cook the carrots in the broth along with parsnips and turnips and serve the dish with bone marrow dumplings (see page 202) and Maldon salt.

For Italian *bollito misto*, cook the meat in water flavored with an onion, carrots, fennel tops, garlic, peppercorns, and bay leaves. Cook baby fennel and celery hearts in the broth and serve with plain boiled potatoes and Leda's Marrow Sauce (page 183).

For a French pot-au-feu, cook the meat in water flavored with leeks, carrots, onions, peppercorns, thyme, cloves, bay leaves, and flat-leaf parsley sprigs. Cook baby turnips and carrots in the broth with pieces of celery root (celeriac) and serve it with Dijon mustard and poached marrow bones and sea salt.

Bone Marrow Tacos

Serves 6

6 marrow bones, presoaked (see page 172)

12 warm corn tortillas

Fleur de sel

Bone marrow tacos are a perfect way to start your meal of Puchero (page 178). Instead of just eating the marrow straight out of the bones, you enclose it, along with a little Fresh Tomato Salsa (page 181), in a warm corn tortilla. Pass out lots of napkins, as these delicious tacos are messy. If you serve the tacos with the puchero, use the marrow bone from the shank and ask your butcher to set aside five more marrow bones of the same size. There is no need to restrict these tacos to a puchero meal, though. You can eat them anytime.

Preheat the oven to 250°F / 120°C.

Drain the marrow bones. Bring a large saucepan of salted water to a boil, add the marrow bones, and reduce the heat to a simmer. Poach the bones gently until the marrow has shrunk from the ends of the bone and is hot in the center, 10 to 15 minutes. To test, insert a metal skewer into the center of the marrow and touch it to your wrist to see if it is hot. There should be no resistance when the skewer is inserted. Transfer the bones to a baking sheet and keep warm in the oven.

Serve the bones on warmed plates with the corn tortillas, Fresh Tomato Salsa (recipe follows), *fleur de sel* or flaky sea salt, and a small spoon for scooping out the marrow, allowing diners to assemble their own tacos.

Fresh Tomato Salsa

The secret to good tomato salsa is great tomatoes. If I have a choice I use Roma tomatoes, because it is easier to remove their seeds, but you can use any type. Draining the tomatoes keeps the salsa from having too much liquid. This simple tomato salsa complements rich bone marrow, makes a great dip for Spiced Pork Crackling (page 76), and goes well with Refried Beans (page 108) or Carnitas (page 109).

Core the tomatoes, cut in half lengthwise, and remove and discard the seeds. Chop the tomatoes and place in a fine-mesh sieve over a bowl. Leave to drain for about 30 minutes.

Remove the stems and seeds from the serrano and poblano chiles and chop them finely. Combine the chiles in a bowl with the drained tomatoes and garlic clove and let stand for 1 hour.

Coarsely chop the cilantro leaves. Remove the garlic clove from the salsa, stir in the cilantro, and season with salt.

Makes about 2 cups / 500 ml

4 to 6 Roma (plum) tomatoes

2 serrano chiles

1/2 poblano chile

1 clove garlic, peeled

1/2 cup / 7 g cilantro (coriander) leaves

Fine sea salt

Roasted Marrow Bones

Scooping the soft, warm marrow straight from the bone is a sensual delight, but it can be a bit difficult if you don't have the right utensil. While marrow spoons are becoming popular again, they are not essential for enjoying marrow. A lobster pick or an espresso spoon are also good implements for extracting marrow, and of course you can always just suck it out. Usually the butcher cuts marrow bones crosswise, but for this recipe ask him or her for bones from the center section of a leg bone cut lengthwise, which will provide easy access to the delicious marrow. Plan ahead for this dish, as the bones must be soaked before you begin (see page 172).

The bread crumb topping is a twist on the classic presentation of marrow. Roasted marrow bones are traditionally accompanied with toast: the diner scoops the marrow from the bones and spreads it on the hot toast. In this recipe the marrow is lifted from the split bone with the bread crumb topping so there is no need for toast. Follow the bones with a green salad tossed with a good acidic dressing.

Preheat the oven to 425°F / 220°C.

Finely grate the zest from the lemon and combine it in a bowl with the bread crumbs, parsley, and mustard. Squeeze 2 tablespoons of juice from

Serves 4 as an appetizer

1 lemon

1/2 cup / 1 1/2 ounces / 40 g fine fresh bread crumbs

1 tablespoon chopped fresh flat-leaf parsley

1 teaspoon dried mustard

Freshly ground black pepper

1/2 teaspoon fine sea salt

4 veal or beef marrow bones, each about 8 inches / 20 cm, split in half lengthwise and presoaked (see page 172)

the lemon. Add the juice to the bread crumb mixture with lots of pepper and the salt. The bread crumbs should just hold together when squeezed; if not, add a little more lemon juice.

Drain the marrow bones and pat dry.

Place the bones cut side up in a roasting pan and top evenly with the bread crumb mixture. Roast until the marrow is warm in the center, 15 to 25 minutes. To test, insert a metal skewer into the center of the marrow and touch it to your wrist to see if it is hot. There should be no resistance when the skewer is inserted, and a little of the marrow should have melted and started to leak from the bones. Serve the marrow bones hot.

Leda's Marrow Sauce

- -

A mutual friend introduced me to Leda. We first met at her apartment, which is a wonderful place, full of bookshelves from floor to ceiling, but there are still not enough of them to contain her large collection of books, which spill into piles on the floor and cover every flat surface. Many of her books are old Italian cookbooks, and we spent the afternoon leafing through her books, drinking good coffee, and talking about food. Leda gave me this recipe for marrow sauce, which she serves with the meat and vegetable course of her pot-au-feu. I also use this rich and delicious sauce to make Marrow Crostini (recipe follows).

Makes 1 cup / 250 ml

$1 3/4$ ounces / 50 g bone marrow, prepared and diced (see page 172)

$1/4$ cup / 60 ml dry white wine

$3/4$ cup / 2 ounces / 60 g fine fresh bread crumbs

1 cup / 1 ounce / 30 g very finely grated Parmesan cheese

$3/4$ cup / 175 ml cooking liquid from pot-au-feu or beef stock

2 tablespoons chopped fresh flat-leaf parsley

Sea salt and freshly ground black pepper

In a saucepan over low heat, cook the bone marrow until it begins to color lightly, about 3 minutes. When the marrow is no longer white, add the wine and deglaze the pan, using a wooden spoon to scrape up any bits on the bottom. Gradually stir in the bread crumbs and the cheese.

Stirring constantly, slowly add the cooking liquid to the saucepan a couple of spoonfuls at a time. This is a bit like making risotto: once the mixture has absorbed the liquid, add some more. When all the liquid is added, about 7 minutes, you should have a thick sauce. Stir in the parsley and season very well with lots of black pepper and a little salt. Serve hot.

Bone Marrow Crostini

- -

Leda's sauce makes the most wonderful marrow crostini. These are great served as an hors d'oeuvre with drinks, but you can also serve them with a pot-au-feu, in soup, or with a salad.

Makes 20 crostini

20 baguette slices

1 cup / 250 ml Leda's Marrow Sauce (see above)

Heat the broiler to high.

Place the bread slices on a baking sheet and toast them under the broiler on one side only. Turn the bread toasted side down and spread each slice with a spoonful of marrow sauce. Return the crostini to under the broiler and cook until the topping is hot and golden. Serve warm.

Steak and Kidney Pudding

Serves 4 to 6

Filling

1 pound / 450 g chuck or shoulder steak

Coarse sea salt and freshly ground black pepper

3 tablespoons beef dripping or rendered beef fat

1 onion, chopped

1 carrot, peeled and cut into $1/4$-inch / 6-mm dice

1 celery stalk, halved lengthwise and sliced

2 large sprigs rosemary

1 fresh bay leaf

1 large portobello mushroom

$1/4$ cup / 60 ml port

2 tablespoons flour

1 cup / 250 ml beef stock

2 teaspoons dried mustard

2 teaspoons Worcestershire sauce

12 ounces / 375 g trimmed veal kidney

1 recipe Suet Pastry for Steaming (page 186)

While the thought of steaming a pudding for 2 hours may dissuade you from trying this recipe, don't let it. Steaming is no more difficult than baking. You will need to glance at the pudding occasionally to make sure there is always enough water in your pot, but then again, you need to check in the oven to make sure a pie isn't burning, too. As this is a winter dish, all the steam will put some much-needed moisture back into the air of your heated home. If you really can't wait the two hours, you can bake the filling under a pastry cover as Steak and Kidney Pie (page 187). Veal kidneys are mild in flavor, but if you don't like kidney you can just replace them with more meat. If you are unfamiliar with kidney as an ingredient, read Preparing Veal Kidney on page 190 for encouragement.

While metal pudding molds are common, I always cook my pudding in a china pudding basin. It is steeper and more tapered than a regular mixing bowl and it has a raised rim to hold the string that secures the aluminum foil in place. Its glazing protects it from the heat.

A green vegetable like Brussels sprouts or rapini is a good accompaniment for pudding, but pass on the potatoes, since you will be serving this with a suet crust.

Preheat the oven to 300°F / 150°C.

To make the filling, remove any sinew from the steak and cut it into $1/2$-inch / 1-cm dice. Season the meat with salt and pepper. In a Dutch oven or flameproof casserole with a lid, heat 1 tablespoon of the dripping over high heat. Add the meat in batches and brown quickly, adding more dripping as necessary. Transfer the browned meat to a plate.

Add the onion, carrot, celery, rosemary sprigs, and bay leaf to the pan and lower the heat to medium. Cook, stirring, until softened slightly, 3 to 5 minutes. Remove the mushroom stem and set aside for stock. Cut the mushroom cap into $1/2$-inch / 1-cm dice and add to the pan. Add the port and deglaze the pan, using a wooden spoon to scrape up the browned bits from the bottom. Return the meat and its juices to the pan and sprinkle with the flour, stirring to coat the meat.

In a small bowl, stir together the beef stock, mustard, and Worcestershire sauce. Pour the mixture into the pan and bring to a boil, stirring. Cover the pan with a piece of wet parchment paper (see page 185) and the lid, transfer to the oven, and cook for 1 hour.

Uncover the pan and remove the parchment paper, stir the meat, and continue to cook, uncovered, until the meat is barely tender, about another 30 minutes.

Place a colander over a large bowl and pour in the meat mixture. Discard the remains of the rosemary sprigs and the bay leaf. Transfer the meat mixture to a bowl and pour the liquid into a measuring cup; there should be about $1/2$ cup / 125 ml. If you have less liquid, add some water. If you have more, boil it to reduce it. Taste and adjust the seasoning. Leave the meat and liquid to cool separately.

Cut the veal kidney into 1/4-inch / 6-mm pieces and season with salt and pepper. Heat 1 tablespoon of the remaining beef dripping in a frying pan over high heat. When it is hot, sear the kidney pieces quickly, leaving them pink in the center. Add the kidney to the meat mixture.

To assemble the pudding, grease a 6-cup / 1.5-l pudding basin or mold with the remaining beef dripping and place a round of parchment paper in the bottom of the basin.

Remove the pastry from the refrigerator. Cut off one-quarter of the pastry and set aside. Roll the remaining pastry into a 14-inch / 35-cm circle about 1/4 inch / 6 mm thick. Drape it over your fist and invert the pudding basin onto it. Flip the basin and line the pudding basin with the dough, leaving a 1-inch / 2.5-cm overhang.

Mix the cooled cooking liquid into the meat and kidney mixture. Fill the pastry-lined basin with the meat mixture. Roll out the remaining pastry into a circle the same diameter as the top of the basin. Fold in the overhanging pastry and brush it with water. Top with the pastry circle, making sure not to trap any air in the pudding, and seal the edges well.

Place another circle of parchment paper on top of the pudding and then cover the top of the basin with a large piece of heavy-duty aluminum foil folded to make a pleat about 1/2 inch / 1 cm deep in the middle (this is to allow the foil to expand with the pudding during cooking. Secure the foil under the rim of the bowl with a length of string to make sure no water can drip into the pudding. If you don't have a steaming basket, extra string can be tied around the basin to make a makeshift handle, or use a piece of cloth (see tip, below).

Place the pudding in a steamer or on a trivet in a large stockpot. Fill the pot with enough water to come three-quarters of the way up the sides of the basin, cover, and bring to a boil over high heat. Lower the heat so the water boils gently and steam the pudding for 2 hours, adding more boiling water as necessary to maintain the same level.

Remove the pudding from the pot by lifting out the steamer basket and let stand for 10 minutes. Remove the foil and parchment paper and turn the pudding out onto a warmed plate. Cut into wedges and serve.

TIP If you don't have a steamer basket that fits in your pot you'll need to put a handle on your pudding basin. Place a large square of cloth over the top of the pudding basin. Make a pleat in the center and then tie the cloth securely with string under the lip of the basin. Fold up the four corners of the cloth and tie them in a knot. Use this knotted cloth as a handle to remove the basin from the hot water.

If you are going to eat fat, eat enough so that it runs down your chin! (Ukrainian)

The fat's in the fire.

To be as fat as a monk: to be very fat (French)

PARCHMENT PAPER

Parchment paper is a great way to protect the meat and keep the moisture in a dish. I wet the paper first so it softens and sits down on the meat. This also means I can just tear off a piece and don't have to cut it precisely to fit my pan. When the dish is cooked, I leave the parchment on top of the cooling meat to prevent its surface from drying out.

Suet Pastry for Steaming

Makes enough for one 6-cup / 1.5-l pudding

$2^{1/2}$ cups / 10 ounces / 300 g flour

$2^{1/2}$ teaspoons baking powder

$1^{1/2}$ cups / 5 ounces / 150 g finely grated suet

2 teaspoons finely chopped fresh rosemary

$1/2$ teaspoon fine sea salt

About 1 cup / 250 ml cold water

This is the pastry to use when you're making a steamed steak and kidney pudding, but you can also use it for any steamed savory pudding. Line the pudding basin with the pastry and add any precooked meat filling, like a beef and vegetable stew or a lamb stew. The pastry is best made no more than an hour before using it. If you prefer to bake your filling, use the Suet Pastry for Savory Pie (recipe follows).

Sift together the flour and baking powder. Stir in the suet, rosemary, and salt. Using a fork, stir in enough of the water so the mixture forms a dough that pulls away from the bowl. Turn the dough out onto a floured surface and knead gently until smooth. Wrap the pastry in plastic wrap and refrigerate for 30 minutes.

SUET LATTES

In her book *Food in England*, Dorothy Hartley recommends the following cure for a bad chest cough: whisk a tablespoon of very finely grated suet and a pinch of salt into a pint of steaming hot milk and pour it into a glass wrapped with a napkin. It sounds like the perfect drink for an upscale coffee chain, but there might be one drawback. Hartley notes that not only does the drink relieve a chest cold, but it is also an "emollient and laxative."

Suet Pastry for Savory Pie

Makes enough for a top crust for a 9 to $9^{1/2}$-inch / 23 to 24-cm pie

2 cups / $8^{3/4}$ ounces / 250 g flour

2 teaspoons baking powder

$1^{1/3}$ cups / $4^{1/2}$ ounces / 125 g finely grated suet

2 teaspoons finely chopped fresh rosemary (optional)

$1/4$ teaspoon fine sea salt

About $2/3$ cup / 150 ml cold water

This suet pastry for making pie is exactly the same as the pastry for making steamed pudding, but the recipe makes a smaller quantity. This pastry can be used to top any sort of savory pie, although you might want to vary the herbs according to the dish. If you are making a chicken pot pie, for example, you might replace the rosemary with chopped tarragon or flat-leaf parsley.

Sift together the flour and baking powder. Stir in the suet, rosemary, and salt. Using a fork, stir in enough of the water so the mixture forms a dough that pulls away from the bowl. Turn the dough out onto a floured surface and knead gently until the pastry is smooth. Wrap the pastry in plastic wrap and refrigerate for 30 minutes.

Steak and Kidney Pie

Even though I am a big fan of steak and kidney pudding, I like pie, too. The same filling works in both, so which one you make really depends on how much time you have. Suet pastry can be baked (though the recipe varies a bit depending upon whether you are baking or steaming it), but I do like my pie with puff pastry too, so I've given that as an option here.

Prepare the filling as directed for the Steak and Kidney Pudding (page 184). When the filling and cooking liquid are cool, mix them together and pour into a 9-inch / 23-cm pie dish.

Preheat the oven to 425°F / 220°C. Beat the egg with the water.

On a floured work surface, roll out the pastry into a circle about 1/2 inch / 1 cm larger in diameter than the pie dish. Cut a strip of pastry 1/2 inch / 1 cm wide from the outside edge of the circle and fit it around the rim of the pie dish; this forms a collar to anchor the pastry top. Brush the pastry strip with some of the egg mixture and top the pie with the pastry circle, pressing to seal the edges. Brush the pie top with the egg mixture and let dry. Place the pie on a baking sheet and brush again with the remaining beaten egg. Cut a slit in the center of the pie to allow the steam to escape and bake until the pastry is golden and the filling hot, 25 to 30 minutes.

Serves 4 to 6

1 recipe Steak and Kidney Pudding filling (page 184)

1 egg

1 tablespoon water

1 recipe Suet Pastry for Savory Pie (page 186) or 12 ounces / 350 g Puff Pastry (page 33)

DR. ATKINS'S HERO

Vilhjalmur Stefansson was promoting a carbohydrate-free diet long before Dr. Robert Atkins became famous for his low-carb eating plan. Born in Canada in 1879, Stefansson spent long periods in the Canadian and Alaskan Arctic at the beginning of the twentieth century. He was an explorer, but he also spent his days recording the life and culture of the Inuit. During his time with the Inuit, Stefansson ate their diet of fish, meat, and fat. Despite not eating any fresh fruit or vegetables, he, like the Inuit, had no problems with his health or his teeth, nor did he succumb to scurvy. Stefansson wrote about his experiences and championed an all-meat diet as the way to good health. He was, understandably, met with much skepticism, since what he preached went against the prevailing medical opinion. In 1928, to silence his skeptics, he checked himself into the Bellevue Hospital in New York City to follow his meat-only diet for a year under medical supervision. Almost immediately Stefansson fell ill, and his doctors gloated. Stefansson quickly realized, however, what was wrong, since he had encountered the same problem in the Arctic: the meat he was eating didn't have enough fat. He demanded well-marbled meat with a good coating of fat (he would have loved Wagyu beef) and had no further health problems. After he had spent a year eating nothing but fatty meat, the doctors could find nothing wrong with his health.

Grilled Steak with Red Wine Sauce and Bone Marrow

Serves 6

2 cups / 500 ml red wine

4 shallots, chopped

1 carrot, peeled and sliced

3 sprigs thyme

1 fresh bay leaf

$1/2$ teaspoon black peppercorns, crushed

2 cups / 500 ml concentrated veal stock

2 bone-in rib steaks, each 3 inches / 7.5 cm thick

Sea salt and freshly ground black pepper

6 pieces whole bone marrow (see page 172)

It really doesn't get much better than this, well-marbled rib steak served with a red wine sauce and topped with rich bone marrow. The rich, fatty marrow melts over the warm steak slices, enriching the beef and melting into the wine sauce, adding another layer of beef flavor. Although meat always has more flavor when cooked on the bone, you could also serve this sauce with six individual boneless steaks. Concentrated veal stock is not hard to make. Take a good veal stock, preferably homemade, that has no salt and boil to reduce it and concentrate its flavor. To make the 2 cups / 500 ml needed for this recipe, start with 4 cups / 1 l of stock. You can make the sauce up to a day in advance, reheating it while the steaks are resting.

Combine the wine, shallots, carrot, thyme, bay leaf, and peppercorns in a saucepan over high heat and bring to a boil. Reduce the heat and boil gently until the liquid is reduced to $2/3$ cup / 150 ml, 15 to 20 minutes. Add the veal stock and continue to boil gently until the liquid is reduced by half. Strain the sauce through a fine-mesh sieve, pressing hard against the solids to extract all the liquid. The sauce can be stored for up to a day in the refrigerator.

One hour before cooking, remove the steaks from the refrigerator.

Preheat the grill or broiler to high.

Season the steaks with salt and pepper. Sear the steaks for 1 minute per side. Lower the heat or move the grill rack farther away from the heat and continue to cook the steaks, turning once, until a kitchen thermometer registers 120° to 125°F / 48° to 51°C for rare or medium-rare, 10 to 14 minutes. Let the steaks rest, loosely covered with aluminum foil, for 10 minutes. Remember, during this time the internal temperature of the steak will rise by about 5°F / 2°C.

While the meat is resting, reheat the sauce over medium-low heat. Slice the marrow into $1/2$-inch / 1-cm slices and poach them in simmering salted water until translucent and no longer pink, about 2 minutes. Drain the marrow on paper towels.

Cut the meat from the bone and slice it thickly. Top the sliced meat with the poached marrow and serve with the sauce.

Pemmican: extremely condensed thought or writing

PREPARING VEAL KIDNEY

You will need to have a chat with your butcher before roasting a veal kidney in its fat, because the kidney will be a special order. In Paris my butcher prepared for me one kidney with a thin coating of fat, so I had no work to do. In Toronto I ordered a veal kidney in its fat, and I received both the animal's kidneys with all their fat. If you are adventurous, I recommend buying your kidney this way, because it provides you with a large amount of suet, which you can grate or render for other uses, and it results in a better wrapping of fat around your kidney. Use the other kidney for Steak and Kidney Pudding (page 184) or freeze it for up to 3 months.

To prepare a kidney for Whole Roasted Veal Kidney (below), first separate the kidneys, and then pull off the papery membrane and trim off any large pieces of fat. Each kidney will be about three-quarters enclosed in fat. Cut away and discard any blood vessels and connective tubes. Continue trimming the fat until you have about 1/4 inch / 6 mm covering each kidney. The layer doesn't have to be precisely uniform; the aim is simply to have a thin covering of fat over most of the kidney. Because kidney fat is hard and brittle, the covering won't be smooth but will have cracks and fissures. Don't worry if there are a few spots with no fat. The fat (suet) you have removed can be grated and refrigerated or frozen for use in other dishes (see page 171).

Whole Roasted Veal Kidney

Serves 2

1 veal kidney with its fat, about 1 3/4 pounds / 800 g when trimmed (see above)

Sea salt and freshly ground black pepper

1 tablespoon rendered suet, beef fat, or dripping

1 shallot, finely chopped

1/4 cup / 60 ml Madeira

1 cup / 250 ml veal stock

1 heaping tablespoon Dijon mustard

This is a recipe for two kidney lovers. The kidney is left whole with a coating of suet still surrounding it, which melts and bastes the kidney as it cooks, keeping it from drying out. There will be quite a lot of fat left around the kidney when you slice it, but I don't expect you to eat it. Just cut it away; its work is done. The kidney should be served medium-rare; overcooked kidney, even when it is wrapped in fat, is tough and dry. The best way to judge when the kidney is cooked is to use a kitchen thermometer. When you order this from your butcher, remember that kidneys always come in pairs and be specific. Good accompaniments for kidney are boiled potatoes or Suet Dumplings (page 202) and a green vegetable.

Allow the kidney to come to room temperature. Season the kidney well with salt and pepper. Preheat the oven to 150°F / 65°C.

In a flameproof casserole or Dutch oven, melt the beef fat over medium-low heat. Add the kidney and cover the pan. Cook the kidney gently, turning every 10 minutes, until a kitchen thermometer inserted into the kidney registers 120°F / 48°C, about 30 minutes.

Transfer the kidney to a dish, cover loosely with aluminum foil, and place in the oven. Turn the oven off.

Pour all but 1 tablespoon of fat from the pan, setting the extra fat aside for another use. Add the shallot to the pan and cook over medium heat, stirring, until softened. Add the Madeira and bring to a boil. Deglaze the pan, using a wooden spoon to scrape up the browned bits from the bottom. Add the veal stock and boil until the liquid is reduced to about $1/3$ cup / 75 ml, about 5 minutes. Whisk in the mustard and season with salt and pepper.

Remove the kidney from the oven and pour any juices from its dish into the sauce. Strain the sauce through a fine-mesh sieve.

Slice the kidney into $1/4$-inch / 6-mm slices and serve with the sauce.

FAT THURSDAY AND LES BOEUFS GRAS

In Bazas, a town south of Bordeaux, they celebrate the festival of Les Boeufs Gras, or the Fat Beef, on Fat Thursday, the day after Ash Wednesday. This tradition began in 1283, when King Edward I of England, who was also the Duke of Aquitaine, proclaimed that all butchers must donate a bull to the church. In return, they were given permission to parade their cattle through the town. While the church was on the receiving end of this decree, the butchers made the best of it and turned the event into a celebration, which continues to this day. The festival now promotes the local breed of cattle, called Bazadaise. Slaughtered between the ages of $3^{1}/2$ and 4 years old, these large beasts produce wonderfully marbled meat with a thick coat of fat that is enhanced with a special diet of cereals during their last 6 months of life.

The animals still file through the town during the festival, but this is no running of the bulls. These beasts are massive, weighing up to 1 ton / 1,000 kg, and while they are known for being docile, they are still firmly attached, in pairs, to the back of flatbed trucks to prevent any mishaps. Carefully groomed and decorated with ribbons, each magnificent beast wears a headdress emblazoned with the name of its producer and the butcher shop where it will finish its days. The chosen bulls parade through town with their proud owners, who sport berets and carry heavy wooden sticks to keep their animals in check. Accompanying the procession is the town fife and drum band and a troop of young folk dancers, some of whom are perilously perched on stilts. As the cavalcade wends its way through town, it stops at every butcher shop named on the bovine headgear. While the cattle unwittingly wait outside their future resting place, the participants enjoy a glass of wine, a chat with the butcher, and naturally some grilled Bazadaise beef. Finally the procession arrives in the town square, where a large crowd awaits the selection of the best animal by a jury of cattlemen, butchers, and specialists from the local agricultural college. The festivities conclude with a huge dinner for more than 1,200 guests, during which several lucky people are inducted into the Confrérie Bazadaise du Boeuf. Not only are the inductees allowed to don impressive red and yellow velvet capes, to represent the red meat marbled with yellow fat, but they will also have the honor of leading the parade the following year. And what do the guests and the members of *confrérie* eat? Grilled entrecôtes of Bazadaise beef washed down with Bordeaux wine, of course.

Bone Marrow in Red Wine Butter Sauce

Serves 4

1 recipe Beurre Rouge (page 41)

4 slices brioche or other egg bread, each $3/4$ inch / 2 cm thick

8 pieces whole bone marrow (see page 172)

Although this combination of bone marrow and butter sauce could be used as a sauce for steak, it's really a dish in its own right. The silkiness of the butter sauce pairs with the soft bone marrow, and together they make an amazingly rich dish that shows just how good fat can taste. This recipe requires organization to make, but it's definitely worth the effort for a dinner party, where it will make an impressive starter. Just make sure the main course is simple and stress free, or serve this for lunch followed by a green salad. If you can't find a loaf of brioche, any other egg bread will do very nicely.

Preheat the oven to 200°F / 100°C.

Prepare the beurre rouge and keep it warm in a glass measuring cup in a pan of barely warm water, around 120°F / 48°C over very low heat. Toast the brioche slices, put them on individual serving plates, and place in the oven to keep warm.

Place a saucepan of salted water over low heat and bring to a simmer. Slice the marrow into $1/2$-inch / 1-cm slices. Poach the marrow in simmering salted water until translucent and no longer pink, about 2 minutes. Drain the marrow on paper towels.

Divide the marrow slices among the toasts and spoon over the warm sauce. Serve immediately.

VARIATION Instead of bone marrow you could use cubes of sautéed or poached foie gras.

THE MOST MARBLED MEAT IN THE WORLD: WAGYU BEEF

The highest-grade beef available in Japan is Wagyu beef (*wa* means Japanese and *gyu* means cattle). It is often referred to as Kobe beef because many of the cattle are finished in the Kobe region. The Wagyu breed's genetics combined with special feeding methods produce beef so highly marbled that it can resemble fat marbled with meat. It's the fat in Wagyu that gives the meat its distinctive taste and succulence. Analysis of Wagyu fat reveals that, like bone marrow, it has more monounsaturated fat than regular beef fat, explaining its melt-in-the-mouth quality. Numerous stories abound of Wagyu cattle's pampered lifestyle, and while it is true that they are given beer because it helps their digestion, the piped-in music and daily massage that one hears about is more myth than reality.

Wagyu beef, now raised from Texas to Australia, commands very high prices, but not all Wagyu meat is equal in quality. Thus the Japanese are considering imposing legal restrictions on the use of the term *Wagyu* and limiting its use to cattle raised in Japan, much as the French have done with wine and other foods produced in their country.

INDIAN MUTINY

It was fat that sparked the fires of the Indian Mutiny of 1857, seen by many as the first war of independence waged by the Indians against the British. The British had been in India since the seventeenth century with the East India Company (EIC), a commercial enterprise that was backed by the firepower of 40,000 British soldiers and 200,000 native Indian soldiers, or sepoys. During this time the British imposed their morals, culture, and religion on Indians through the educational system, and serious tensions arose between the colonizers and the various cultures of the subcontinent. The economic exploitation of the native population by the EIC did not help—wages were kept low, compounding the misery from frequent crop failures and food shortages.

In the Hindu caste system, if you crossed the "black waters," or the ocean, you would lose your caste. So when, in 1856, a regulation was introduced requiring all sepoys to serve in Burma, it meant that any Hindu soldier who was sent to Burma would lose his caste. Around the same time the sepoys were issued with new rifles—the Enfield rifled musket. The method for loading this rifle required the soldier to bite open the cardboard cartridge, pour the gunpowder down the barrel, and add the cartridge as a wad before ramming in the musket ball. A rumor spread that these cartridges were greased with a mixture of pork fat and beef tallow to make them easier to load. When the sepoys complained, the British officers responded with the offhand suggestion that if they had a problem, they should make up their own cartridges and grease them with beeswax or oil. This show of indifference only helped to confirm the rumor and managed to offend both the Muslim and the Hindu sepoys. The pork fat was forbidden by the Muslim religion, while the presence of beef tallow distressed the Hindus, who believed the cow was a sacred animal. By the time the British realized their mistake, it was too late. The ensuing rebellion served to end the EIC's control of India: the administration of the subcontinent was taken over by the British government, which instituted many reforms, including the integration of Indians into the government and civil service and an increase in religious tolerance.

Risotto Milanese

Not only does this dish taste good, but it also looks beautiful, with its vivid golden color. A wonderful starter, it is the classic accompaniment for osso buco, and it's also great with a grilled veal chop. Risotto Milanese, however, has been sidelined because of our fear of fat. I never understood why risotto tasted so good in Italy until I saw a chef make it. When the risotto was cooked he added about half a pound of butter. As bone marrow is mainly unsaturated fat and full of important nutrients, you can add it to your risotto knowing that it will taste good and be good for you, too.

Heat the butter in a large saucepan over medium-low heat. Add the diced bone marrow and shallots and cook until the shallots are softened, about 3 minutes. Most of the marrow will melt during this time.

Meanwhile, in another large saucepan, toast the saffron threads over medium heat until fragrant, about 30 seconds. Add the stock and bring to a boil. Lower the heat so the stock barely simmers.

Add the rice to the saucepan containing the butter, bone marrow, and shallots and stir to coat the rice with the fat. Add the wine and stir until it is absorbed by the rice. Now add a ladleful of hot stock, stirring the simmering rice constantly until the liquid is almost completely absorbed. Continue adding the stock, one ladleful at a time, adding more stock only when the previous liquid has been completely absorbed.

After about 20 minutes, the rice will be creamy and cooked but still slightly al dente. Remove the saucepan from the heat, stir in the cheese, and season with salt and pepper. Serve immediately.

Serves 6

1 tablespoon unsalted butter

Six 3-inch / 7.5-cm marrow bones, presoaked and the marrow removed and diced (see page 172)

2 shallots, finely chopped

$1/2$ teaspoon saffron threads

8 cups / 2 l beef stock

2 cups / $10^{1/2}$ ounces / 300 g Vialone Nano or Carnaroli rice

$2/3$ cup / 150 ml dry white wine

1 cup / 30 g very finely grated Parmesan cheese

Sea salt and freshly ground black pepper

PEMMICAN

Pemmican is a Cree word meaning "fat." This Native American food was traditionally made from dried meat, usually buffalo, which was pounded into a paste and then packed into rawhide sacks. Liquid bone marrow was poured over the meat to hold it together and preserve it. Lightweight, long-lasting, and extremely nutritious, pemmican became a staple food for early European fur traders and trappers in North America. Pemmican was also an important source of income for the Native American peoples, who added berries, sugar, and even cereals to the mixture to make it more appealing to European tastes. So vital was pemmican to the survival of fur traders and early settlers in Canada that its supply sparked unrest between the Native Americans and the Europeans.

Lamb Ribs with Flageolets

Serves 4

2 cups / 12 ounces / 350 g dried flageolets, soaked overnight in cold water

2 1/4 pounds / 1 kg lamb breast ribs, trimmed

Coarse sea salt and freshly ground black pepper

2 tablespoons rendered lamb fat or lard

1 onion, chopped

1 carrot, peeled and chopped

1 celery stalk with leaves, sliced

14 ounces / 398 g canned tomatoes

3 cloves garlic, peeled

4 sprigs thyme

1 large strip lemon zest

1 fresh bay leaf

3 cups / 750 ml lamb stock

2 tablespoons freshly squeezed lemon juice

1 cup / 15 g fresh mint leaves, shredded

Lamb breast ribs are a great fatty cut that are perfect for cooking with dried beans, which need fat to give them flavor. Flageolets are small kidney-shaped beans that range in color from pale green to cream and are traditionally served with lamb. They aren't always easy to find, but don't let that stop you from making this dish; just substitute Great Northern beans.

You can keep this dish in the refrigerator, and it reheats well, but don't add the lemon and mint until just before serving, as these flavors must be fresh. Cook the ribs in lamb fat if you can, as this will add yet another layer of flavor. This is a one-dish meal: you don't need to serve anything else with it.

Drain the flageolets, discarding the soaking water, and set them aside.

Preheat the oven to 300°F / 150°C.

Remove the opaque membrane from the bone side of the ribs by loosening it with a sharp knife and pulling it off. Cut the lamb into individual ribs or pairs of ribs, depending on their size. Season the meat with salt and pepper. In a Dutch oven or flameproof casserole, melt the lamb fat over medium-high heat and brown the ribs in batches. As the ribs brown, transfer them to a plate.

Add the onion, carrot, and celery to the pan and cook until softened. Add the tomatoes and their juice and bring to a boil. Deglaze the pan, using a wooden spoon to scrape up the browned bits from the bottom. Add the garlic, thyme, lemon zest, bay leaf, and drained flageolets. Add the stock and then the browned lamb ribs. Bring to a boil and cover with a piece of wet parchment paper (see page 185) and then the lid. Transfer to the oven and braise for 2 hours.

After 2 hours the beans should be just tender. Uncover the pan, remove the parchment paper, and cook, uncovered, for another 30 minutes.

Remove the thyme and zest and add 2 teaspoons salt. Taste and adjust the seasoning. Stir in the lemon juice and mint leaves just before serving.

FATTY HOSPITALITY

Living in the desert, the Bedouins didn't waste their limited water supply on washing their hands. After a meal, their tradition was to wipe their hands on their host's tent flap. The greasier the tent flap, the greater the owner's reputation for a generous table.

"Those of us who were nice would go to the end of the tent where the flap of the roof-cloth, beyond the last poles, drooped down as an end curtain; and on this clan handkerchief (whose coarse goat-hair mesh was pliant and glossy with much use) would scrape the thickest of the fat from our hands." —T. E. Lawrence

Cape Malay–Style Lamb Shoulder

The origins of this dish lie with the Malay slaves who were brought to South Africa by the Dutch. As Muslims, they were happy to cook lamb, mixing it with spices and the sour tamarind from their homeland. I use Spiced Ethiopian Butter (page 25) to cook the lamb in this dish to give it another layer of flavor, but once I finally get my hands on a fat-tailed lamb (see page 206), I'll be using that. I suggest buying a bone-in shoulder of lamb and either boning it yourself or having your butcher do it. Then you'll have all those bones for stock, and you'll be able to cut marbled pieces of lamb shoulder for this dish, saving the rest of the meat and fat for Lamb, Rosemary, and Red Wine Sausages (page 203). Serve with rice or, if you fancy a pan-African meal, couscous.

In a bowl, combine the tamarind pulp with the 1 cup / 250 ml of boiling water; set aside.

Pat dry the lamb and season well with salt and pepper. Place a large deep frying pan with a lid or Dutch oven over medium-high heat and add 2 tablespoons of the butter. When the butter is hot and just starts to color, add half the lamb and brown it on all sides. Transfer the browned lamb to a plate, add another tablespoon of butter to the pan, and brown the remaining lamb. When all the lamb is browned, lower the heat to medium-low and add the remaining butter and the onions and chiles to the pan. Stir, scraping the bottom of the pan, until the onions soften slightly, about 5 minutes. When the onions are soft, add the 1/4 cup / 60 ml water and bring to a boil. Deglaze the pan, using a wooden spoon to scrape up any browned bits from the bottom. When the water has boiled off, remove the pan from the heat.

Using your fingers, squeeze the tamarind pulp together with the soaking water, removing any seeds as you squeeze. Place the tamarind pulp and liquid in a blender, add the brown sugar, and blend until smooth. Pour the tamarind mixture over the onions in the pan and add the garlic, bay leaves, cloves, 1 teaspoon salt, the cayenne pepper, nutmeg, and allspice. Stir to blend. Grind in a generous amount of black pepper, about 20 turns of a peppermill, and add the lamb and its juices to the pan. Bring the mixture to a boil over medium heat, then lower the heat so that it simmers gently. Cover and cook, stirring occasionally, for 1 hour.

Peel the pumpkin and cut into 1-inch / 2.5-cm dice. Add the diced pumpkin to the pan and cook, uncovered, stirring often, until the pumpkin and lamb are tender, about 30 minutes. Sprinkle over the cilantro and serve.

Serves 4 to 6

2 tablespoons tamarind pulp

1 cup / 250 ml boiling water, plus 1/4 cup / 60 ml water

2 pounds / 900 g lamb shoulder, cut into 1 1/2-inch / 4-cm chunks

Sea salt and freshly ground black pepper

1/4 cup / 60 g Spiced Ethiopian Butter (page 25)

2 large onions, thinly sliced

2 serrano chiles, seeded and finely chopped

1 tablespoon brown sugar

3 cloves garlic, peeled and crushed

3 fresh bay leaves

6 cloves

1/2 teaspoon cayenne pepper

1/4 teaspoon ground nutmeg

1/4 teaspoon ground allspice

1 pound / 450 g winter squash or pumpkin (hubbard or kabocha) or sweet potato

1 cup / 15 g cilantro (coriander) leaves, chopped

Braised Oxtail

Serves 4 to 6

5 pounds / 2.25 kg oxtail, cut into pieces

Sea salt and freshly ground black pepper

3 tablespoons beef dripping or rendered beef fat

3 celery stalks, halved lengthwise and sliced

2 onions, chopped

2 carrots, peeled and chopped

1 large orange

1 cup / 250 ml red wine

3 cups / 750 ml beef stock

4 cloves garlic, peeled and crushed

1 tablespoon tomato paste

3 fresh bay leaves

1 teaspoon toasted cumin seeds

2 cloves

1 star anise

Oxtail is a great fatty beef cut that is full of flavor, but it often meets with resistance. People happily eat beef shin, but they are stopped in their tracks by the thought of chewing on a tail. Oxtail is usually sold precut, the pieces becoming progressively smaller as the tail tapers. The meatiest pieces, those from the beginning of the tail, can be substituted in almost any beef stew recipe. While oxtail takes longer to cook than many other cuts of beef, it delivers an intense beef flavor and a wonderful unctuous texture. The secret to preparing oxtail is to cook it a day or two before serving it. This allows all the fat to rise to the top of the dish, making it easy to remove and keep for another use. Serve the oxtail with Suet Dumplings (page 202) cooked in beef stock.

Preheat the oven to 300°F / 150°C.

Pat the oxtail dry and season with salt and pepper. In a Dutch oven or flameproof casserole, heat the beef dripping over medium-high heat and brown the oxtail in batches. As they brown, transfer the pieces to a plate.

Add the celery, onions, and carrots to the pan and cook until slightly softened, about 5 minutes. Remove the zest from the orange in large strips; set the zest and the orange aside. Pour the wine into the pan and bring to a boil. Deglaze the pan, using a wooden spoon to scrape up the browned bits from the bottom. Stir in the stock, garlic, and tomato paste, and then add the orange zest, bay leaves, cumin, cloves, and star anise.

Return the oxtail pieces to the pan and cover with a damp piece of parchment paper (see page 185) and the lid. Braise the oxtail in the oven until the meat is tender but not falling off the bone, 3 to 4 hours. Transfer the oxtail to a platter. Strain the liquid into a large glass measuring cup and leave to cool. Cover and refrigerate both the meat and the cooking liquid overnight.

The next day, remove all the fat from the top of the jellied liquid and any from the oxtail pieces. Set aside to clarify and use for cooking something else.

Preheat the oven to 300°F / 150°C. Squeeze the orange to obtain $1/2$ cup / 125 ml of juice.

Place the oxtail in a baking dish and put the jellied liquid in a saucepan and bring to a boil over medium heat. Continue to boil until the liquid is reduced to 2 cups / 500 ml. Add the orange juice and then pour the liquid over the oxtail.

Transfer the oxtail to the oven and cook, uncovered, turning once, until the oxtail is almost falling from the bone, about 1 hour. Serve with suet dumplings.

Dripping Pastry

This sturdy pastry, ideal for pasties, can be used to enclose any beef or beef and vegetable filling. It freezes very well.

Combine the flour and salt in a food processor and pulse to mix. Add the dripping and pulse until the mixture resembles coarse bread crumbs. Transfer the mixture to a bowl.

Pour $1/4$ cup / 60 ml of the water over the flour and dripping mixture and mix with a fork. Squeeze a bit of the mixture between your fingers. If it holds together tip the dough onto a lightly floured surface; if not, mix in the remaining 2 teaspoons of water and test again.

Gently knead the dough into a ball. Divide the pastry in half and flatten into 2 disks. Wrap each disk in plastic wrap and refrigerate for at least 30 minutes before using.

Makes enough for 9 pasties

4 cups / $17 1/2$ ounces / 500 g flour

1 teaspoon fine sea salt

6 ounces / 175 g beef dripping or diced rendered suet

$1/4$ cup / 60 ml plus 2 teaspoons ice-cold water

THE ORIGIN OF THE PASTY

In Cornwall, England, the home of the Cornish pasty, these sturdy pastries provided the local miners and fishermen with a very portable meal they could take down the mines or on their fishing boats. Each pasty was marked in the corner with its owner's initials, so there would be no confusion when hunger struck. Pasties held any number of fillings, from meat or fish with vegetables to fruit. The pasty not only went down into the mines, but it also traveled with Cornish emigrants across the world to Australia, where lamb with vegetables is the most popular filling, and to the United States. In the United States, the pasty is now considered a regional specialty of northern Michigan. In the 1860s Cornish immigrants came to Michigan to work the copper mines, bringing their pasties with them. The next wave of immigrants to the area, the Finns, saw the pasty and immediately recognized it as a close relation of their *piirakka*, a whole-wheat pastry filled with rice or potatoes, and the *kalakukko*, a mixture of fat and fish cooked in a rye dough. Each new wave of immigrants influenced the Michigan pasty, and now its most popular incarnation is a mixture of beef and vegetables, available at bakeries, grocery stores, bars, and restaurants. The pasty has also migrated beyond the borders of Michigan to Florida and California, where the filling is just as likely to be chicken and chile as beef and vegetables.

Cornish Pasty

A Cornish pasty is a sturdy pastry filled with meat and vegetables. I have a soft spot for pasties because they were the only food I was allowed to eat on the couch while watching television as a child. Pasties have many relatives around the world: empanadas, samosas, and pierogis are all portable pastries containing tasty fillings. For pasties, the raw filling is placed in a pastry circle that is folded in half and then tightly crimped, so that the filling cooks in its own juices. Dripping Pastry (page 199) is the best pastry to use for this dish, as it is strong enough to hold the filling and has a mild beefy flavor. Traditionally, pasties are formed with their crimped edge pointing skyward, but you can bake them lying down, too. Serve these warm or at room temperature with relish, chutney, or tomato sauce.

Preheat the oven to 400°F / 200°C. Remove the pastry from the refrigerator.

Cut the meat into 1/2-inch / 1-cm cubes, removing any sinew, and place in a bowl. Peel and cut the potato, onion, carrot, and turnip into 1/4-inch / 6-mm dice. Add the vegetables to the meat along with the parsley, rosemary, and salt. Season well with pepper and stir. In a small bowl, whisk the egg with the water.

On a floured surface, roll out the pastry about 1/4 inch / 6 mm thick. Cut out nine 6-inch / 15-cm circles, kneading the scraps together and rerolling the pastry as necessary. Take 1 circle and place 1/3 cup / 75 ml of the filling on half of the circle. Brush the edges of the circle with the egg wash and then fold over the pastry to make a half-moon shape. Crimp to seal the edges well and place the pasty on a baking sheet. Repeat with the remaining circles.

Brush the pasties with the egg wash and use a fork to prick the pasties several times on the topside. Bake for 20 minutes, reduce the oven to 350°F / 180°C, and continue cooking another 25 minutes, until they are golden brown and a little cooking juice has leaked from the holes in the pasties.

Makes 9 pasties

1 recipe Dripping Pastry (page 199)

1 pound / 450 g marbled sirloin steak

1 potato

1 onion

1 carrot

1 small turnip

1 tablespoon chopped fresh flat-leaf parsley

1 teaspoon finely chopped fresh rosemary

1 teaspoon sea salt

Freshly ground black pepper

1 egg

1 tablespoon water

A study at Ohio State University looked at the effect of the changing ratio of omega-6 to omega-3 fatty acids in our bodies. The vegetable oils that have flooded our kitchens in recent years are high in omega-6 fatty acids, while our sources of omega-3 fatty acids, such as fats from grass-fed animals, have declined. As a result, we are now getting far more omega-6 in our diet than ever before. Previously, most of us had about two to three times as much omega-6 as omega-3, but today it appears that on average we have between ten and fifteen times as much omega-6 as omega-3, and some of us have even higher levels. The Ohio study concluded that people with at least eighteen times as much omega-6 to omega-3 are likely to be depressed, prone to heart disease, or have damaged immune systems, type 2 diabetes, and arthritis. They concluded that this fatty acid imbalance could be responsible for the increase in these diseases over the past century.

THE WRONG FAT WILL MAKE YOU DEPRESSED AND SICK

Suet Dumplings

Makes 6 dumplings

$^1/_2$ cup / 2 ounces / 60 g flour

$^1/_2$ teaspoon baking powder

$^3/_4$ cup / 2 ounces / 60 g fine fresh bread crumbs

$^2/_3$ cup / 2 ounces / 60 g finely grated suet

2 tablespoons finely chopped fresh flat-leaf parsley

$^1/_2$ teaspoon fine sea salt

1 egg

2 cups / 500 ml stock or water

Sea salt and freshly ground black pepper

Simple to make and amazingly light and fluffy, suet dumplings are the perfect garnish for a beef broth and a great companion to dishes like Braised Oxtail (page 198) and Whole Roasted Veal Kidney (page 190) that have a sauce to sop up. There's no need to restrict dumplings to accompanying meat, however; also try them alongside a dish of grilled or steamed vegetables.

I prefer to cook my dumplings separately from the dish I am serving them with. Although cooking them in water will do, using stock gives them more flavor. Use the stock that matches the meat they are accompanying. You can also add spices to the dumplings, such as a pinch of ground star anise if they are going with the oxtail. This recipe is easily doubled, but you might need to add a tablespoon of cold water to the dough to achieve the right consistency.

Sift the flour and baking powder into a bowl and stir in the bread crumbs, suet, parsley, and salt. Whisk the egg and stir it into the flour mixture to make a stiff dough. Tip the dough onto a floured surface and knead gently for a few seconds. Divide the dough into 6 equal pieces and roll each piece into a ball. Set aside.

Bring the stock to a boil in a wide saucepan and season with salt and pepper if necessary. Add the dumplings, lower the heat so the stock simmers, cover, and simmer gently until the dumplings have doubled in size and are cooked through, 15 to 20 minutes.

Remove the dumplings from the liquid with a slotted spoon and serve in a soup or stew, with a roast, or alongside cooked vegetables.

VARIATIONS To vary the flavor of these dumplings, replace the parsley with fresh chopped chives or cilantro (coriander).

For horseradish dumplings, after rolling each dumpling into a ball, use your finger to poke a hole in it and insert about 1 teaspoon of prepared horseradish. Seal the hole well and cook as directed.

For marrow dumplings, replace the suet with an equal amount of finely chopped raw bone marrow. Add 1 teaspoon of finely chopped shallot and a pinch of grated nutmeg to the dough before adding the egg.

Lamb, Rosemary, and Red Wine Sausages

Lamb, rosemary, red wine, and garlic are a classic combination that make great sausages. When making up your own sausage recipes, think about what ingredients you like to eat with each type of meat and use that as a springboard for choosing your flavorings. Most people simply use pork fat when making any type of sausage, but do try to get some lamb fat trimmings from your butcher, as this will boost the lamb flavor of these sausages. You can make up any shortfall with pork fat.

Cut the lamb and fat into small pieces that will easily fit into your meat grinder, removing any sinew from the meat as you go. In a large bowl combine the meat and fat with the rosemary, salt, garlic, and pepper, and stir to mix. Cover and refrigerate for 4 to 6 hours or overnight.

Place the bowl from your stand mixer and your meat grinder in the refrigerator about 2 hours before starting.

Remove the meat mixture, bowl, meat grinder, and wine from the refrigerator. Using the finest die for your grinder, grind the meat mixture into the chilled bowl. Alternate pushing the pieces of fat and meat through the grinder to ensure that the fat doesn't stick inside. Using the paddle attachment on your stand mixer, mix the ground meat on low speed, adding the cold red wine. When the mixture is homogenous and sticky, after about 2 minutes, form about 1 tablespoon of the mixture into a patty, cook it in a frying pan, and taste to check the seasoning, adding more salt if necessary. Refrigerate the ground meat mixture until well chilled, about 2 hours.

While the meat mixture is chilling, soak the sausage casings in warm water for 1 hour. Rinse the casings in cold water, then run water through the casings. I slip one end of the casing over the tap and gently turn on the water to let it flow through the casing. Place the casings in a fine-mesh sieve to drain; you want them to be moist when you fill them.

Attach the sausage stuffer to the grinder and push the damp sausage casing over the tube until about 4 inches / 10 cm is hanging from the end and tie a knot in this piece. At this point it is a good idea to rope in a friend to help you, especially if it is your first time making sausage.

Add the chilled mixture to the grinder on low speed and slowly stuff the sausages, trying to minimize the air pockets in the casings. As filling enters the casing, it should slowly slide off the tube.

If there are two of you, one can concentrate on putting the mixture in the grinder while the other can devote his or her attention to easing the meat into the casings. Once all the mixture is used up, ease any remaining casing off the tube. Roll the sausage on a damp surface to distribute the filling as evenly as possible and then form the sausage into links by twisting the casing at 6-inch / 15-cm intervals. Twist each link in the opposite direction to prevent them from unwinding.

Cover the sausages and refrigerate for up to 3 days. They can also be frozen. To cook the sausages, see page 106.

Makes ten to twelve 6-inch / 15-cm sausage links

$2^{1}/4$ pounds / 1 kg fatty lamb shoulder

$1/2$ pound / 225 g lamb or pork fat

$1/4$ cup / 6 g fresh rosemary leaves, chopped

0.8 ounce / 25 g coarse sea salt

3 cloves garlic, peeled and finely chopped

1 teaspoon freshly ground black pepper

$1/2$ cup / 125 ml red wine, chilled

6 feet / 2 m sausage casing

Fat cat

Fat of the land: the best or richest part

Suet-brained or suet-headed: stupid

Lamb Fat and Spinach Chapati

Makes 8 chapatis

1 bunch spinach

2 cups / 8¾ ounces / 250 g whole wheat flour, sifted

2 teaspoons cumin seeds, toasted and crushed

1½ teaspoons fine sea salt

3 tablespoons rendered lamb fat, melted (see tip, below)

About ¾ cup / 175 ml water

To get the fat out of one's cabbages: to reap the benefit from something (French)

My friend Lynn makes great Indian food. I knew she made lots of flat breads, so I asked her for a recipe. Lynn gave me her spinach chapati recipe, and I thought it would be improved with a little lamb fat. Now, I doubt that Lynn, who is a vegetarian, would be too keen on my addition, or that any Indian chef would use lamb fat. I took my inspiration from the steppes of Asia, where they make many types of flat bread brushed with melted rendered lamb fat. If you don't have any lamb fat, you can use Ghee (page 24) with Lynn's approval.

The simplest of all flat breads, chapatis are traditionally cooked on a cast-iron plate called a tava, but a cast-iron griddle or frying pan works just as well. Your pan needs to be just a little larger than the size of your chapatis. Don't worry if they don't puff on your first attempt; they will still be good to eat.

Rinse the spinach well and remove the stems. Transfer to a colander to drain. Place a large frying pan over high heat and, when it is hot, add the spinach. Cook, stirring, until the spinach wilts. Tip the spinach back into the colander and refresh under cold running water. Squeeze out the water and chop coarsely; you should have about 1 cup / 250 ml.

Combine the spinach, flour, cumin, and salt in a food processor and pulse to mix. Add 1 tablespoon of the lamb fat and pulse to blend. Tip the flour mixture into a bowl, add the water, and stir with a fork to make a soft dough. The amount of water needed will depend on your flour and the amount of water left in the spinach. Tip the dough onto a floured surface and knead for 5 to 10 minutes to make a soft, pliable dough. Let the dough rest, covered, for 30 minutes.

Line a baking sheet with waxed paper. Divide the dough into 8 balls of equal size. Working with one ball at a time and leaving the rest of them covered, roll the ball into an 8-inch / 20-cm round and place on the prepared baking sheet. Continue with the remaining balls, layering a piece of waxed paper between each dough round in the stack. Keep the dough covered with a cloth.

Heat a cast-iron frying pan over medium-high heat. When the pan is hot, add a dough round and cook until small bubbles form and the bread turns brown in spots, about 1 minute. Turn the bread over and cook the other side until the bread puffs up, about 1 minute. You can encourage the bread to puff by pressing down on the air bubbles as they form with a clean towel. This will help the air expand through the dough and puff it up.

Brush one side of the cooked chapati with some melted lamb fat and wrap in a clean towel to keep warm and soft. Repeat with the remaining dough rounds and serve immediately.

TIP To yield enough lamb fat for this recipe you'll need to render about 4 ounces / 115 g of lamb fat.

THE QUEST FOR THE FAT TAIL

It all began with a simple line illustration of a sheep that I saw in a book. This wasn't just any sheep, but one endowed with a huge tail. And as if that weren't odd enough, the sheep's large tail rested on a small wooden cart attached by a harness to the animal's chest. At first I thought it was a joke, but it turns out this was an illustration of a fat-tailed lamb based on a description penned in the fifth century B.C. by the Greek historian Herodotus.

> There are in Arabia two kinds of sheep worthy of admiration, the like of which are nowhere else to be seen. One kind has long tails no less than four and a half feet long, which, if they were allowed to trail on the ground, would be bruised and develop sores. As it is, the shepherds have enough skill in carpentry to make little carts for their sheep's tail. The carts are placed under the tails, each sheep having one to himself, and the tails are then tied down upon them. The other kind has a broad tail which is at times 18 inches across.

Fat-tailed sheep, found mainly in the Middle East, North Africa, Central Asia, and northern India, account for more than a quarter of the world's sheep population. The fat in their tail provides them with a store of food, rather like a camel's hump. As these sheep are often found in extreme climates, it has been speculated that their tail fat was nature's response to their difficult living conditions. However, there are two problems with this conclusion; all wild sheep are thin tailed, and if you dock the tail of a fat-tailed sheep, its fat is then deposited all over its body, just like a thin-tailed sheep. It turns out that fat-tailed sheep were deliberately bred to deposit fat in their tails. But why?

Lamb fat is valuable to the inhabitants of harsh climates, where the choice of fat is limited. Soft lamb fat is particularly prized, as it melts easily and its lower saturation gives it a more pleasant mouthfeel. The consistency of a sheep's fat depends on where it is found on the animal's body. As the sheep's tail is exposed to the ambient temperature on all but one side, the fat found there is softer than other types of sheep fat. A fat sheep's tail is either wide and fat, rather like a beaver's, or long and thick, resembling a kangaroo's, and it can weigh up to one-sixth of the animal's total bodyweight. There's also a fat-rump sheep that stores fat on its buttocks. Fat-tailed lambs are prized in the Arab world, where they are often served at weddings. In the Gulf States they are roasted whole with their tail folded back over the body to baste the meat. Tail fat is sometimes used much like bacon, threaded onto skewers with other meats to add flavor and keep them juicy, or melted and drizzled over dishes to enrich them. In the mountains of Lebanon, lamb fat is rendered with spices and herbs and then preserved with salt, the main ingredient of *qawarma*, a type of lamb confit. Some authorities insist that a spoonful of rendered tail fat added to the butter is the secret to a good baklava and that lamb fat is excellent for frying sweet fritters. While traveling in Syria, my friend David, at my urging, ate fat-tailed lamb. His favorite dish was skewered cubes of the fat grilled until crisp on the outside and meltingly soft in the center, served with hummus. Cooking with fat-tailed lamb is not restricted to the Arab world; in parts of China, lamb fat flavors rice dishes, while in South Africa it was an important ingredient in early Cape cooking. Although fat-tailed sheep are still being raised—they are good milk producers and their wool is woven into carpets—their tail fat is declining in use. The sheep are suffering from the modern fear of fat, and the association of fat-tailed sheep with old-fashioned cooking styles is making it less popular with the younger generation.

Since seeing that illustration I have been on a quest to eat the fat of a fat-tailed lamb. I almost succeeded once in Australia, where it is known as saltbush lamb. Friends put me in touch with a Melbourne chef who served fat-tailed lamb in his restaurant. We were talking about how wonderful the meat tasted when I asked him how he used the tail. He looked at me blankly and said, "I don't. I throw it away."

Horrified, I proceeded to make a case for its use, even though I'd never tasted it. He gave me the name of his supplier in Sydney and I ordered my own fat tail. Since it came with a lamb attached I organized a lamb barbecue for my friends.

In Sydney, I drove across town with my friend Liz to pick up my lamb. There it hung in full splendor, wrapped in a protective cloth. I hadn't considered that it wouldn't be broken down. How would I ever get it in Liz's refrigerator? Perhaps I could just take the tail? I eagerly looked for the prized piece, but, to my horror, discovered my lamb was tailless!

"There's no tail!" I screamed.

My supplier jumped up, looked at the carcass, and grabbed his cell phone. Several calls later the sad story emerged. It was indeed a fat-tailed lamb, but the farmer had been forced to change abattoirs at the last minute. The abattoir workers, not familiar with the breed, had cut off the tail and thrown it away, just like that Melbourne chef. I was out of luck, the barbecue was canceled, and I have yet to taste lamb tail fat.

I haven't given up my quest, however, and I continue to dream of those crisp cubes of tail fat with their soft fatty centers. Wistfully I gaze at the illustration, and wonder if there are still shepherds fashioning wooden carts to support their sheep's tails. Then I imagine a flock of sheep, carts attached, rolling across the fields toward me and my barbecue.

An essential ingredient for steamed puddings and mincemeat, suet is much more versatile than even I had imagined. This really shouldn't be surprising. Like leaf lard (see page 70), suet is a kidney fat, so it imparts a great texture. Suet's big advantage is that you don't need to render it. I recommend suet pastry to first-time pastry makers or anyone who thinks making pastry is difficult. Suet pastry is fast and easy to make, and it holds its shape well, which is good news for anyone who likes to decorate their pies. My biggest revelation came when I used suet instead of butter in a tea biscuit recipe; never had I made such light biscuits.

Marrow is also useful in the dessert kitchen; I use it in very small amounts to enrich sweets. It was popular in the past, when it was often added to desserts and puddings instead of butter. Marrow also doesn't need to be rendered, but it does take some time and effort to prepare (see page 172).

SUET, MARROW, AND DESSERT

Marmalade Pudding

I have a passion for both good steamed puddings and marmalade, and in this recipe, adapted from one by Arabella Boxer, the former cooking editor for British Vogue *magazine, the two come together. In this easy recipe the pudding steams in the oven in just 1 1/2 hours. Conveniently, once this dessert is made, it can wait for you in a turned-off oven for a good 45 minutes with no problem. It's important, however, to use a top-quality, not-too-sweet Seville orange marmalade.*

Preheat the oven to 325°F / 160°C.

Lightly butter four 1/2-cup / 125-ml ovenproof ramekins and place a disk of parchment paper in the bottom of each one.

In a bowl, mix the bread crumbs, suet, sugar, cardamom, and salt. Finely grate the zest of the orange and stir into the bread crumb mixture. Squeeze the orange to obtain 1/4 cup / 60 ml juice. In a small bowl, whisk 2 tablespoons of the juice with the egg and 3 tablespoons of the marmalade, setting the rest of the juice aside. Stir the egg mixture into the bread crumb mixture and mix until well blended.

Divide the mixture among the 4 ramekins. Press the mixture into the ramekins and cover each one with a square of aluminum foil. Place them in an ovenproof dish and fill the dish with enough boiling water to come three-quarters of the way up the sides of the ramekins.

Bake the puddings for 1 1/2 hours, then remove from the oven and transfer the pan with the puddings to a wire rack and let stand for 5 minutes.

While the puddings are baking, combine the remaining marmalade and the cream and whiskey in a small saucepan. Add the remaining 2 tablespoons of orange juice and bring to a boil over high heat. Lower the heat so the sauce boils gently and boil until the mixture is reduced to 1/2 cup / 125 ml, about 12 minutes. Keep warm, or set aside and reheat to serve.

Take the puddings from the hot water and remove the foil. Run a sharp knife around the puddings to loosen them and turn out onto warm plates. Remove the parchment paper from the top and pour over the marmalade sauce. Serve warm.

Serves 4

Unsalted butter, softened, for greasing

1 1/4 cups / 3 1/2 ounces / 100 g fine fresh bread crumbs

1 cup / 3 1/2 ounces / 100 g finely grated suet

1/3 cup / 2 ounces / 65 g superfine (caster) sugar

1/2 teaspoon ground cardamom

Pinch of fine sea salt

1 orange

1 egg

1/4 cup / 60 ml plus 3 tablespoons Seville orange marmalade, chopped

1/2 cup / 125 ml whipping (35 percent fat) cream

2 tablespoons whiskey

THE HISTORY OF PUDDING

"Ah, what an excellent thing is an English pudding! To come in pudding time, is as much as to say, to come in the most lucky moment in the world."
Henri Misson

Pudding is one of the great British contributions to the culinary world. While today the term is generally applied to anything sweet served at the end of a meal, the ancestors of pudding were savory. Puddings began as mixtures of meat, fat, and spices packed into animals' intestines or their stomachs. These large sausages were boiled in huge pots that were hung over the fire. Some of these early puddings, including haggis and black pudding, are still around today. In the Middle Ages puddings based on cereals, suet, and bread crumbs began to appear, and as dried fruits arrived from the East, they were added to the mix. The big advance in pudding history was the introduction of the pudding bag or cloth. Cooking the pudding in a cloth meant you no longer had to wait for an animal to be slaughtered for its stomach or intestines, so you could cook pudding anytime you wanted. Sometimes the pudding cloth was lined with a suet pastry. These dishes developed into savory puddings, the most famous of which is Steak and Kidney Pudding (page 184). At other times, the pudding mixture would be packed directly into the cloth. These puddings tended to consist of a thick, porridgelike mixture of cereals, bread crumbs, and suet, and in the seventeenth century, as sugar became more affordable, they were often sweetened. This is the origin of sweet suet puddings, the best known of which is Traditional Christmas Pudding or plum pudding (page 211). Since little fresh fruit was available in the winter, mixtures of dried fruits were popular at Christmas. Plum pudding, for example, never contained fresh fruit, but only dried plums (prunes). Because "plum" was a generic term applied to all dried fruits in the Middle Ages, however, there is no way of knowing when raisins and currants replaced dried prunes in plum pudding.

The traditional day for making Christmas pudding (at least since the middle of the nineteenth century) is "Stir-up Sunday," the Sunday before Advent, or five Sundays before Christmas. Like many recipes that are almost entirely made with dried fruits, Quincemeat (page 214), or fruitcake, Christmas pudding is made at least a month in advance so the flavors of the fruits and spices have time to blend. Every member of the family takes a turn stirring the pudding mixture and making a wish. If you think it sounds Dickensian, you're right. Charles Dickens's tale *A Christmas Carol* did much to romanticize Christmas, turning foods like goose and pudding into part of Christmas lore. Pudding's prestige was also helped by Prince Albert, Queen Victoria's husband, who had a fondness for rich steamed puddings. A German, Prince Albert also popularized the German tradition of a Christmas tree. A tree, a goose, and pudding have now all become an essential part of an English Christmas.

As suet fell out of favor in the kitchen, many recipes substituted butter for the beef fat, but they weren't as light as the original, and puddings gained a reputation for being stodgy. Today, puddings both savory and sweet are enjoying a resurgence in popularity and are now appearing on restaurant menus, especially in England and Australia. They are no longer made in pudding cloths but steamed in anything from a specialized ceramic pudding basin or mold to an individual soufflé dish or cake pan.

Traditional Christmas Pudding

For me, it isn't Christmas unless there is a Christmas pudding. It's not simply a dessert; it's a tradition. We always made our pudding on Stir-up Sunday (see page 210), stirring in the silver coins and making a wish. Our pudding contained silver sixpences and threepences, until the currency went metric and the silver disappeared from the coins, forcing us to replace the money with silver trinkets. After an initial steaming, our pudding was wrapped in cloth, then hung in the laundry room to mature until Christmas Eve.

Ritual demands that the cooked pudding be placed on a serving dish, the lights dimmed, and the pudding doused with hot rum and set alight, often a dangerous act at the end of a long celebratory meal. The pudding is then cut and served, starting with the youngest person at the table and ending with the oldest. Serve the pudding with Rum Butter (page 27).

Combine both types of raisins, the currants, and the candied peel in a large bowl. Chop the almonds coarsely and add them to the fruit along with $1/4$ cup / 60 ml of the rum. Stir to mix, cover, and then leave to marinate at room temperature overnight.

Prepare a 6-cup / 1.5-l pudding basin or mold by buttering the inside and placing a circle of parchment paper at the bottom.

Sift the flour, *quatre épices*, salt, and cinnamon into a bowl. Toss the suet with the bread crumbs and add to the flour, stirring to mix. Pour the flour mixture over the fruit mixture and add the finely grated carrot. Finely grate the zest from the lemon and add to the mixture and then squeeze 2 tablespoons of lemon juice.

Blend the lemon juice, eggs, and sugar and pour into the bowl with the flour and fruit mixture, stirring to mix very well. This is the time to have family and friends stir and make a wish and add any silver coins or trinkets.

Pack the mixture into the prepared basin or mold. Place another circle of parchment paper on top of the pudding and then cover the top of the basin with a large piece of heavy-duty aluminum foil folded to make a pleat about $1/2$ inch / 1 cm deep in the middle (this is to allow the foil to expand with the pudding during cooking). Secure the foil under the rim of the bowl with a length of string to make sure no water can drip into the pudding. If you don't have a steaming basket, extra string can be tied around the basin to make a makeshift handle, or use a piece of cloth (see page 185).

Place the pudding in a steamer or on a trivet in a large stockpot. Fill the pot with enough water to come three-quarters of the way up the sides of the basin, cover, and bring to a boil over high heat. Lower the heat so the water boils gently and steam the pudding for 2 hours, adding more boiling water as necessary to maintain the same level.

Remove the pudding from the pot by lifting out the steamer basket and let stand for 10 minutes. Cool the pudding and then refrigerate in the

Serves 8 to 12

4 ounces / 115 g golden raisins (sultanas)

4 ounces / 115 g seedless Thompson raisins

4 ounces / 115 g currants

2 ounces / 60 g mixed candied citrus peel

1 ounce / 30 g blanched almonds, lightly toasted

$1/2$ cup / 125 ml rum

1 teaspoon unsalted butter, softened

$3/4$ cup / 3 ounces / 90 g flour

1 teaspoon quatre épices (see page 91)

$1/4$ teaspoon fine sea salt

$1/4$ teaspoon ground cinnamon

$1 1/4$ cups / 4 ounces / 115 g finely grated suet

$1 1/4$ cups / $3 1/2$ ounces / 100 g fine fresh bread crumbs

1 small carrot, peeled and finely grated

1 lemon

3 eggs

$1/2$ cup / 3 ounces / 90 g firmly packed brown sugar

mold, still covered with the parchment and foil, for at least 4 weeks and up to 6 weeks. The pudding can be frozen for up to a year.

When you are ready to serve the pudding, remove it from the refrigerator and steam as before for another 2 hours. If it steams for a little longer, no harm will be done; you cannot overcook it.

Remove the pudding from the pot and carefully take off the foil and parchment paper. Turn out the pudding onto a warm serving dish and remove the second parchment paper disk.

In a small saucepan, heat the remaining $1/4$ cup / 60 ml rum over medium heat until hot. Pour over the pudding and set alight using a long match.

Let the flames die down, then cut the pudding into wedges and serve.

TREASONABLE FAT

In 1914, long before he became president of the United States, Herbert Hoover found himself in London when war broke out. He was instrumental in organizing the repatriation of thousands of Americans trapped in Europe by the hostilities. He then turned his attention to organizing food relief to Belgium, where supplies had been cut off by the Germans and the British blockade. This experience resulted in his being appointed to head the U.S. Food Administration when the United States entered the war in 1917. In this role he kept food prices under control and prevented food rationing in America while ensuring adequate supplies to the troops. Hoover promoted the idea of the body as a machine, saying, "I am an engineer, and I am not using my body. An engineer does not stoke the engine unless there is a considerable amount of power to be exerted. So, I eat as little as I can to get along." He also employed a clever propaganda campaign that appealed to his fellow Americans' patriotism. The idea was simple: if you wasted food, you were helping the enemy, and wasting fat was treasonable. Some of the campaign slogans were:

"Food will win the war."

"Do not help the Hun at meal time."

"Gospel of the clean plate."

"Food is sacred. To waste is sinful."

With this strategy he managed to convince Americans to observe "meatless Mondays" and grow their own vegetables. At the end of the war he was famous as the man that fed Europe, and then as head of the American Relief Administration, he sent aid to the starving people in Central Europe and Russia, despite much criticism that he was aiding Bolsheviks.

Fruit Cobbler

Most people make cobbler with a buttery tea biscuit or scone mixture. Here, however, the topping is made with suet. You won't believe how light it is until you try it. Once you do, I bet you'll be using suet all the time, or at least substituting it for some of the butter in your favorite biscuit recipe. You can make this with any combination of fruit you like. I have raspberries growing in my garden, so I end up throwing them into everything in the summer. Rhubarb makes a good filling in the spring, and apple and blackberries are a great option in the autumn, but when you include apples reduce the cornstarch by half. If you don't feel like making cobbler, you can just make the suet biscuits, split them while they are warm, and serve with whipped cream and fresh fruit preserves.

Preheat the oven to 425°F / 220°C.

To make the filling, bring a large saucepan of water to a boil. Drop in the peaches and leave for 1 minute, then transfer immediately to a bowl of ice water. Using a paring knife, remove the skin from the peaches; it should peel off easily. If it doesn't, drop the peaches back into the boiling water for another 30 seconds.

Cut each peach into sixths or eighths, depending on its size, and discard the pit. Place the peach slices in a large bowl with the raspberries and sugar and toss gently to combine. In a small bowl, mix the cornstarch with about 2 tablespoons of the juice released by the fruit, add the lemon juice and salt, and pour over the fruit. Stir to mix and then place the fruit mixture in a 9 by 12-inch / 23 by 30-cm baking dish.

To make the biscuits, sift the flour, granulated sugar, baking powder, and salt into a bowl and stir in the suet. In a small bowl, whisk together the egg and milk and add to the flour mixture. Stir with a fork to make a soft dough. Transfer the dough to a floured surface and knead gently, just until the dough comes together.

Pat the dough out to a thickness of 1/2 inch / 1 cm and, using a 2 3/4-inch / 7-cm biscuit cutter, cut out rounds of dough. Press any leftover dough together and cut again; you should have about eight rounds. Arrange the rounds evenly on top of the fruit; there will be space between them. Brush the tops of the biscuits with the cream and sprinkle the Demerara sugar on top. Bake until the filling is bubbling and the pastry is puffed and golden, 20 to 25 minutes.

Let cool and serve at room temperature.

Serves 6 to 8

Filling

2 pounds / 900 g peaches

1 pound / 450 g raspberries

1/2 cup / 3 1/2 ounces / 100 g sugar

2 tablespoons cornstarch

A squeeze of lemon juice

Pinch of sea salt

Suet Biscuits

2 cups / 8 3/4 ounces / 250 g flour

3 tablespoons granulated sugar

1 tablespoon baking powder

Pinch of fine sea salt

1 1/4 cups / 4 ounces / 115 g finely grated suet

1 egg

1/2 cup / 125 ml milk

1 tablespoon whipping (35 percent fat) cream

1 1/2 tablespoons Demerara sugar

Quincemeat

Makes about 4 cups / 1 l

6 ounces / 175 g seedless Thompson raisins

4 ounces / 115 g golden raisins (sultanas)

2 ounces / 60 g mixed candied citrus peel

$2/3$ cup / 4 ounces / 115 g firmly packed brown sugar

1 cup / $3^{1}/_{2}$ ounces / 100 g finely grated suet

3 tablespoons brandy or aged rum

2 small quinces

1 orange

1 lemon

$1/2$ teaspoon ground cardamom

$1/2$ teaspoon ground cinnamon

$1/2$ teaspoon ground mace or nutmeg

Fine sea salt and freshly ground black pepper

My friends call me the "Queen of Quince" because I am always cooking with them. Quinces magically turn deep red and lusciously tender when cooked, and they add an amazing perfume to anything they come in contact with. Apples are the fresh fruit most commonly added to mincemeat, but I prefer quinces, as they impart a special aroma and flavor to the mixture, which I call "quincemeat." From the Middle Ages through the Renaissance it was common to mix dried fruits with ground meat. The fruit added flavor and made the meat go further. The meat portion of mincemeat, however, gradually declined, and now all that is left is the suet. Make the quincemeat at least a month before you want to use it so the flavors can blend.

Coarsely chop both types of raisins and the citrus peel. Combine them in a large bowl and add the brown sugar, suet, and brandy. Peel and coarsely grate the quinces. Finely grate the zest of the orange and lemon. Blend the grated quince and zests into the fruit mixture.

Squeeze the lemon to obtain 2 tablespoons of juice and add it with the spices to the fruit mixture. Add a pinch of salt and a few grindings of pepper, mix well, cover, and leave at room temperature for a day.

Stir the mixture again and then pack it into a clean glass jar. Cover and refrigerate for at least a month before using. The longer the quincemeat sits, the better the flavor, and it will keep for up to a year refrigerated.

A CULTURE OF FAT

Not everybody wants to be thin, as shown by the tale of the *pishtaco* (see page 216), and in some cultures being fat—even very fat—is seen as desirable. In Africa, where food has always been scarce, there is a long tradition of fattening young girls before marriage. Fat is a sign of beauty and wealth: the fatter a man's wife, the richer he is. In the Muslim societies of Niger and Mauritania obesity is revered, and young girls are given more to eat than boys so they can gain weight. Fattening young girls is often taken a step further, and girls as young as seven years old are sometimes force-fed a diet of couscous and dates to make them gain weight. Although this practice is dying out, the Mauritanian government estimates that 10 percent of young girls in the country undergo this treatment today. The practice is having economic effects in this poor country, as the large number of obese women, who have a high incidence of arthritis, heart disease, and diabetes, is putting a serious strain on the local health system. This, and a worrying new trend toward young girls taking steroids meant for cattle in order to gain weight quickly, has forced the government to launch a campaign against the practice. The campaign has not been very successful, although perhaps the pervasive influence of Western culture, which is obsessed with thinness, may succeed in curbing the practice where the Mauritanian officials have failed.

Quincemeat Tarts

According to one tradition, if you eat a mince pie every day between Christmas and January 6, Twelfth Night, you will have a happy year. Now that's a good reason to eat them! Since quincemeat is very rich, it is best served in small amounts. Instead of making a large double-crusted quincemeat pie, then, I make little tarts with a pastry circle on top. You'll easily be able to eat one of these tarts for 12 days. If you prefer to make a single 9-inch / 23-cm tart, you will probably need a little more filling.

Lightly butter a 12-cup muffin pan. Roll out the pastry on a floured surface about $1/4$ inch / 6 mm thick. Using biscuit cutters, cut out twelve 3-inch / 7.5-cm circles and twelve $1 1/4$-inch / 3-cm circles, pressing any leftover pastry together and rerolling as necessary.

Press the larger circles into the bottom of the muffin tins and fill each one with 1 tablespoon of quincemeat. Top the tarts with the smaller pastry circles and refrigerate for 30 minutes.

Preheat the oven to 375°F / 190°C.

Bake the tarts until the pastry is set and lightly colored, about 20 minutes. Transfer them to a wire rack and, once cool, store in an airtight container.

Makes 12 small tarts

Unsalted butter, softened, for greasing

1 recipe Suet and Butter Pastry (recipe follows)

$3/4$ cup / 6 ounces / 175 g Quincemeat (page 214)

Suet and Butter Pastry

I love this pastry. It is simple to make and easy to use, and it shows just how useful suet can be in the dessert kitchen. The suet makes a wonderfully crisp and flaky pastry, while the little bit of butter adds flavor and helps it color. You don't have to restrict it to making mince pies. Use it for a fruit tart, or double the recipe and make a pie.

Combine the flour and salt in a food processor and pulse to mix. Add the butter and pulse until the mixture resembles very coarse bread crumbs. Add the suet and pulse again just to mix the suet into the flour. Tip the mixture into a large bowl.

Add the water and stir with a fork. Squeeze a bit of the mixture between your fingers. If it holds together, transfer the dough to a lightly floured surface; if not, add another couple of teaspoons of ice water and test again.

Gently knead the dough into a ball and flatten into a disk. Wrap the disk in plastic wrap and refrigerate for at least 30 minutes before using. This pastry also freezes well.

Makes enough for a 9 to $9 1/2$-inch / 23 to 24-cm pie or 12 small tarts

1 cup / $4 1/2$ ounces / 125 g flour

Pinch of fine sea salt

2 tablespoons unsalted butter, diced

$3/4$ cup / $2 1/2$ ounces / 75 g finely grated suet

$1/3$ cup / 75 ml ice-cold water

Quincemeat Soufflés

Makes 6 soufflés

3/4 cup / 6 ounces / 175 g
Quincemeat (page 214)

2 tablespoons brandy

Unsalted butter, softened,
for greasing

1/3 cup / 2 ounces / 65 g
granulated sugar

6 egg whites

Confectioners' (icing) sugar,
for dusting

I often have quincemeat lingering in my refrigerator long past Christmas. Once, when I was looking for a way to use my quincemeat other than for baking tarts and pies, I was inspired by a Delia Smith recipe, and quincemeat soufflés were born. This is a great way to lighten up rich quincemeat. Don't be scared off by the word soufflé*: this is a ridiculously easy dessert that can stand a lot of abuse.*

Serve these soufflés with Brown Butter Ice Cream (page 50) in a separate dish for a wonderful hot-and-cold effect.

Combine the quincemeat and brandy in a heatproof bowl and put in a warm place or a pan of hot water to soften.

Butter six 3/4-cup / 175-ml ovenproof ramekins. Use about 2 tablespoons of the granulated sugar to coat the insides of the ramekins.

Preheat the oven to 350°F / 180°C.

Place the egg whites in a bowl and whisk until white. Gradually add the remaining granulated sugar and continue to whisk until the egg whites are thick and glossy, with soft peaks.

Remove the quincemeat mixture from its warm spot and add a large spoonful of the beaten egg white to it. Stir well to lighten the quincemeat, and then add the lightened quincemeat mixture to the remaining beaten egg whites. Using a spatula, gently fold them together. Divide the mixture among the ramekins and transfer them to a baking sheet. Bake until the soufflés are puffed and golden, about 12 minutes.

Dust the tops of the soufflés with the confectioners' sugar and serve immediately.

PISHTACO

High in the Andes Mountains, you might hear a folktale about a terrifying white stranger who attacks unsuspecting Indians during the night, and drags them into a cave, where he strings them up and removes their fat. He either kills them by beheading and dismembering them, or he removes their fat with such precision that when the victim awakes, he has no marks on his body or any memory of what happened. However, two or three weeks later, without his fat to sustain him, the Indian dies. This evil stranger is called a *pishtaco*.

According to sociologists, the *pishtaco* tale first surfaced after the arrival of the Spanish conquistadors and clergy in South America, and it parallels the history of the colonization and exploitation of the Andean Indian. For the indigenous peoples of the Andes, fat is a positive attribute. Like any population living under difficult conditions, they see their body fat as beautiful and know that they cannot survive without it. Losing your fat equals losing your health, beauty, and vitality. In the tale of the *pishtaco*, the Indian doesn't simply lose his precious fat, but it is stolen from him by a white man who then sells it for profit.

The Indians were horrified when they saw the Spanish cutting out the fat from enemy corpses and using it to treat their wounded soldiers. (Fat has a long tradition of medicinal use, especially as an ointment.) They believed that the clergy, too, stole Indian fat to use in their churches, as fuel for the lamps, to polish the statues, and to grease the bells. This explains why the first *pishtaco* figures in the legend were priests and soldiers. As the power structure changed, so did the *pishtaco* figure. In later versions of the story he rode a horse and wore leather chaps like a rancher, and in the twentieth century he appeared in overalls and stole Indian fat to grease his airplanes and machinery or to sell it to the pharmaceutical industry. Today the myth is still alive in some remote rural areas, although now the *pishtaco* is likely to drive an SUV, wear mirrored sunglasses, and use his mobile phone to extract the fat from his unwilling victims.

The *pishtaco* tale has had a negative effect on development projects in the region. An aid program to feed children attending school was seen by the Indians as a way to fatten up their children to make them more desirable to the *pishtaco*. It took a long time to persuade them that this was not the aim of the program. Slowly the *pishtaco* legend is being discredited, but only when the Indians have power over their economic livelihood will the *pishtaco* disappear completely.

Marrow Rice Pudding

My husband loves rice pudding, but I don't, so I rarely make it, much to his chagrin. When we are in Paris he always buys rice pudding from our neighborhood charcuterie. The owner recently retired and, knowing how much my husband loved her pudding, she gave me her recipe. Here is her recipe, enriched with bone marrow and flavored with vanilla; sometimes I just can't stop myself from reworking recipes. Instead of making a caramel that sets hard on the cold pudding like the charcutière, I serve it with Salted Caramel Sauce (page 54); that way, my husband can eat the pudding while it is still warm.

Pour the milk into a medium-size saucepan, and add the rice, vanilla bean, and salt. Bring to a boil over medium-high heat, stirring constantly. Lower the heat, cover, and simmer very gently, stirring from time to time, for 40 to 45 minutes, or until the mixture is thickened and the rice is cooked. Remove the vanilla bean.

Whisk together the sugar, eggs, and rum, then add the bone marrow and stir the mixture into the rice. Bring slowly to a boil over low heat, stirring constantly. Lower the heat so the rice simmers, and continue to cook, stirring, for 5 minutes. Serve the rice pudding warm or cold, with Salted Caramel Sauce.

Serves 6

4 cups / 1 l milk

2/3 cup / 4 1/2 ounces / 125 g Arborio rice

1 vanilla bean, split

Pinch of sea salt

3/4 cup / 5 ounces / 150 g sugar

2 eggs

1 tablespoon dark rum

1/4 cup / 1 ounce / 30 g finely diced prepared bone marrow (see page 172)

1 recipe Salted Caramel Sauce (page 54)

bibliography

Achaya, K. T. *Indian Food: A Historical Companion*. Delhi: Oxford University Press, 1994.

Alexander, Stephanie. *The Cook's Companion*. Melbourne: Viking, 1996.

Ayrton, Elizabeth. *The Cookery of England*. Harmondsworth: Penguin Books, 1977.

Ayto, John. *The Diner's Dictionary: Food and Drink from A to Z*. Oxford: Oxford University Press, 1993.

Bayless, Rick. *Rick Bayless's Mexican Kitchen*. New York: Scribner, 1996.

Becker, Marion Rombauer. *Joy of Cooking*. Indianapolis: Bobbs-Merrill, 1978.

Behr, Edward. "Cleanness, Freshness, and the Butter Wrapper." *The Art of Eating*, No. 65, 2003.

————. "The Most Famous Fatback in the World." *The Art of Eating*, No. 75, 2007.

Bilson, Gay. *Plenty: Digressions on Food*. Melbourne: Lantern, 2004.

Borer, Alain. *The Essential Joseph Beuys*. Cambridge, MA: MIT Press, 1997.

Boxer, Arabella. *A Visual Feast*. London: Random Century House, 1991.

Brillat-Savarin, Jean-Anthelme. *The Physiology of Taste*, translated by M. F. K. Fisher. Washington, D.C.: Counterpoint, 1994.

Buford, Bill. *Heat*. Toronto: Doubleday, 2006.

Campos, Paul. *The Obesity Myth: Why America's Obsession with Weight Is Hazardous to Your Health*. New York: Gotham Books, 2004.

Clark, Samantha, and Samuel Clark. *Moro: The Cookbook*. London: Edbury Press, 2001.

Clements, Carole, and Elizabeth Wolf-Cohen. *The French Recipe Cookbook*. London: Lorenz Books, 1975.

Colquhoun, Kate. *Taste: The Story of Britain Through Its Cooking*. London: Bloomsbury, 2007.

Conran, Terence, and Caroline Conran. *The Cook Book*. New York: Crown, 1980.

Corriher, Shirley. *CookWise*. New York: William Morrow, 1997.

Davidson, Alan, ed. *On Feasting and Fasting*. London: Macdonald Orbis, 1988.

———. *The Oxford Companion to Food*. Oxford: Oxford University Press, 1999.

Detienne, Marcel, and Jean-Pierre Vernant. *The Cuisine of Sacrifice among the Greeks*, translated by Paula Wissing. Chicago: University of Chicago Press, 1989.

Dumas, Alexandre. *Dumas on Food*, translated by Alan and Jane Davidson. London: Folio Society, 1978.

Enig, Mary. *Know Your Fats: The Complete Primer for Understanding the Nutrition of Fats, Oils, and Cholesterol*. Silver Spring, MD: Bethesda Press, 2000.

Enig, Mary, and Sally Fallon. *Eat Fat, Lose Fat*. New York: Hudson Street Press, 2005.

Fallon, Sally, and Mary Enig. *Nourishing Traditions*. 2nd rev. ed. Washington, D.C.: New Trends, 2001.

Fearnley-Whittingstall, Hugh. *The River Cottage Meat Book*. Berkeley: Ten Speed Press, 2007.

Fernández-Armesto, Felipe. *Near a Thousand Tables*. Toronto: Key Porter Books, 2002.

Fitzgibbon, Theodora. *The Food of the Western World*. New York: Quadrangle, 1976.

Forman, H. "The Butter Gods of Kum Bum." *Canadian Geographic*, January 1948.

Froud, Nina, and Charlotte Turgeon, eds. *Larousse Gastronomique*. London: Hamlyn, 1961.

Gage, Fran. *A Sweet Quartet: Sugar, Almonds, Eggs, and Butter*. New York: North Point Press, 2002.

Garavini, Daniela, ed. *The Goose*, translated by Kate Clayton. Cologne: Könemann, 1998.

———. *Pigs and Pork*, translated by Isabel Varea. Cologne: Könemann, 1999.

Gratzer, Walter. *Terrors of the Table: The Curious History of Nutrition*. Oxford: Oxford University Press, 2005.

Grigson, Jane. *Charcuterie and French Pork Cookery*. Harmondsworth: Penguin Books, 1977.

———. *European Cookery*. New York: Athenaeum, 1983.

———. *The Observer Guide to British Cookery*. London: Michael Joseph, 1984.

Guérard, Michel. *L'Art et la manière d'engraisser et de confire les oÿes et les canards*. Paris: Cairns Editions, 1999.

———. *La Cuisine gourmande*. Paris: Robert Lafont, 1978.

Hartley, Dorothy. *Food in England*. London: Little, Brown, 2003.

Jaine, Tom, ed. *Oxford Symposium on Food and Cookery 1986: The Cooking Medium*. London: Prospect Books, 1987.

Keller, Thomas. *The French Laundry Cookbook*. New York: Artisan, 1999.

Klein, Richard. *Eat Fat*. New York: Pantheon, 1996.

Kulick, Don, and Anne Meneley, eds. *Fat: The Anthropology of an Obsession*. New York: Tarcher/Penguin, 2005.

Kumove, Shirley. *Words Like Arrows: A Collection of Yiddish Folk Sayings*. Toronto: University of Toronto Press, 1984.

Kurlansky, Mark. *Salt: A World History*. New York: Alfred A. Knopf, 2002.

Levenstein, Harvey. *Paradox of Plenty: A Social History of Eating in Modern America*. New York: Oxford University Press, 1993.

Mallet, Gina. *Last Chance to Eat: The Fate of Taste in a Fast Food World*. Toronto: McClelland & Stewart, 2004.

McCullough, Fran. *Good Fat*. New York: Scribner, 2003.

McGee, Harold. *The Curious Cook*. San Francisco: North Point Press, 1990.

———. *On Food and Cooking*. New York: Scribner, 1984.

Mennel, Stephen. *All Manners of Food*. New York: Basil Blackwell, 1987.

Montagné, Prosper. *Larousse Gastronomique*. London: Hamlyn, 1974.

Morton, Mark. *Cupboard Love*. Toronto: Insomniac Press, 2004.

Oliver-Smith, Anthony. "The Pishtaco: Institutionalized Fear in Highland Peru." *Journal of American Folklore*, No. 82.

Perry, Charles. "Crazy for Milk Scum." *Los Angeles Times*, July 7, 2000.

Planck, Nina. *Real Food: What to Eat and Why*. New York: Bloomsbury, 2006.

Rhodes, Gary. *New Classics*. London: Dorling Kindersley, 2001.

Robuchon, Joël. *Les Dimanches de Joël Robuchon*. Paris: Chene, 1993.

———. *Ma Cuisine pour vous*. Paris: Robert Laffont, 1986.

———. *Le Meilleur et les plus simple de la pomme de terre*. Paris: Robert Laffont, 1994.

Romans, John, William Castello, Wendell Carlson, Marion Greaser, and Kevin Jones. *The Meat We Eat*. Danville, IL: Interstate Publishers, 1985.

Root, Waverley. *Food*. New York: Simon and Schuster, 1980.

Ruhlman, Michael, and Brian Polcyn. *Charcuterie: The Craft of Salting, Smoking, and Curing*. New York: W. W. Norton & Company, 2005.

Sahni, Julie. *Classic Indian Cooking*. New York: Morrow, 1980.

Samuelsson, Marcus. *The Soul of a New Cuisine*. New York: John Wiley & Sons, 2006.

Schott, Ben. *Schott's Food & Drink Miscellany*. New York: Bloomsbury, 2003.

Schwartz, Hillel. *Never Satisfied: A Cultural History of Diets, Fantasies and Fat*. New York: Anchor Books, 1990.

Seid, Roberta Pollack. *Never Too Thin: Why Women Are at War with Their Bodies*. New York: Prentice Hall, 1989.

Serventi, Silvano. *La Grande histoire du foie gras*. Paris: Flammarion, 1993.

Slater, Nigel. *Appetite*. Toronto: Random House, 2002.

———. *Real Cooking*. London: Michael Joseph, 1997.

———. *Toast*. London: Fourth Estate, 2003.

Spencer, Colin. *British Food: An Extraordinary Thousand Years of History*. New York: Columbia Press, 2003.

"Spoilt for Choice: A Survey of Food." *The Economist*, December 13, 2003.

Stachelhaus, Heiner. *Joseph Beuys*, translated by David Britt. New York: Abbeville Press, 1991.

Steingarten, Jeffrey. *It Must Have Been Something I Ate*. New York: Knopf, 2002.

———. *The Man Who Ate Everything*. New York: Knopf, 1998.

Stevenson, Burton. *The Home Book of Proverbs, Maxims and Familiar Phrases*. New York: Macmillan, 1948.

Strang, Jeanne. *Goose Fat & Garlic*. London: Kyle Cathie, 2003.

Szwarc, Sandy. "Food Is Good." *IACP Food Forum*, First Quarter, 2006.

Tannahill, Reay. *Food in History*. New York: Stein and Day, 1973.

Taube, Gary. "What If It's All Been a Big Fat Lie?" *New York Times*, July 7, 2002.

This, Hervé. *Casseroles & éprouvettes*. Paris: Pour La Science, 2002.

Tisdall, Caroline. *Joseph Beuys*. London: Thames and Hudson, 1979.

Toussaint-Samat, Maguelonne. *History of Food*, translated by Anthea Bell. Oxford: Blackwell Publishers, 1992.

USDA Economic Research Service. *Food Data Consumption and Availability*. 2007.

Visser, Margaret. *Much Depends on Dinner*. Toronto: McClelland & Stewart, 1986.

Walker, Harlan, ed. *Oxford Symposium on Food and Cookery 1994: Disappearing Foods*. Totnes: Prospect Books, 1995.

———. *Oxford Symposium on Food and Cookery 1998: Food in the Arts*. Totnes: Prospect Books, 1999.

———. *Oxford Symposium on Food and Cookery 2002: The Fat of the Land*. Bristol: Footwork, 2003.

Wheaton, Barbara Ketcham. *Savoring the Past: The French Kitchen and Table from 1300 to 1798*. New York: Touchstone, 1996.

White, Florence. *Good Things in England*. London: Futura, 1974.

White, Marco Pierre. *Wild Food from Land and Sea*. London: Ebury Press, 1994.

Willan, Anne. *La Varenne Pratique*. Toronto: Macmillan, 1989.

Willoughby, John. "Understanding Butter." *Martha Stewart Living Magazine*. 1998.

Wilson, Gail Henderson. "Butter Clarified." *Cooks Magazine*, September/October 1985.

Wolfert, Paula. *The Cooking of South-West France*. New York: Dial Press, 1983.

———. *Couscous and Other Good Food from Morocco*. New York: Harper & Row, 1973.

Ziegler, Dominic. "In Praise of Gluttony." *The Economist: Intelligent Life*, Summer 2005.

acknowledgments

As I began working on this book, I discovered the world is divided into two opposing camps: those who love and appreciate fat, and a much larger group who are horrified by fat in any form. This book was almost stillborn, and would not have come into being without the heroic struggle of my agent, Liv Blumer. She loved the idea of *Fat* right from the get-go and worked tirelessly to sell it. Thank you, Liv, for all your hard work, for believing in my unusual ideas, and for always being there.

In a surprisingly fat-phobic cookbook world, it took a Canadian, Doug Pepper at McClelland & Stewart, to take the plunge. Soon after, he was followed by Aaron Wehner at Ten Speed Press. Both these men love fat and understand its importance to taste. So from nothing, *Fat* gained two enthusiastic champions and the support of two great publishing teams. Bill Blumer deserves a special thank you for working through the contractual complications of having one book with two publishers.

The love of food unites people; it creates and sustains friendship, and I would like to express my gratitude to friends and colleagues who boosted my spirit through the difficult times. A special thank you to Laura Calder, Jeffrey Alford, Naomi Duguid, Harriet Bell, Pat Holtz, Miriam Rubin, and Heather Trim.

I have met many people who generously took time to answer my questions and share information, and their contacts, with me. All of them, friends and strangers, willingly contributed their knowledge, passed on recipes, and sent me interesting fat facts.

In North America, I would like to thank Lynne Clare, David Field, Brenda Garza, Steve Isleifson, Ihor Kuryliw, Fran McCulloch, Lieve de Nil, Walter Staib and Paul Bauer, Bree Seeley, Nancy Shanoff, Oksana Slavyutich, Molly Stevens, Hiroko Sugiyama, Keijo Tapanainen, and Nach Waxman.

In Europe and the UK, I extend a thank you to Olivier Assouly, Michel and Marie-Jo Bablot, Bénédict Beaugé, Thierry Breton, Stéphane Davet, Anne Dolamore, Frédérique Fromentin, François Gerard, Cyril and Maryse Lalande, Melinda Leong and Frerk Meyer, Christianne Muusers, Leda Vigliardi Paravia, Antonio Rodrigues, Laura de Turckheim, and Judy Witts.

In Australia, New Zealand, and India, thanks are due to Jane Adams, Liz Adsett, Vinod Advani, Alister Brown, Richard Cornish, Ritu Khanna, Ruby Leong, Cheong Liew, bon vivant Matt Preston, and the very supportive Cherry Ripe.

All these people were exceedingly generous with their time and knowledge and, best of all, many of them are now good friends.

Thank you to my mother, Claudine, for instilling in me a love of animal fat, and to my many fat-loving friends, who willingly ate their way through this book without fear or complaint. Thank you to Laura Calder, Colin Faulkner, David Field, Rob and Daniela Fiocca, François and Caroline Gerard, Eric and Marie-line Incarbona, Val and Ilze Lapsa, Karen Lim, and Vincent and Lindsay Wong, who all happily ate anything I put in front of them and told me exactly what they thought of it. It is not an easy task pinpointing why you like or dislike a dish, and it requires fortitude to criticize the cook—those who know me well will realize just how brave these individuals are.

While knowledge and experience are fundamental to cooking, a cook is nothing without good ingredients. So I'd like to thank all my suppliers, especially Leila Batten and Stanley Janecek at Whitehouse Meats, Elizabeth and Peter Bzikot at Baa Sheep, Stephen Alexander at Cumbrae Farms, and Wayne Kienitz of Wayne's Meat Products. Thank you also to all my Paris suppliers, especially my butcher, who deserves a special mention. Joël Lachable is passionate about his profession and he treats every piece of the animal, including its fat, with care, love, and respect.

I was doubly lucky to have two great editors working with me on this book, Clancy Drake at Ten Speed and Jenny Bradshaw at McClelland & Stewart; thank you both. And Clancy, please know how much I appreciate your maintaining my vision of this book and working to make it stronger and more focused. Thank you to the teams at both publishing houses, especially copy editor Sharron Wood. My food styling genes are strong, so the visuals of this book are extremely important to me. A big thank you to the hardworking team of photographer Leigh Beisch, prop stylist Sara Slavin, and food stylist Dan Becker, who demonstrated just how delicious fat looks. Thank you also to designer Betsy Stromberg at

Ten Speed for putting the images, the recipes, and my words into such a stylish, sophisticated, and beautifully designed book.

I am saving until last the person to whom I owe the biggest debt of gratitude, my husband, Haralds Gaikis. Writing a book is like enduring a long illness, and spending time with a self-absorbed, suffering patient is no fun. He has now survived two books and is enthusiastically encouraging a third! Best of all, he has proved what I always knew: that he is no Jack Sprat. Thank you, Haralds. I couldn't have done it without you.

Jennifer McLagan
Toronto, 2008

index

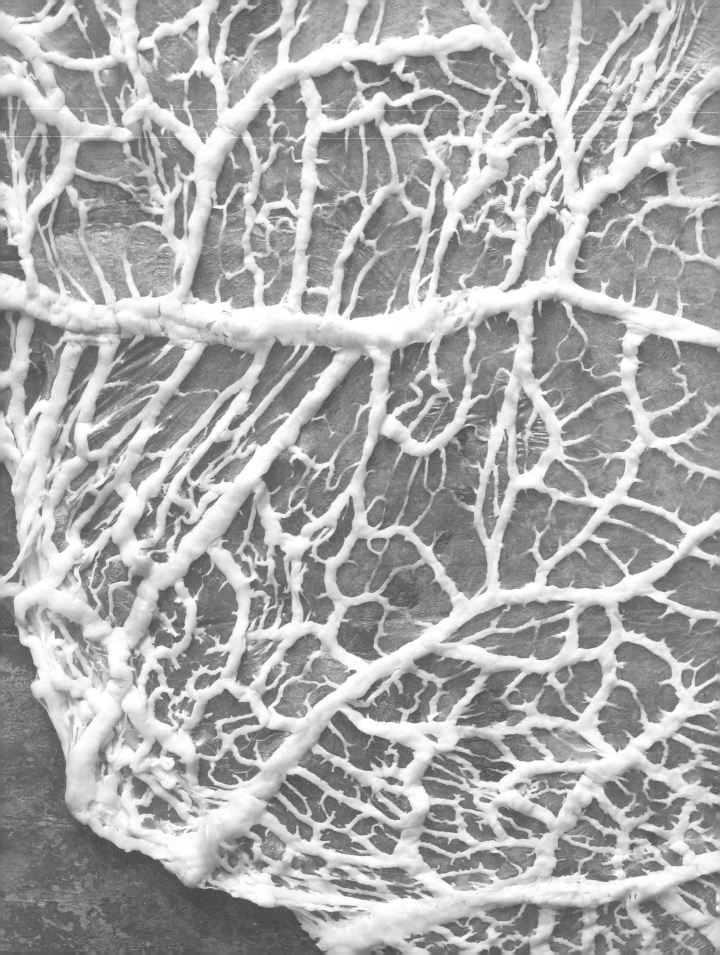